THE SCIENCE
INSIDE THE CHILD

In this engaging book, psychologist Sara Meadows shares the fascinating story of what happens when we're growing up, showing how science can deepen our understanding of how children develop. The book also describes some of the ways in which children's development is linked with health and happiness in later life.

Filled with entertaining anecdotes, the book presents an accessible overview of the different scientific perspectives on child development. There are chapters looking at children's individual development within the development of our species, at the influence of genes and the environment, and the role of the hormone systems that flood our bodies. It also describes the neuroscientific processes at work within children's brains and considers what we can learn about development by looking at the patterns of behaviour in large populations.

The Science Inside the Child will be an informative and enriching read for all parents, educators, and carers and for anyone interested in how children develop to be emotionally balanced, socially skilled, and enthusiastic seekers of knowledge.

Sara Meadows works in the Graduate School of Education at the University of Bristol. As a psychologist, she uses the concepts and the methods of developmental psychology as a way of understanding what children are experiencing at home and in their other social settings and the ways in which they grow up as effective social actors. Much of her current research is with the Avon Longitudinal Study of Parents and Children (ALSPAC), also known as the 'Children of the Nineties' study.

THE SCIENCE INSIDE THE CHILD

The story of what happens
when we're growing up

Sara Meadows

Routledge
Taylor & Francis Group

LONDON AND NEW YORK

First published 2016
by Routledge
2 Park Square, Milton Park, Abingdon, Oxon, OX14 4RN

and by Routledge
711 Third Avenue, New York, NY 10017

Routledge is an imprint of the Taylor & Francis Group, an informa business

British Library Cataloguing in Publication Data
A catalogue record for this book is available from the British Library

Library of Congress Cataloging-in-Publication Data
Meadows, Sara.
  The science inside the child : the story of what happens when we're
growing up / Sara Meadows.
    pages cm
  Includes bibliographical references and index.
  1. Child psychology.   2. Child development.   I. Title.
  BF721.M4237 2015
  155.4—dc23
  2015008872

ISBN: 978-1-138-80066-3 (hbk)
ISBN: 978-1-138-80067-0 (pbk)
ISBN: 978-1-315-75532-8 (ebk)

Typeset in Joanna
by ApexCovantage, LLC
Printed in Great Britain by Ashford Colour P

MIX
Paper from
responsible sources
FSC   FSC® C011748
www.fsc.org

CONTENTS

◆

1

---◆---

INTRODUCTION

In which I explain why this is not an advice
book and why it is worth your attention

Nursery rhymes sometimes, disconcertingly, say something that is obviously nonsense and at the same time subversively true. Consider the 'sugar and spice and all things nice' versus 'slugs and snails and puppy-dog tails' assertion about what girls and boys are made of. Part of what is going on here is the implication that children are both 'all things nice' and 'some things nasty'. In my experience of being a parent, it could feel like this: being a parent involves anxiety and fear and loss of self-confidence and exhaustion and anger and love and excitement and delight and satisfaction and pride and wonder – absolutely simultaneous feelings as well as amazingly strong ones. My offspring was in the very same single moment the best and brightest and most beautiful thing that there has ever been in the entire universe, and the source of my sleep deprivation, my anxieties about feeding and health and staying out late, some singularly aversive high-pitched or bass-heavy noises, and yet another sticky and indelible stain on the carpet or a demand for new clothes or an emptied fridge or a borrowed-and-lost hairbrush. Sugar and spice, indeed, but snail trails were lurking.

I had been a developmental psychologist by trade for years by the time she was born, and I was used to reading, researching, and teaching the science of child development. This helped, I think. But although the bits of my mind that were not sleep-deprived or irritated or panicked valued the science – and there were occasional tips for very specific things to do, a lot of tips for things to avoid doing if possible, and a sense of 'good enough' parenting being good enough for the child, and better than perfect parenting in the sense that it was achievable – the science rarely functioned as a source of advice.

I do think it enriched my sense of what was going on. Even when what the science told me to do was 'obvious', I understood the parenting dilemma differently; and when it said there is no single right thing to do (which happened much more often), that tended to reduce the anxiety and guilt and to increase my confidence that no single action would be catastrophic or a guarantee of total success and that we would have second chances to do things better and to muddle through in the end. My child has grown up to be indeed the best and brightest and most beautiful thing that there has ever been in the entire universe, and efficient, conscientious, stylish, witty, compassionate, and much loved to boot, but I don't think that makes me an expert who can offer advice on how to bring up children.[1] My motivation for writing this book is something different.

This is not a book about how to bring up your child. It is a book about the ways in which science describes and explains children. These descriptions and explanations may or may not be helpful to parents, caregivers, and educators. I would be very pleased if they were helpful, but that is not the main point. The point is that there is a lot of science about children, much of it very new and not especially well-known. I thought it would be useful and interesting to bring it together and see how the scientific picture compared with the everyday one we all have. We've all been children and had parents, many of us have had children and are parents, and we may feel completely certain of what is going on or we may be puzzled and bemused. Science may not tell us what to do in a moment of despair and panic about our child – for that we may need to have recourse to an advice book – but it can correct too much certainty (such as you may well find in some advice books) and clarify a fog of confusion and doubt (such as you may develop if you read too many advice books). This is not a user's manual or a recipe book, but it could be a guide to what we might think about while we live alongside children.

I believe that science is one of the glories of human activity. I believe that we should all have access to scientific understanding and know how science works. I believe that scientific pictures of children are interesting in themselves. I believe that people concerned with the practicalities of bringing up children might enjoy the bringing up more if they knew what 'the science inside the child' says. This is not so much because the science helps when we don't know what we should do (though sometimes it does), but for its own sake, and for the sense of a deeper and wider perspective that it gives.

I do also know that there is a lot to be enjoyed in nonscience and a lot to be learned from it. I've read novels and biographies that illuminate the human condition quite as vividly as science does, but they are not what this book is about. I've also had good advice from nonscience sources (for example my mother, my daughter's childminder, my friends) and from sources (such as Dr Benjamin Spock) who had a lot of science behind them but presented mainly experience-based advice. I've even read advice books that felt very helpful. My advice on advice is this: relax; see if the action that's being advised feels comfortable to you; think about whether there would probably be seriously bad consequences from not doing what's advised; think about whether the person advising you is really trying to sell you something; be prepared to try things and not blame yourself if they don't work; know some experts to go to for urgent help or if things feel wrong; have a support system (and a support system for the first support system, and ideally a support system for the second support system, too); remember you have needs and rights yourself, as well as responsibilities; and again, relax. Mostly the children of intelligent and conscientious persons turn out quite well. You, as a parent, will probably be nicer to them than the rest of the world will be, so you don't need to tell yourself the usual story of the conscientious person: 'It's all my fault'. Instead, reflect on the other set of stories that I am going to tell you on behalf of science.

Humans are inveterate storytellers, but for me one of the important things about science is the particular sorts of stories it tells. It's impressive how science has enabled us to describe and analyse and appreciate and marvel at, and in some cases predict and control, an enormous range of phenomena – how the universe came into being, how old its components are, how life evolved, how the body works, why a tsunami happens, how to eradicate smallpox, why there are fewer bees and more cases of cancer, and so on. We simply understand our physiology better than previous generations did. Scientific knowledge deepens and widens and becomes more precise in ways that I don't see in nonscience stories. A sixteen-year-old pupil doing science today will have a much better understanding of the menstrual cycle than Queen Victoria's gynaecologist did (a 'top' doctor of the time, he thought women should not be educated beyond a very cursory minimum because the stress of it would upset their menstruation and make them infertile). A novelist writing now, early in the twenty-first century, does not 'know' more or write 'better' novels, which is one among the thousands of reasons that we should still be reading *Middlemarch* and *Persuasion* and *The Turn of the Screw* (each of which still tells us things about parents and children, though that's not the main thing to be gained from reading them).

What I am going to do in this book is present some of the science that could help us to understand what children's development is made of. This is going to mean looking at children's individual development within the development of our species, at genes, at how genes express themselves during children's development, at the hormone systems that flood our bodies, at the neuroscience of children's brains, at how there are clues to better and worse development in the patterns of behaviour you can see in large populations – at the scientific disciplines, therefore, of evolutionary theory, genetics, epigenetics, endocrinology, neuroscience, epidemiology, and psychology. There will be some discussion of the basics of these scientific disciplines, but I am going to concentrate on the science that is tightly relevant to children and their development, and especially the science that is near the cutting edge of discovery.

To help ground this science, I'm going to begin with a psychological model[2] of how parenting and child development fit together that first took my fancy when I began teaching developmental psychology, and then proved useful again when I became a parent. The centre is the idea of 'functional frames' that parents provide for their offspring as part of the social systems that the child inhabits. This model is probably going to look as though it comes from the school of the 'bleeding obvious', and at this point it's not going to be specified in detail, but I think it's useful. This book is about the evolution, the genetics, the epigenetics, the endocrinology, the neuroscience, the epidemiology, and the psychology that feeds into it. That interdisciplinarity is important.

All over the science that studies children we will see evidence of the importance of development in determining our chances of health and happiness. On one level we all know this. We know that lack of cuddles is a bad thing, that lack of conversation is a bad thing, that patience and negotiation are good things, that it's good if we get enjoyment out of each other's company. But the science I'm going to talk about shows why and how development happens, that development affects our behaviour and our emotion and our thinking, as we all know, and also our brain cells, our stress hormones, and even our genes, as we may not have thought it would. I am not saying that the 'inside the skin' levels are more important than what's obvious in our behaviour and our society, but I am saying that it is worth knowing what is going on at multiple levels.

Although children's development is very predictable, no outcome is completely fixed in someone's ancestry or at someone's conception or birth; whatever is specified at an early point in one's existence is capable of being modulated to some degree at later points, as one adapts to the way things happen to be. It's never just nature, never just nurture; conceptually and practically, what we have is an interplay of both – *epigenetic* and *developmental* are the terms you are going to see. This is the first bleeding obvious point: children's development means that they are living a predictable set of changes, with some things more stable and others more volatile, with some things fast and some things gradual, with some things affecting a long period of life and other things more transitory. Some useful science describes and explains a lot of this.

The second obvious point: many different influences coexist in shaping children and their lives. It's not just their parents, or their schools, or their genes, or their economic situation or their social class. When the prime minister says that the reason that young people went out and rioted and looted in British cities in the summer of 2011 is 'criminality, pure and simple', the only pure and simple thing you can say is that this statement is wrong and stupid (intellectually and morally). When we see the exam results of a school and blame (or praise) the school for the level of achievement, we are – in large part – wrong. When we bask in how wonderful our children are, we are wrong to feel that is all down to us (although that's such a lovely feeling it's hard to give it up – one of the unsung benefits of breastfeeding is that for several months you can look at your wonderful and rapidly plumping-up baby and say 'apart from a sperm, a vitamin K injection, and some few spoonfuls of water, all this came from my body'). Concentrating on only one factor and ignoring others is pretty much always a mistake in child development. And since the different factors may be studied in different sorts of ways by different sorts of scientists, we need to coordinate a lot of different types of understanding.

All over the science, we are going to see evidence of the importance of other people in the development of each individual child. Maternal licking and nuzzling of the infant rat and monkey affect the expression of their genes, how their brains get wired up, how their hormones are balanced, their emotional states, their social bonds to others. Position in the social hierarchy, partly inherited from your parents, affects stress reactions, access to food, alliances with others the same age, reproductive success. How much your parents discussed other people's feelings with you when you were a small child – how often they explained that 'nobody likes someone who snatches their toy', 'the baby really likes it when you hold him gently', 'would you have liked it if someone treated you like that' – predicts whether you will develop a subtle understanding of other people's emotional lives. How much they read to you and talked with you and sang you nursery rhymes will predict not just your success in learning to read and all through school, but also whether the adults who know you think you have behaviour problems. How they help you deal with success and failure will affect your attitude to challenge and how confident you are. What comes through loud and clear from the basic science is that adults are crucial to the development of children. We can see this at the level of genes and of the endocrinological stress system, in the development of the brain, in the pre-natal and postnatal development of the child, in evolution, in epidemiology. Children grow from parents' bodies and parents' behaviour.

But in every one of these influences, the parents are part of a network of other influences acting together – sometimes neatly adding together, some-times cancelling each other out – over life from conception to the time when the outcomes is measured. Parenting behaviour is important, and you can see its effects *all other things being equal*. But it is not the only factor in child development. Most importantly, the child itself is an active agent with influence on what it experiences. Beyond that, other people get involved – friends, teachers, schoolfellows, employers, policy makers, and so forth.

Which gets me back to my big developmental psychology model, frames. *Frames* are ways of describing the parenting relevant to child development operating within the wider and deeper context of biological and social sys-tems. We will see some parental framing that is essential, some that is better than the alternatives, some that should be avoided if possible. There is a lot of good natural history here – categories and descriptions derived from obser-vations, using both biological and cultural contexts, making comparisons between different species. There are also a certain number of experiments – interventions in which parents (or others) did something differently, and there was a change in the children's behaviour from before to after.

There are always different ways to categorise complex phenomena such as parenting. What follows is a hybrid of different models.[3] I've chosen them because they rest on good science as I understand it; because they are cur-rent and influential; because there is strong evidence; and because I feel they work. Certain other models, which don't have so much supportive science or which don't feel right, I have ruthlessly ignored. In particular, you should note that I have not been prepared to tolerate theories involving blaming mothers – both self-interest and feminist principles came in here.

This is a very brief description, intended to be enough to ground the hard science chapters that follow. Just to note, I'm going to prefer to talk of *parents*, by which I mean whoever is doing the parenting – mother, father, grand-parent, professional carer – without specifying their gender or their relation to the child except where that is very specific in the evidence.

The first sets of parenting frames centre on the child's need for protec-tive care – for safety, nourishment, and comforting. These are universal in humans and apparent in many other species of animal. While an individual is immature, it may not be able to feed itself, protect itself from dangers, cope with stress. (Even when we are mature, we may benefit from help with these things.) Parents *nurture* their children, meeting their needs for nourishment and comfort, both physical and emotional. Parents feed their offspring, clean them, keep them warm, cuddle them, reassure them, try to keep them healthy. They *protect* children from harm, so far as they are able. They try to *modulate* their arousal, comforting the sad child, calming down the over-excited child, distracting the child who is doing something the parent doesn't want him or her to do, encouraging the child to be reflective and not give in to every impulse. Parents *help* or act as instruments, either doing for children things they cannot yet do themselves or modifying the wished-for activities or objects so that the child can achieve them – cutting up food, providing a hand to steady the child's step, giving the young adult an interest-free loan as a deposit for the purchase of a house. Analogous behaviours (except the loan for house-buying) have been seen in other species as well. For example even in the restricted range of this book we will see mother rats licking the pup they have been separated from and parent gulls regurgitating part-digested fish to feed their chicks. It may only be a matter of time before something equivalent to subsidising the next generation's mortgage is seen in a nonhuman species.

All of this nurturing is far from being a completely top-down process: both parent and child are active participants. Essentially, parents need to be responsive to their child, and preferably they should be proactive. In order to do what is most appropriate to deal with a child's need for nurturing, you as parent have to identify what it is. To do this, you use the situation and any clues it offers. There is history about what caused upset and what worked in the past. There is other people's advice. There are the child's own signals: babies use behaviours and features, such as an expressive face,[4] or cries that vary according to their needs, or patterned activity that the parent can fit in with, to signal what they need. Evolution has probably shown a preference for individual children who could communicate in these ways and for parents who could understand and act on these communications. You get patterned, coordinated behaviour building up. With success in this interaction, children develop further ways to ask for what they want, and they also learn about the possibilities of doing things cooperatively with their parents. As the child develops language skills and social skills, communication about need becomes more complex and more acculturated on both sides. If a history of needing, asking, and being given builds up, it allows and enhances communication and mutual understanding (*intersubjectivity* or *mutuality*). Again, there is evidence of some of this sort of thing happening in nonhuman animals who live in stable social groups with time to build up memories of other people's behaviour. These frames look like evolved behaviours.

Parents react to the child's expression of need, but they can also anticipate where the child is shortly going to be and get in there first. Are there signs of incipient hunger? Have food to hand. Is the tower of bricks about to topple down, hitting the builder on the way? Warn about it, steady the construction, be there to catch the bricks or to cuddle the hurt away. Is there conflict on the horizon about the teenager continually asking for money for clothes? Give the teen a budget which is under his or her control and is not topped up by parents – once it's spent, it's spent. A friend of mine said that being a successful parent included choosing your battles; being proactive and seeing what may be coming and preempting it is the same sort of good advice.

Ideally, protective nurturing of children works while still allowing them to do things that are not yet quite within their competence – the lioness crippling a small prey animal so that her cubs can practise their hunting skills on it, the adult human letting the toddler walk along a low wall while walking alongside ready to help if there are wobbles. I'll argue that this bolsters the child's success rate and helps with the child's sense of being able to do things effectively. It also involves children learning to nurture and protect themselves, preferably learning a range of ways to do this. What can you do if you're upset? Seeking a cuddle from Mummy is fine, provided she is there, but she isn't always available. Thus, feeling that someone else can cuddle you, or that your comfort blanket can comfort, or that you can do it yourself by taking slow deep breaths, or you can distract yourself, or you can talk about it to a trusted friend, will be a useful stress relief toolkit.

I think the science shows that the long-term consequences of receiving good nurturing framing, experienced as gentle care and good opportunities for practising talking together and playing together, could include the fine-tuning of stress reactions and emotion regulation, the building up of positive ways of working with others (including altruism), and contentment, trust, and bonding with others – and, of course, simply survival. The long-term consequences of not getting good protective care include risks to all these aspects of the well-being of the individual. Science is examining the mechanisms of what is going on, and these include changes in gene expression and programming, changes in the endocrinological stress response system, changes in the behaviour of the child, changes in social experience beyond the family. There are effects at so many levels that good experiences may protect in many ways, and it may be hard to recover from bad experiences. Science, properly read, would tell us that we should not just blame people when they succumb to risks, and that prevention might be easier than cure. The detail on this is going to come up in later chapters.

There are further parenting frames that widen the social world. Parent and baby may cuddle together, but they are affected by other social partnerships – other family relationships, the parent's employment, the nation's policies on health care and education. Humans have evolved as social animals, and we spend most of our lives as members of groups. In order to manage being in groups we have to engage in *coalition* – the acquisition and sharing of resources, the development of group identification and in-group behaviours, the development of mutual defence against threat and against out-groups. We learn the markers that identify which group someone belongs to, and we categorise people as group members or not. We develop fear of exclusion from the group, a situation which would be seriously damaging to social animals' chances of surviving and reproducing. Children learn where they 'belong', who is an ally and who is a stranger or potential enemy, and how 'people like us' behave. They learned about how to get on with their parent figures; next they have to learn how to get on with people who are not so close and eventually with people who are distant strangers or even enemies. Gradually they move from early favouring of the 'in-group' to later hostility to the 'out-group', generally picking up their parents' prejudices. Biological systems such as mirror neurons and imitation may form a basis for being able to achieve and maintain coalitions; teaching from parents and others, and everyday observation of them, will also be enormously important. Again, there's interesting science here in evolutionary theory, endocrinology, neuroscience, epigenetics, and psychology.

In a well-functioning social group there may be a high degree of *mutuality* – sharing, reciprocity, intimacy, friendship, collaboration, group identification. The basic tools are joint attention, imitation, cheat detection, language – all skills which would foster group cohesion and have very probably evolved because of this. I'm going to describe the research that suggests that parent–infant communication and shared behaviour early on facilitate later communication and shared behaviour – mutuality and co-regulation – between friends. Co-regulation with friends leads to positive emotions and increased feelings of belonging to the group. The ability to develop and maintain close relationships with other people is an important component of the growth of self-definition and autonomy, and again for controlling stress and depression. I'll look later at the biological and psychological bases of this.

There is an interesting role here for imitation. Human beings, and particularly young ones, often copy other people's behaviour, and in lots of games they make it an enjoyable form of play. Young children, even as babies, tend to do a lot of imitation. Sometimes they seem to be 'catching' someone else's behaviour. For example, when amazingly young, literally only a few hours old, children have been seen to imitate facial gestures such as opening mouths wide or sticking out tongues.[5] Babies engage in games with parents that involve turn-taking in imitation. They observe actions that achieve desirable outcomes, and they do the same. Interestingly, they have been seen to imitate actions exactly, even when the actions are obviously inefficient and could easily be modified to work better. This is a contrast with chimpanzees, who are more likely to observe a human's stylised action, pick up on the goal and change the action to reach the goal more effectively.[6] This suggests that the children's imitation is a combination of a biologically programmed set of imitative skills and a social or cultural engagement in doing exactly the same as one's model, as you would in many parent–infant games.

There is relevant science about this. A tendency to learn from others' behaviour could be a very cost-effective contributor to development, and consequently we might have evolved brain structures which make it easier. Our ancestors had behavioural traits which made it easier for them to survive and reproduce successfully. If these are not inherited, they would have to be reinvented in each generation. But if the offspring have inherited an ability to imitate, they may copy their parents' behaviours and pick up behaviour that previously enhanced their ancestors' reproductive success. This might increase their fitness if the environment they have to adapt to is much the same as their ancestors' was. A propensity to imitate and learn from imitating might be a cheap, quick, and highly effective way to adapt – especially in a species which has a lot of highly complex stuff to learn and a culture to pass on. Research on evolutionary theory and children's development is going to come up later, as is research in neuroscience about brain features that make this possible and research in endocrinology about the hormonal base.

I've been talking about the benefits of belonging to a social group and fitting in with other members, and about how useful it will be to understand and imitate others. But social groups tend to have internal structure, with top dogs and lower members of the pack. Individuals have to deal with the hierarchy of their social group, and in many groups each individual has a place that he or she must keep to, if the group is to accept or protect the person. Individuals will also react differentially to others depending on how much of a threat they may be. Knowing about social status is a condition of safety, thus low-status individuals will employ wariness, submission, and 'don't hurt me' signals. Typically, infants and children also show some of these signals and reactions to others' signals. Infants show great sensitivity to sounds produced by others; for example males' voices are more likely than females' to frighten them, and signals from higher status adults inhibit older children's exuberance and exploration. In social interaction with others, young individuals prepare for dominance, competition, and their place in the group hierarchy.

In many species, this place is dependent on the status of your parents. Dominance and kinship and social status have a strong influence on who does what to whom in most animal groups. They predict who grooms whom, who shares food with whom, who gets first go, and who has to wait. Obviously human groups have hierarchies, too, some more powerful than others, some steeper and longer than others. What these are, how they work and where you are in them influence your stress levels, your achievements, your happiness, how long you live – and many aspects of your childhood and your parenting. Inequality in societies tends to be associated with worse health and less prosperity for everyone, even the top dogs.

I've been talking about parental behaviour that affects children's functioning as emotional and social beings, but we have already seen that behaviour is mixed with language and thought. What parents provide for their children's development is often explicitly cognitive as well as social and emotional. Basically, it may be an advantage to the young if other people organise the world of objects, people, and events for them in ways that reduce potential chaos to something nearer intelligible order. Good nurturing will allow and enhance communication and mutual understanding. Protection from harm may include explanations of what should be sought after or avoided. But we deliberately talk to children in ways that help them understand what is going on in the ways we want them to understand. This brings me to some more frames.

It can be hard to see what matters in the 'blooming buzzing confusion'[7] that confronts us. The parent provides *feedback* on the child's actions so that consequences can be more consistent or more salient or less disruptive than they would appear to be without the parent's action: 'Darling, don't tease the cat, she will scratch you'/'The cat scratched you because she doesn't like being teased'; 'You played really well in that match, your ball control was especially good'/'You need to be more aware of where the other players are, that's why your passing didn't work.' How this framing is done may, as we will see, have profound effects on children's confidence as thinkers and learners; the metaphor that has been used is *scaffolding*. Opportunities to stretch your capabilities a little bit and succeed, precise feedback, expression of confidence in the child to succeed if he or she tries, and encouragement to do as well or better next time can combine to produce someone who believes in his or her ability to be effective, and is right to believe this.

As well as providing feedback on events and actions, parents *model* and provide demonstrations of skills and actions. This is not always intentional. I once overheard my small daughter fiercely telling off her dolls in a horribly familiar voice – a far too exact imitation of my own. But often the parent does intend it, and often it is part of a joint activity. I learned about flower-arranging from my mother, about history from my father on Sunday afternoon walks, about clothes and pop music from my sister, about not scrubbing off your eye makeup from my oldest sister-in-law. In my turn, I've modelled things to my daughter. Up to a point, she imitated at least some of them. Imitation may seem a very human activity, but we will see that it is possible other animals do it – even, amazingly, ants.[8]

Parents *invite* participation in culture. We all know that children may inherit allegiance to a particular football team or enthusiasm for reading or habits of arguing from family members. Parents and others push children to play musical instruments or join the Boy Scouts or go to church or eat noodles rather than potatoes because of a cultural preference for the activity and a feeling that the child needs to take part in it to be a member of the culture or to gain or express advantages over others by being seen to be part of a prestigious group – perhaps not altruistically.

For a number of reasons, children may benefit from their parents' fostering the child's involvement in *productive activity*. As I will examine later, human beings seem to like to have their curiosity satisfied and to achieve a feeling of mastery as a result of having made a bit of an effort. The key idea is that there are positive results from getting engaged with a challenge and succeeding through your own efforts. The child develops a sense of agency, a sense of control, and a sense of success. If they've met the challenge with the approval and support of another person, that can lead to a sense of the benefits of working with other people. Children with a history of engaging with activities successfully and productively may feel such activities are enjoyable, rewarding, and manageable, and that they themselves are competent and in control.

Parents and children also go in for a lot of talk about each other. Parents support and encourage *discourse*, which is a means of sharing and enhancing understanding (and can be seen to be an effective basis for understanding other people). Language development proceeds well if child and parent do a lot of talking to each other in a normal conversational way (and a lot of listening to each other). As I'll describe, there are biological bases for language development, and there is genetic involvement, but the evidence is overwhelming that the ways that parents use frames determine many aspects of language competence and language use.

Parents act as a *memory* for the child, and this helps in the organisation of knowledge and in the fulfilment of plans and in the co-construction of family stories about who people are and what they're like and how they belong together. Parents are the archive for young children's memories, telling them things which happened before the child was old enough to remember them, reminding them of things they had forgotten, construct-ing a biographical narrative for them. 'When you were little, you used to. . .' can become a family story. My family has a story of how the toddler me was found banging on the door of the fridge and shouting 'meat', and this was my first word. I've told my daughter about how she was riding on her father's shoulders when they saw some dogs chasing around, and he said 'Look at the bow-wows', and she responded with her first word, 'wow'. There are event stories such as these, and stories about what we are like, and joint pretend stories, and family jokes.

The core is simply warm participation in socially and intellectually stimu-lating interactions, with adults showing reciprocity with children, being responsive to them, and providing emotional support, but also providing some structured, directed experiences with encouragement and praise. Pos-sibly, the child participant in such interaction derives an enhanced sense of being competent and effective as well as receiving good cognitive oppor-tunities and helpful interpretations and support from the adult; it is worth noting that maternal intrusiveness, being very directive and controlling, is associated with the child doing less well. (But this may be somewhat dif-ferent in other cultures – we could look at the case of Chinese parents' belief in making intensely high demands on their children to be the best ever.[9]) I will discuss how it does seem to be the case that if the parent–child interaction is characterized by positive emotional support, high cognitive stimulation, and low parental intrusiveness, the child is likely to do well in terms of both cognition and confidence, while the reverse of this pattern is associated with the child doing badly. Parenting and the environment of the home are the first bases of individuals' approaches to learning challenges and achievement.

To do all this framing for children really well is a gigantic task. It requires a great deal of adult sensitivity to what the child is feeling and doing, and a great deal of patience, as many, many, many repetitions of various frames will be required for all that the child has to learn. It isn't – it can't be – a one-way or an unchanging process. Parents do things for children, but chil-dren may have elicited the parental behaviour and will respond to it, and both partners build up a history of how to interact and what it means; their roles and functions are interdependent. In their partnership, both sides are causes of each other's behaviour. Their power levels may be asymmetrical, but it is by no means the case that parents have all the power and the child has none. Goodness knows the powerfulness of the child is obvious to most parents: oddly, it hasn't always been obvious to researchers!

Also, every parent–child relationship will change over time. Partly this is because any relationship will change as it develops a history, but also it is because the child is growing up and changing in skills, understandings, and needs. There is a lot of interesting science about this developmental change. This science helps to specify what children are going to be like right now, what they can and can't be expected to do, what they are very probably going to be like in a year or so. Part of what parents have to do is adjust their parenting to the child's changing skills and the child's changing world, accommodating these and anticipating them and maybe working towards expected goals. Part of what children have to do is help parents realise what adjustments and accommodations are needed, which parenting habits they have to give up. My daughter has trained me to say not 'Put your coat on before you go out' but 'I think you may have a coat in the spare bedroom, if you need one', for example.

Frames are about the detail of interaction between child and parent (or parent figure, teacher, mentor). I think they are vastly important. But we also have to remember that children have their own characteristics, inside their skin – genes, nerves, hormones, memories, habits, expectations – and they live within multiple social systems. These affect each other: your parents' employment affects how much they can be present in your family; whether they can supply the latest fashion in trainers, or whether you have to face the playground fashion competition in old trainers that never were the fashion; whether the family's life contains a lot of anxiety about making ends meet. And there are the gigantic culture-level circumstances or beliefs that shape the lives of everyone in that culture; for example how important schooling is for social mobility, how the society discriminates between males and females, the degree to which there is economic inequality. Later we'll see how these different systems fit together in children's development. Expect, please, to see many physiological and psychological systems coexisting inside and beyond the child's skin.

So this book is about understanding the science that helps us understand parents and children, which helps us provide good conditions for children to grow up in. I'm going to begin with a brief discussion of why science is a good thing in this context and how it differs from the accumulated practical experience of professionals (one basis of parenting books like Gina Ford's oeuvre or of Super Nanny's prescriptions) or personal experience (the basis of different types of books about parenting, for example Amy Chua's *Battle Hymn of the Tiger Mother* or Julie Myerson's *The Lost Child*, both memoirs, or Sarah Moss's bleak and very funny novel *Nightwaking*, or Karen Joy Fowler's *We Are All Completely Beside Ourselves*[10]). Then I get into the science, discipline by discipline. These chapters will necessarily include some research that may seem not to be about children, but bear with me, as ultimately I will show you that it is relevant.

2

SCIENCE'S STORIES

In which we have a look at different ways of knowing

Science has rules for what count as good stories – rules which mean that scientific wisdom genuinely improves over time. Science is a continual process of questioning, data-seeking, and struggling to clarify and refine the current answers. It is not easy. It may not be what we naturally tend to do. We can be very good at something without doing it scientifically or using the scientific work of others. But what science has achieved is extraordinary. So I want to point out some of the advantages of science and some of the different ways of doing it. I begin with two points made half a century apart that say effectively the same thing. First, the psychotherapist and personality theorist Carl Rogers:[11]

> Scientific research needs to be seen for what it truly is; a way of preventing me from deceiving myself in regard to my creatively formed subjective hunches which have developed out of the relationship between me and my material.

More recently, the science writer and epidemiologist Ben Goldacre:[12]

> When it comes to thinking about the world around you, you have a range of tools available. Intuitions are valuable for all kinds of things, especially in the social domain. . . . But for mathematical issues, or assessing causal relationships, intuitions are often completely wrong, because they rely on

shortcuts which have arisen as handy ways to solve complex cognitive problems rapidly, but at a cost of inaccuracies, misfires and oversensitivity.

It's not safe to let our intuitions and prejudices run unchecked and unexamined: it's in our interest to challenge these flaws in reasoning wherever we can, and the methods of science and statistics grew up specifically in opposition to these flaws. Their thoughtful application is our best weapon against these pitfalls, and the challenge, perhaps, is to work out what tools to use where.

The sort of science I am including in this book is concerned with checking its hunches, refining its observations, and continually testing its assertions. It involves commitment to a set of four values: objectivity, generalisation, prediction, and replication. I'm going to say a little about each of these in preparation for the 'science inside the child' that follows.

First, good science tries to ensure that what is said is, if not fully objective, at least not heavily dependent on the idiosyncrasies or the actions of the researcher. It is not good scientific practice to ignore the possibility that you have influenced the outcomes. It is not good scientific practice to assert something but not provide evidence for your assertion. It is probably impossible to be completely objective once you get into studying something emotionally important (such as children), but good science strives to constrain how our subjective values and assumptions might have influenced what we see and what we say. The ideal is that there should be minimal influence of the observer/researcher on the results, and the ways in which the results might have been influenced should be conscientiously examined. As Rogers and Goldacre say, you need to check your hunches, even if they are the result of a lot of wisdom and experience, even if they work. And you need to allow others to check on your hunches, hence science's emphasis on activities such as publishing results, sharing data, and peer review.

The second value, generalisation, places a priority on trying to find out what is true of others beyond the small set of cases you are focussing on. A really deep understanding of an individual is a precious thing, and it may be exactly what we need when dealing with that individual. But it is obvious that we (like most other animals) tend to generalise from our present knowledge; it would be very inefficient not to. Thus, if we prioritise going for generalisable knowledge – not just the particular individual boy Joe, but boys in general, or mammals in general, or whatever – we make our tendency to generalise more explicit and testable than if we are only interested in a particular case. Again, we check on our intuitions and prejudices. And we can examine what we base our generalisation on, which might be quite interesting in itself.

In my list, the third value of science was prediction. Generally, scientists want to be able to predict future results. A one-off may be very interesting, but most scientists want to know if the one-off will still be true for the next case you look at. Again, this tendency to predict is something we all casually do when we generalise from what we 'know' and build up expectations of whether it will continue to be like that. We need to do this because if we were continually faced with unpredictable events, we would not be able to function. It leads to great economies of effort if we remember what sort of food we have liked and do not have to taste every single food item as if for the first time. It would be dangerous if we had not learned what is likely to happen when traffic lights change. Yes, we may miss out if we are unwilling to go beyond what we already know and try something unpredictable – it was only *after* I had tried wasabi, mastic, and tripe (not simultaneously!) that I knew for certain that I would rather not eat two of the three ever again but the remaining one was delicious. But just as we inevitably generalise we inevitably predict, and we might as well recognise that and do it properly.

Using prediction as a specific tool also opens up the possibility of developing ways of doing it with greater and greater precision. All the way from betting on future events, such as horse races, to anticipating what might help our toddler not wake us up in the night, if we have more information and a clearer analysis of what is relevant that will help us predict how to get the results we want just a little more often. Science has developed systematic ways of making predictions and testing how good they have been. In particular, assessing how reliable our predictions are is one of the basic functions of statistical analyses. Things do happen by chance, and a lot of statistical analysis is about working out how likely it is that something did not happen by chance but was a really significant event that tells us something reliable. This helps counterbalance our intuitions.

Science emphasises clarity and replication. A scientific study or a scientific theory must be expressed as clearly as possible so that it can be examined and replicated by other researchers. It will have little credibility if it is not clear or if other scientists cannot observe the same phenomena or get the same results. A scientific study can use various means of expression, but it often involves measurement, or at the very least counting, and precision is more important than the gist or the broad sweep. It has to deal with different types of description and explanation, for example coordinating levels or modifying one level in the light of another. Science is demanding rather than casual, invigorating rather than relaxing, produces new questions rather than certainties.

Especially in the social sciences, there is a lot of debate about how you should do science and about whether what scientists really do actually fits how they 'should' be doing it. I am not going to address the issues raised in these debates. But I am going to write a little about Karl Popper's view of what good science is[13] in general, and then about some of the ways of doing Popperian science that are typical of the different research traditions that I want to discuss in detail.

Popperian science involves a repeated cycle of having a theory, developing a prediction, forming a precise hypothesis, testing the hypothesis, examining the results of the test, and adjusting the theory accordingly. What I see as an especially strong point for Popper is that 'testing the hypothesis' always involves looking extra hard for evidence that could falsify it. One justification for this is logical. If our hypothesis is the classic 'all swans are white', then seeing another white swan tends to support our hypothesis, but it is really only just another example of something we expected anyhow. We cannot tell whether all swans really are white, or merely that all the swans we have seen so far or have heard about are white. Our generalisation that all swans are white is certainly more robust if we have seen a hundred or a thousand white swans than if we have only seen two, so we will be interested in repeating our experiments and observations to see if the same thing happens again. If other people find the same thing happening again, then that adds conviction because it would help to rule out the possibility that we personally are getting it wrong in some way. But even repeated confirmations cannot give us complete certainty for ever and ever. On the other hand, seeing a single pink or blue or black or tartan swan instantly *disproves* our hypothesis that all swans are white. If even one swan is a different colour, it is not true that all swans are white, though it may still be true that most swans are white or that all the swans I have ever seen with my own eyes are white.

Having found negative evidence which does not fit our hypothesis, we need to do some further thinking and investigation. Some negative instances can be set aside – if the pink swan was actually a flamingo, for example, it is not relevant to the question of the colour of swans. Some might be the result of poor observation conditions – we saw our swan at sunset and its feathers looked pink in the sunset light, but they are actually white. But ultimately, if negative instances that we cannot set aside build up in number, then we really ought to reject our hypothesis and modify our theory. Then the cycle goes round again. We develop a new theory, make a new prediction, design a new test, gather new data, consider the implications of our data for our theory, revise the theory, and so forth. We never reach complete certainty, *proof*, that our theory is right, but we can *disprove* and discard theories, and we can retain and *improve* theories, and we can get to a position where a theory can be accepted not as proved but as quite a good approximation of the truth, even as 'good enough' for everyday action, because it works pretty well and better than any other competing theory.

This leaves room for some bright spark to come along and improve on our theory. Our observations and the results of our experiments always need to be regarded as imperfect. We have to cope with measurement error, with definition problems, with ambiguities. Popperian science carries with it a procedural checklist:

- Consider the implications of your results for your theory.
- Carefully consider possible sources of error.
- Acknowledge the limitations of your study.
- Compare your findings with other studies' findings.
- Do not overinterpret your findings.
- Try to replicate.
- Don't resist modifying or even abandoning your theory if there is a lot of evidence against it.

In short, bear in mind what Oliver Cromwell said to his Scottish allies when they were contemplating changing to the other side in the Civil War of the 1640s: 'I beseech you, in the bowels of Christ, think it possible that you may be mistaken.' This asking 'am I possibly mistaken?' is essential when war is a possible outcome, but even in peaceful scientific activity – and in childrearing – this is excellent advice.

Everything I have said so far applies to all branches of science. But there are various different ways of seeking good scientific data, and they crop up in different amounts in different disciplines. Careful systematic observation and recording is the basis of all science. Experiments where a few measures of interest are systematically controlled and manipulated (for example, do changes in how often parents read to children fit with improvements in children's vocabulary?) will tell us something. Examination of possible combinations of factors as they occur (for example, if parental reading is associated with children's vocabulary, is this still the case if you allow for how much parents and children talk to each other?) helps sort out the relative importance of different factors, and how they fit together in the real and complex world. Whether you get the same pattern under a slightly different set of circumstances is another important thing to look at. My different scientific disciplines use all these in different quantities. There can be tensions between them because of differences in methods. For example epidemiology uses very large samples – thousands of cases – to detect patterns across individuals who differ in real-life experiences, and it can be looked down on by experimental endocrinologists who rely on precise lab measurements. The Human Genome Project sequenced the genome (that is the sequence of genes across all our chromosomes) of a very small number of individuals and is having to retreat from its proclamation that the human genome was 'mapped' as further individuals are added to the data (and differences in what's on the map turn up). The number of brains looked at in any single neuroscience study is generally quite small. And no measurement technique is perfect for everything you might want it to do. Science is expensive, and scientists have to make careers, and what is researched and what is published are sometimes influenced by financial considerations[14] to the detriment of the science itself. There are sometimes bitter arguments about what issues like this do to the trustworthiness of the findings, and it's not always easy to find solutions.

The solutions I have used are these. I've done my best to find research studies systematically, usually using online databases. I've read them with a constant attention to quality control: do the methods, the samples, and the analyses look sound? How does this set of findings fit, or not, with other studies? Are the findings in proportion to the quality of the study? Has the research been published in high quality journals using systematic peer review? There are sometimes systematic reviews (meta-analyses) of available studies which do this sort of quality control review, and they have always been a useful first step, but I've generally gone back to the original studies, too.

There is some bias in this. My personal tolerance for reading poor quality work is low; papers which were grandiose or stuffed with jargon to an unnecessary degree were read irritably and mostly quickly discarded. Studies by researchers who I respect for a sustained contribution to the field probably got read more carefully. But all of my examples are of recent science that clarifies our views of childhood. The studies vary in scale and they vary in method. They vary in the amount of evidence that there is for them (and against them). They vary in whether they apply to everyone all the time or whether they are more local and individual. They vary in how closely they apply to practice. But all of them do theory building and theory testing via observation, measurement, and patient replication. Every one of them earns its place here because of its intrinsic interest. Every one of them looks, right now, like a contribution to knowing the truth, but for every one of them, future truth may look slightly or even considerably different.

So, this is not a how-to book about parenting. (If anything, it should undermine any parenting book that is rigid and doctrinaire about what you 'should' do or individuals who smugly proclaim that their experiences with their own children shows that they know it all.) It is a celebration of science about children (and about parenting). And for every theory, your child may be the exception or may conform to a theory which is not the one that you prefer. Part of the delightfulness of children is how often they can surprise you. What they do and what they are can be far more interesting (and impressive) than you expected. My experience, and my hope, is that knowing more about the science enhances this sense of wonder more than it gets in the way of it.

3

EVOLUTION

In which we pootle around in deep time and consider how evolution and children fit together

I am going to begin by teasing out the relevance to child development of evolutionary theory. Charles Darwin's theory of evolution by natural selection is one of the biggest scientific theories there has ever been. To pick up a phrase from Richard Dawkins, this is 'the greatest show on earth'.[15] It is a brilliant and insightful explanation of life, and it is a fascinating example of how science works. It has also been the object of attacks by nonscientists, which very vividly illustrates how important it is for nonscientists to develop a better understanding of science. This chapter describes some of what we need to know about evolution as it applies to the development of children.

'Adaptation' and 'evolution' had become words to think about by the early 1800s. Darwin picked them up and used them, but he made two gigantic contributions. As an exuberant young man, he had the adventure of his life employed as a scientific observer sailing around South America.[16] He saw geological formations, animals, and plants unfamiliar to Europeans and creatures, which differed from place to place but were clearly related to each other, suggesting they descended from a common ancestor. From this he developed the idea that the demands of the environment naturally 'selected' individuals that could meet these challenges. Individuals whose characteristics did not fit the demands of the environment had fewer offspring, and therefore, over successive generations, they had fewer and fewer descendants until their lineage dwindled away; they were selected against. Individuals who were well fitted to the demands of the environment had more descendants, and gradually the population in that environment would contain mainly individuals who had inherited the adaptive characteristics of the well-adapted ancestor. In geographically separate areas, as in the Galapagos Islands, the successful descendant finches or tortoises on one island might differ so much from the descendant finches or tortoises of another island that they would no longer be able to breed together, and thus would technically be separate species. This was the origin of species.

Back in England after his voyage, Darwin spent a couple of decades working out his theory. He took a long time over it, partly because his health was very poor after the voyage and his youthful exuberance declined, partly because of the second gigantic contribution he modelled for science. He realised the controversy that would be produced by his theory, which contradicted many of the received beliefs of Victorian England, and he was very sensitive to the probability that undermining established beliefs would cause feelings of distress and hostility to many in his audience. To ensure that his theory could not be easily dismissed, he spent decades collecting evidence from every possible source, including both observations and experiments extending over geology, botany, and animal breeding, to name but a few. This example of patient, careful, systematic, and insightful research, carefully presented so as to answer the objections of critics even before the critics had formulated them, is exactly how good science should be done.

The essence of the Darwinian account of evolution is that, for about the last 4 billion years, individual organisms have had slightly different characteristics from each other. Some of these variations they have inherited from their parents (and we now know that genes have the central role in this), others may just have occurred by chance (genes may still be the means of inheritance), and yet others may have been acquired after birth (in which case genes are very much less involved, as we shall see). None of the genetically based differences was *intentionally* formed during evolution. Some characteristics just happen to fit the environment in which you have to live, and individuals who have them tend to survive and flourish and have better reproductive success. Over many millennia, the fit of differences in individuals with differences in environmental demands has led to the diversification of forms of life from a remote original life form into a multiplicity of different forms, each with ancestors who have reproduced successfully in environments whose particular demands have made particular variations adaptive.[17] Some diversification has led to dead ends where adaptation of organism to environment was impossible and the lineage died out. Some lineages have maintained the same characteristics for ages and ages because they fitted their environments really well and did not need to change in order to adapt. Other lineages have undergone comparatively

Figure 3.1 Charles Darwin and his son William Erasmus Darwin

rapid or radical change. The point is not progress towards a 'higher form' or even towards 'better adaptation', but a diversification into 'endless forms most beautiful and most wonderful', as stated in the lovely phrase Darwin wrote at the end of *The Origin of Species*.

This appears to be a universal process that has applied to all living creatures. There is brilliant and extensive evidence[18] of how it happened, even if there are debates about detail, and there is no strong alternative theory.

Once we accept that evolution is the best theory of the development of life on earth that we have, certain consequences follow. These consequences are for two sorts of development: the development of species, or *phylogeny*, and the development of individuals over their lives, or *ontogeny*.

Once we agree with the idea that humans and other species are descended in different lineages from common ancestors (phylogeny), it makes sense to look carefully at the ways in which we and other species are similar and different. If we find similarities in our bodies or our genes or our brains or our behaviour, these may work in similar ways in ourselves and in other animals, and this may justify comparing ourselves with them. Quite a lot of the genetics, the endocrinology, and the neuroscience that I'm going to present to you comes from animal studies. I'm going to take it as incontrovertible that this angle of investigation is very important and that we can usefully study other species in order to understand ourselves. However, it is also clear that we will need to think carefully about what else might apply when we look at humans using animal models.

A number of characteristics seem to make humans different from other species,[19] even from species such as chimpanzees, who are close relatives (we had a common ancestor around 6 million years ago). Some of these are very relevant to infancy and childhood, and I will discuss them later, for example the trajectory of brain development, the timing of birth, being able to produce speech sounds, being able to digest cows' milk way beyond infancy, and believing that we and other people have minds and mental states such as beliefs and desires. Some may be less obviously relevant to children's development: walking on two feet, hyperactivity of the T-cells in our immune system, extra-long and muscular thumbs, being able to keep running for a long time instead of just in short sprints. We will see that there are some very interesting things going on here in our developmental history.

So what do we know about the phylogeny of humans,[20] especially of child humans? The database of fossils that tells us about the anatomical evolution of humans is growing all the time, but our direct evidence of the very early young humans and prehumans is still sparse. There are, famously, fossilised footprints[21] which look as though they were made by individuals with small feet (possibly young) walking with larger (presumably older) ones and in less straight lines, suggesting that very early human young frisked about, much like contemporary children, while their parents plodded onwards. There are a few fossil skulls, mainly incomplete, which may allow estimates of brain size or even brain structure, and a small proportion of these probably belonged to immature individuals. The way bones fit together may tell us about how our ancestors moved, or how they could have held things, or the size of baby they could have given birth to. Bone scraps, shells, other food debris, and signs of fires suggest what they ate and, consequently, something about the amount of time they would have had to spend finding food. From times later on, there begin to be artefacts such as tools or items, such as cut or scraped bones, on which tools have been used. Eventually, there is art and religion and written material. Very occasionally, these can be interpreted as related to children's lives.

The scantiness of the evidence leads to very varied estimates of how particular behaviours evolved. For example,[22] the emergence of language has been put at 2 million years ago, in homo habilis, or perhaps only 100,000 years ago, when the first symbolic artefacts were (probably) made. New discoveries often push back the date at which there is evidence of behaviour. An archaeological analysis[23] of food residues in fragments of pottery made 6,000 to 7,000 years ago in what is now Libya showed residues of cows' milk in the pots. That the early humans who had made the pots had put milk in them strongly implies that they had begun to domesticate cattle and that they thought the milk worth keeping, presumably because they found it nutritious. This is evidence of very early agriculture and food storage.

It is also evidence of an environmental selection process which is very recent in evolutionary terms. There is no doubt that the availability of milk from domesticated cattle would have helped the very young; your babies might be more likely to survive and grow up strong with this nutritious food. But the genes that allow you to digest milk (or more precisely lactose) switch off after infancy in many humans, and then they have difficulty digesting milk (lactose intolerance). Dairy farming would be of more direct benefit to an adult population if those adults could tolerate lactose and get nutritional benefits from milk. The gene whose effects allow us to digest lactose is now more common in European and African populations with a history of dairy farming than in East Asian populations that have never made much use of cows for milk. The evidence suggests that taking to dairy farming made the presence or absence of the gene much more relevant to successful digestion and development: if you had it, you could continue to enjoy the nutritional advantages of cows' milk throughout your life; if you didn't have it, you couldn't, and you were restricted to fermented milk products such as yoghurt and cheese. Lactose tolerance or intolerance wouldn't matter for reproductive success if there was no supply of cows' milk to consume. The cultural adoption of dairy farming would have had implications for diet and, therefore, for digestion and health, and would have been a selective pressure for the evolution of lactose tolerance.

Arguably, other cultural adoptions would have changed the environment and selective pressures on individuals, and hence the course of evolution.

Several of the human-specific changes between ourselves and other great apes are related to the genes involved in innate immunity to infection and pathogens.[24] Increased immunity is largely a good thing, but it does increase the risk of autoimmune disorders when the body reacts to its own functioning as if it was being attacked (allergies would be an example). It's been argued that stronger immune system responses were an advantage because early humans lived on scavenging more, made more contacts with unrelated groups, and began to domesticate animals, all of which would increase contact with other people's germs (or animals' germs).

Another example is the invention of cooking, which made many foods more nutritious, less likely to spoil, and easier to chew. This changed our digestion, our food-seeking habits, and the musculature of our jaws—changes to be seen in our bodies to this day. Arguably, it enabled us to have large, energy-expensive, creative brains, rather than being the sort of animal that has to spend hours every day lying around passively digesting its last meal. If this is the case, it would have changed us culturally: we had more time for social and technological activity and bigger brains to recognise individuals in our social group and interpret and imitate their behaviour. Our need for containers to carry things in would have increased if we were storing and cooking food, and no doubt having stores of food affected our food sharing, too. Some writers argue that being able to carry stuff (including small children) was one of the reasons why our ancestors changed from moving on four legs to being bipedal.

Just as a lot about our physical nature can be traced back well before the first species of *homo* (see later sections on neuroscience, cortisol, embryology, and genetics), so can a lot of our psychology; basic emotional states, some ways of learning, working memory,[25] nonverbal communication, and face recognition are some of the obvious examples. Parallels to how humans have emotions, learn, remember, and so forth can be seen in other species. But a lot of thinking about evolution tends to concentrate on the more recent years – the around 6 million years since our lineage separated off from the lineage that has led to modern chimpanzees, or the even shorter period between us and early humans. When they consider the possible psychological adaptations of early human parents and children, quite a lot of evolutionary psychologists have relied heavily on evidence from present-day hunter-gatherers, who they assume to be living lives not very different from the early humans living in the Pleistocene period, that is, they assume that the hunter-gatherers' present-day lives show us what their ancestors' lives were like thousands of years ago. It's not just evolutionary psychologists who are willing to assume that there has been no significant change over a very long period of history. Some advice books also present the parenting practices of hunter-gatherers as the 'natural' and desirable way to bring up babies and young children – skin-to-skin contact, feeding on demand, co-sleeping, and so forth.

There is some good in this, but there is also a lot that is problematic about this approach. If we were looking for the earliest ancestor common to us and to the other species who also fear, love, learn, remember, and so forth, we would have go back far beyond the earliest human, probably back to or beyond the earliest mammals. Maybe not back the full 4 billion years of life on Earth, but nearer that length of time than the less than 2 million years that there have been creatures we are now prepared to label as homo something-or-other. If we concentrate on tracing our ancestors who lived during the Pleistocene, we might miss examining which 'human' character-istics might be seen in our ancestors from before there were humans.

A second set of problems stems from the assumption that evolutionary changes have happened for us and our lineage, living as we do in predomi-nantly urban, literate, globalized, and rapidly changing societies. But things did not change much over the same period of time for the hunter-gatherers; we tend to believe that almost everything about them is pretty much the same as life was for their remote ancestors. This can result in romanticising them and their lives or in disparaging them as something that 'we' have moved beyond – both intellectual and moral mistakes. We simply do not know how to what extent the assumption of stability in other people's life-styles is true, and we can't know, given that there is usually little in the way of historical record and not much that is archaeological.

A further problem is thinking of the EEA as a single typical environment. Commonly it seems to be thought of as resembling the environments lived in now by hunter-gatherer groups like the Kung San or the Efe in southern or central Africa. I have read claims that the theoretical EEA (environment of evolutionary adaptedness) is a 'statistical average' of contemporary hunter-gatherer environments. But that makes no sense unless you explain what exactly you have 'averaged', and how you did it; and I suspect not much sense even then. The Pleistocene period lasted for 2 million years or so, and the climate did not remain unchanged (indeed changes in climate may have been associated with changes in selection pressures and hence in what were useful characteristics to have). Early hominins lived as hunter-gatherers in a range of different ecologies – dry savannahs, denser forests, seashores, and riversides – and in climates that were tropical, subtropical, and even quite cold, such as on the seacoast of what is now South Africa. Food resources and needs for shelter and protection from predators would have varied enormously.

Selection pressures could not have been constant over the whole period and the vast geographical area. And adaptations need not be the same everywhere and every time, either. For example we've evolved or invented many ways to cope with a wide range of environmental demands – some people's ancestors lived in hot and desiccated deserts; some of mine lived on isolated islands in the bleak wet North Atlantic; I live now in a densely populated city. The firmest generalisations we can make about the nature of human functioning during the EEA are probably that it was an advantage to be adaptable, to be able to change even when you are well adapted to your current circumstances; that social groups were generally small, and their members knew each other; and that children depended on their parents and parents looked after their children. Much of this we share with other related species.

It seems to me that it is also wrong to concentrate on how some piece of psychological functioning was adaptive in the EEA as if that is all that needs to be said about why it occurs now. Attachment between infant and parent, or acquiring language to communicate with other people, might well have been advantageous in the EEA. It could be true that they are indeed much the same and advantageous in the same ways now. Or they might be subtly different, having responded to selection pressures over the many millennia since they first emerged. If adaptability itself was selected for because individuals had to cope with variation in the environments they lived in, an adaptation now might not be quite the same as an adaptation then. Adaptations might have been selected for originally because they gave a reproductive advantage in a particular way, but they persisted for some different reason – because they gave some different advantage, for example, or because they can combine with other adaptations to create a new massive advantage.

A good example is reading and writing. We now expect all children to learn to read and write, and we see it as a problem if they can't, but historically this is very new. For a few thousand years, a minority of people have become literate in many societies, but there is little evidence that those who were literate achieved social advantage and left more descendants than those who were not. There were other ways of reaching the social heights or having lots of descendants. The literate elite might even be expected not to have descendants, for example if they were members of a celibate class of priests. All in all, literacy skills are probably not an evolved package as such.

However, literacy skills depend on abilities to see, to hear, to coordinate movements, to speak, and to remember, and these abilities are themselves adaptations dating very much earlier in the development of the species. Brought together, this set of abilities results in capabilities and behaviour that have transformed our cognition, our social functioning, and our world. Because we can read and write, we become very practiced at fine visual discriminations at a particular range of distance from our eyes. Because we can read and write, we store information in written form and make less use of other ways to remember it. Because we can read and write, we can make precise records of who owns how much of what and tax them on their possessions. Because we can read and write, we can know about the distant stars, the extinct dinosaurs, and the Higgs Boson (and things that have never existed, such as fairies, dragons, and interplanetary travel). We are born with some simple adaptations and abilities and with the crucial adaptation of an ability to learn, but when we apply these to the tasks of learning to read and write, we are engaging with a set of new adaptations, not at all what the adaptations were first advantageous for. The ways in which something is adaptive now need not necessarily be the same as the ways it was adaptive earlier. The same is true of more recent technological inventions, such as using the Internet, and here we have not even begun to understand what new skills we might be using (and what we are not using) and what the consequences might be.

It is also very evident that many animals, and in particular human beings, learn stuff (facts and behaviours) during their lifetimes. Could that learning be passed on to their descendants and become something they no longer needed to learn? The pre-Darwin evolutionary theory of Jean-Baptiste Lamarck famously proposed that descendants could inherit characteristics that their ancestors had acquired during their lifetimes – that an ancestral giraffe had elongated its neck by stretching for leaves high on the tree and then its babies were born with elongated necks, or an ancestral blacksmith had developed substantial arm muscles by bashing out horseshoes in the forge and the blacksmith's sons and grandsons inherited big biceps. This theory does not fit what we now know about the mechanisms of inheritance; as I will discuss in the chapter about genes, we inherit exactly the genetic material that our parents were born with, apart from some errors in copying and some mutations. What the ancestral blacksmith had was genes which gave him the potential to develop hefty arm muscles, and his descendants will have inherited the same potential, not the arm muscles themselves. However, recent developments in epigenetics do suggest that experience may affect the *expression* of your genes. Maybe we have experiences which bias what our descendants will do through developmental mechanisms.

A linked question is, do we have instincts? Or is each generation born without any of the learning that helped the ancestors to survive, a *tabula rasa* with no inherited knowledge at all?

Evidence from animals such as birds, bees, and caterpillars, as well as mammals and primates, strongly suggested that many animals are born with strong tendencies to behave in particular ways, sometimes very complicated ways. Darwin saw these 'instincts' as susceptible to natural selection in the same way as physical structures. Working out whether instincts were categorically different from learning took another century; the answer was that typically instinct and learning were tightly entwined in the development of the individual. The complex behaviour that makes up an impressive 'instinct' is often built up from much simpler behaviours, and the production and coordination of these components tends to be the result of practice during development. For example,[26] a herring gull chick gets food from its parents by pecking at the bright red spot on the parents' beaks. The chick pecks at the beak, then grasps it and strokes it downwards. After a while, the parent regurgitates food that the chick eats. This is complex instinctive behaviour; the parent gull and the gull chick do it successfully from the very first time. But practice improves the accuracy with which the chick pecks the beak; accuracy is also improved if the novice chick has an opportunity to observe a more experienced one. I hope this reminds you, as it does me, of feeding one's own baby. The newborn baby has an instinct to suckle, but its way of suckling adapts to the mother, and to its own needs, as time goes by. It gets easier for the parent to get the spoonful of food into the baby's mouth as the baby opens wide and adjusts to the incoming angle of the spoon – until the baby learns to swipe it out of the parent's hand, refuse to eat, play at smearing rather than eating, and so on. So far as I know, baby gulls don't deliberately disrupt the efficiency of the process – but then they probably have less indulgent parents.

Some things we may be preset to learn more easily than others. In another classic piece of work, it was shown that laboratory rats could learn to associate a new food with a mild electric shock and thus to avoid it ever after, but typically it took several trials. Learning to associate a new food with being sick was learned in one trial, so one could avoid ever eating the sick-making food again. Using taste to show us the edibility of food seems to be something programmed in to our behaviour (and I present some evidence about this in humans later), but we all know we can modify our views on what food tastes good. There is some evidence from epidemiological studies that early food experiences are associated with food preferences later in life; I will present this later.

Human babies seem to have a strong preference for looking at faces, built on preferences for symmetry, light/dark contrast, and eye-like patterns. This leads them to gaze at their parents with apparent devotion – which leads the parent to gaze back in an equally besotted way – and that leads to all sorts of benefits for emotional, social, and cognitive functioning. The tendency to engage in the simple behaviours may be instinctive and capable of being inherited; the fine-tuning, the coordination, the person specificity, and the meaning are all influenced by learning. The new animal is not a *tabula rasa*, but it does start off with some constraints and predilections in what it can learn. Psychologists have demonstrated what some of these are for humans, and I'll come back to them later.

Evolutionary theory was invented to explain *phylogeny*, the development of species, but it can help us understand *ontogeny*, the development of the individual through the lifespan. Evolutionary theory got into the study of child development in a variety of different ways. First, it became obvious that child development could be studied in a systematic, careful way; childhood would now be of interest to professional scientists, not only to mothers and nurses. Darwin (who was an admirable father) made observations[27] of his sons and daughters, a 'natural history of babies' which tried to provide more precise descriptions of development, and more exact ages, than previous work. In these writings there are speculations about how and when the babies developed their various skills, consideration of how his children differed from each other, debate about what was instinctive and what was learned, and a lot of paternal pride and delight. His books, his notes, and his letters all show that he thought that children's development was interesting in itself, that it reflected evolutionary factors, and that studies of evolution and of child development could complement each other.

Second, if evolution worked through differences in reproductive success, might behaviours and characteristics related to childhood be determining the degree of such success? Might what children are like influence their chances of growing up to have children themselves? Might parents be 'programmed' in some way to treat children in ways that facilitated their fitness? Might the social structures you use have evolved to support your children growing to reproductive maturity? Are there points in the life cycle when individuals are selected by evolutionary pressures more than at other times? What (exactly) is the balance between nature and nurture in development and in reproductive success? Has child development itself evolved, and, specifically, how does it compare in humans and in other species? If humans evolved over millennia, has childhood changed over that time? Do we have characteristics or expectations that suited our species earlier in evolution but are less adaptive now?

There has been a powerful idea, dating back to the late nineteenth century (though not Darwin's idea), that ontogeny recapitulates phylogeny, that the developing child goes through successive stages of resembling earlier ancestor species. This idea of *recapitulation* is one that we have to be cautious about. The development of humans does resemble the development of other species, and we now know that genetic control of development through an individual's lifespan is based on genetic mechanisms that are essentially highly similar across all living creatures. In the earliest stages of development, human embryos do look very much like embryonic fish, monkeys, or apes. But to see humans early on in their development being like *adult* fish or monkeys – to suggest that human infants are recapitulating the ancestral fish when they enjoy splashing in the bath, or recapitulating the ancestral monkey when they climb trees or rush round shouting – is a mistake. Nor are they recapitulating hunter-gatherer societies when they pick blackberries in hedgerows or scrump apples from the neighbours' orchards or shoplift from neighbourhood shops, or early capitalism when they barter and swap collectable objects. The apparently similar development of young individuals of different species up to and after birth is because they share a common ancestor and are still using ancestral genes to control development (more about this later). This may well have led to similarities in behaviours and bodies, for example similarly wired-up brains (more about this later too), but the different species have diverged and are not recapitulating each other's adult states.

Another problem for recapitulation theory is that it picked up the idea that evolution led to progress, that we were 'better' in important ways than our ancestors or the species we had diverged from. You probably have seen the picturing of the evolution of man from a stooped, shaggy, and unimpressive ape-like character to an upstanding Caucasoid young male, almost complete with briefcase, bowler hat, and furled umbrella. The idea of progress implied that evolutionary development added on further developments to what already occurred; for example human development went 'beyond' the development of other primates to add on achievements that the other primates were never going to reach. This model also often implied that the earlier stages of development, which we shared with other animals, were compressed and accelerated in us to give us room for our more advanced stages. The idea would be that we started off like apes or primitive humans and grew out of their less adequate characteristics. This model fitted in nicely, of course, with our long-standing (and regrettable) tradition of regarding ourselves as better than other animals, or even as totally different from them. It also fitted in with a view of children as needing to grow up and get beyond their childish ways; when St Paul said 'when I was a child I saw like a child, I thought like a child, but now I am a man I have put away childish things', he saw this as an improvement, not something to be regretted.

More recently, an opposite theory of how evolution has changed our rate of development has been proposed. This idea is that one of the most important things about our evolution is change in the timing of human development, so that we are born more immature, reach maturity relatively late, and retain the characteristics of juveniles for much longer. This holding on to the characteristics individuals had when they were younger gives the theory its name: *neoteny*.[28] It's a debated concept in biology, but at the very least it looks as though something quite profound has happened to our development (we're beginning to understand about the genes that control the developmental timetable, as I discuss later). Some aspects of our development certainly look like neoteny. Compared with other animals, we retain infant-like faces, with big round eyes and jaws that do not protrude as other apes' jaws do and dogs' snouts do; we have large heads for our body size, long legs for our bodies, and long-continuing brain growth; we are slow to reach sexual maturity and be able to reproduce ourselves. Neoteny, and especially prolonged brain growth, may have allowed relative overdevelopment of some characteristics, so that for example we can spend longer using our still-developing brains to learn, with more knowledge and more flexibility in our behaviour as a result. Neoteny goes along with characteristics such as play and long-lasting relationships with our parents and siblings (attachment), which would also shift our development into new evolutionary paths. It allows more time for socialisation by our parents and others. But not all our development is neotenous:[29] our toe bones are underdeveloped compared with apes, and we cannot use our toes so effectively to climb trees or pick up objects, while our foot bones are overdeveloped, which may make flat-footed walking on only two legs easier for us than it is for other primates.

So far as child development is concerned, whatever biological ways of thinking about our rate of development we go for, I think there are some important points. First, our bodies are changing according to a preset timetable programmed by evolution, and we just have to live with this, however much we might want our baby to give up nappies, or our toddler to lose interest in rushing about incessantly, or our teenager to be able to get up before lunchtime. We might be able to make some difference to the speed of development, but it's not completely within our control. Second, letting things go at their own pace may be beneficial because postponing maturity and its demands gives you more scope for learning (and for fun). You can get frustrated at your preschool children's insistence on getting from place to place very slowly because they stop to examine everything that catches their eyes en route, or you can relax, allow the journey as much time as it needs, and have lots of conversations about whether that's a friendly dog, or where the creepy-crawly lives, or why it is not a good idea to try to pick up dropped cigarette ends or step in the dog poo. Third, it is silly to blame an individual at an early stage of development for being different from the later stage. In order to get to be a well-adapted butterfly, you have to be a well-enough adapted caterpillar for as long as it takes, though I agree it is hard to realise this with teenagers' behaviours.

Evolution can be thought of as having structured the way the life of the species is organised. Different species differ in how fast and how large individuals grow, in how long they live, and in how their lifespans are divided into a prereproductive phase, a reproductive phase, and a postreproductive phase. We humans have a long period prereproduction and a long period after it for modern females, which enables a lot of grandparenting. There's some possibility that social stresses speed this process up in ways we disapprove of – teenage pregnancies, for example, are associated with socially hostile environments.[30]

Species also differ in how many offspring individuals are likely to have and how the parents provide for their young. All of this variation has evolved: it has a species history and it is affected by the demands and constraints of the environment. In some species (for example dandelions or frogs), individuals are small at birth and throughout life, grow quickly to reproductive maturity, have many offspring per litter, do not invest much parental care in these offspring, and die young. This r-selection reproductive strategy produces a large number for the next generation rapidly, and it can result in rapid population growth. If the environment is hostile and full of risks, for example if there is a large number of predators, then r-selection may be effective in keeping the individual's bloodline going. A strategy of 'live fast, live small, die young' is relatively cheap for the individual and may produce a good number of descendants by spreading lots of offspring around; at least some of them may survive to reproduce themselves, even if the majority do not get that far. At the other extreme there is K-selection; some species are large at birth and grow to a large adult size, reach reproductive maturity slowly, have few offspring per litter, invest a lot of parental care in these offspring, and die at an older age. This reproductive strategy may work best in environments where resources are not unlimited but their availability is predictable and where mortality rates are low.

There may be a trade-off between different possibilities, for example between getting your genes into the next generation by having a large number of offspring with each getting little parental care and thus each child having a higher risk of mortality, versus having fewer offspring and investing more in each, thus increasing each offspring's chances of reproducing successfully. It is important to recognise that different characteristics will tend to vary together, for example it takes longer to grow something to a large size than to grow to a smaller one, so larger animals tend to reach maturity later than small ones; and growing larger will cost more in food as well as time (and there are protection costs while the immature individual is too small to protect itself), so you need to live longer after maturity to make the investment in offspring successful. Obviously, high parental investment requires that the parents survive well into the lives of their offspring, rather than, as in the case of some insects, fish, and reptiles, never being seen again or even dying off after producing fertilised eggs.

It seems clear that humans are a K-selected species: large and long-lived, with a high degree of parental investment in caring for their infants after birth. Of course, within the human species, there are differences in when people start to have offspring and how many offspring they have; this is now far more a matter of choice than ever in history, with increased availability and acceptability of reliable contraception. Evolutionary theory would predict a shift towards starting earlier and having more offspring if the prospects of the survival of parents (to parent) and of the offspring (to be carefully brought up) are relatively poor. Evolutionary psychologists and 'life history' theorists see this as happening in the decisions people make about when to begin having children, as do some economists studying the effects of educating women on the age at which they have children and the rate of survival of those children to adulthood. It looks as though more education (and economic power) for women reduces the number of children they give birth to but increases the survival rate of the children who are born.[31]

What is more the case with us than with any other species is that human females survive (at least nowadays) for an outstandingly long time after they have ceased to be fertile, with social consequences of various sorts including the availability of people who have already raised children to help with and advise on the rearing of the children's children. Older females in other species are involved in care of the young – for example high-status baboons quite often 'kidnap' babies of lower-status baboons, presumably for the fun of playing with them. (I haven't got there myself yet, but I am beginning to invest in the idea of Granny Power and reminding myself not to plan to take over.) The consequences of reproductive strategy are another thing that we will come back to.

Humans have also evolved large brains for their body size. Larger animals tend to have larger brains, in part because brains process body sensations and control body movements, and if there is more body having these sensations and making these movements, then by and large more brain is needed to process them. But human brain–body ratio is out of line even with other large intelligent animals. There is debate about what functions the very large brain serves, with one possibility being that large brains help with recognition of faces and emotions and thus help with living in a larger social group.

Having a large brain gives us more scope (probably) for more complex cognition (this is not to decry the cleverness of other animals, however, who are eminently capable of the cognition they need to function in their environments).[32] Having a large brain also uses up a lot of energy which we have to get from what we eat, which means we need to eat efficiently for energy, not rely on chomping grass for hours and hours every day. As I said earlier, our digestive systems have adapted for this, and our adoption of cooking also helps. What nutrients we get from breast milk and other later foods, such as oily fish, can have long-lasting effects on our physical and psychological development, as we'll see from the neuroscience and the epidemiological evidence.[33]

There is an example here of two evolutionary developments occurring more or less together and proving somewhat incompatible, with an evolutionary fudge of a solution. Relatively early in the evolution of the human lineage, as distinct from the ape lineages, our ancestors changed from moving on all four limbs to walking upright. We don't know exactly why it happened, but there must have been benefits that outweighed costs – maybe exposing a smaller surface to the hot African sun (just the tops of the head and the shoulders, instead of the whole back), safer foraging amid tall grass, being able to carry things, seeing other people's faces at a better angle. Whatever advantages were key, in order for upright walking and standing to work, body shape had to change. Compared with our ancestors, the human head sits above the top of the spine and the face is oriented forward at right angles to the line of the spine; human legs became longer and arms shorter; human feet are flatter and toes less prehensile; human knees needed to be below the pelvis in order to balance on only two feet, so we are knock-kneed. The evolutionary fudge comes in because the shape of pelvis that worked well for upright walking is more bowl-shaped than that of apes. Its shape works well for containing the guts and allowing the legs to move efficiently, but ergonomics mean that the pelvis has a smaller hole between its two sides, and hence a smaller birth canal. This limits the maximum size that the baby's head could be allowed to reach before birth, as an infant whose head was too large might get stuck in the smaller opening. If this happened, the infant would die, and so would its mother – and so, quite quickly, would the species.

The main solution to this problem has been babies being born before their heads grow too big. There are ancillary solutions; for example the cartilage that holds the mother's pelvis together softens during labour so that the pelvic bones can move apart a little more than usual, and the bones of the baby's skull are not completely fused together so that the skull plates can slip over each other a little when compressed in the birth canal. But giving birth is still far more difficult for humans than for other primates (and extremely painful, let me tell you).

Effectively, although it is in the interests of both mother and infant to have a safe birth, it would be advantageous to the baby – and to its father's genes[34] – to be able to develop in utero for longer and be born in a more mature state (a pregnancy length of around 21 months has been suggested as ideal for baby, though again I think this would be intolerable for the mother), while it would be in the interests of the mother to give birth to a smaller child in a less painful and dangerous birth. The trade-off fudge of a solution that evolution has arrived at is a relatively early birth for the human infant, born with much brain growth still to come postnatally, but with a head size compatible with the mother having a good chance of a safe delivery and the baby of surviving birth. This trade-off means the infant is very immature. Brain growth postnatally takes years, which means that the infant needs a lot of parenting for a relatively long time but also maybe has more openness to learning.

Parents need offspring to carry their DNA forward into the next generation. Offspring need parental care to survive and flourish and achieve parenthood themselves. So parents have an interest in investing in their offspring, and offspring have an interest in evoking investment from their parents. It is essential for the immature young to survive in a world where they are, compared with adults, rather helpless. It is in their interests to be good at learning and at evoking conditions in which they can learn. It is important for them not to be pushed aside (or worse) by other more mature individuals. Because of all of this, many species have evolved characteristics that signal that babies and children are young (and so not yet competitors), that signal that they need help from related individuals (who should invest in them in order to enhance the survival of the genes that they share), and that enhance their ability to learn what they need to learn (often well before they actually need to use the skills and knowledge). We are familiar with these characteristics of the young – smallness, big shiny eyes, high foreheads, soft skin, plump cheeks, round and chubby feet and hands, smell of milk, tendency to cuddle up, high-pitched voices, uncoordinated movements, cuteness, playfulness, activity, enthusiasm for learning new things, and so on. More mature individuals react to these evolved characteristics by defining the young as nonthreatening. They may, if well-meaning, go further and provide the experiences that they think will give the immature individual a good chance of healthy development (parental frames, for example).

Some signals, particularly early on, may be more subtle than adults can consciously recognise. Once it became possible to film infants and watch their behaviour frame by frame, it was possible to see recurring patterns in both infant and parent. Lynne Murray's[35] work on infants has provided charming visual records of tiny babies showing emotions and attention that could signal their needs to their caretakers. No one would claim that this is what the baby *intends* to do – signals where the baby knows what it wants to express and what its audience needs for the signal to work will come later – but the baby's behaviour may be more eloquent than a lot of us had consciously recognised.

The effect of signals like these is to mark the young individual as non-threatening, as noncompetitors, as deserving more tolerance and more nurturance than an adult. Adults respond in framing ways which protect the young, allow them to learn necessary skills, and become members of the social group. Infants have evolved behaviour that enhances their chances of protection and loving care, too. From very early on, infants selectively attend to human faces and voices and discriminate the familiar voices and smells of their mothers from the voices and smells of other nonfamiliar women. Such a preference and such discriminations are likely to convince parents that they are special to their babies. Infants' vocalisations and movements, which do to some extent reveal what they are feeling, are interpreted by adults as sort-of-intentional expressions of feeling. Caregivers and adults treat the infant as an individual who is intending to communicate, as a social being with needs and wishes and intentions that are not unlike their own; and the infant rapidly develops its own social cognition, attachment relations, and emotion regulation. If the adults cannot or will not fit in with the baby in this way, then the baby may be at risk of less positive adaptations to the world. Attachment theory is one of the big accounts of how this happens, and I'll discuss it later.

Conflict, however, can result if the two sides want to give and to receive different amounts or different types of investment or do so at different times. The best worked-out example of this is in sibling competition for parental investment. All siblings have received all their genes from their parents, so all siblings are equally related to their parents, and parents will have the same amount of interest (in evolutionary terms) for supporting the survival of the one as the other. But each sibling has inherited half the genes of the mother and half the genes of the father, so at one extreme, a pair of sibs might have inherited exactly the same genes from both parents, or, at the other extreme, exactly the half share of genes which their sib didn't get. This means that if a parent's investment goes to your sibling rather than you, your genes may get less benefit than if it had come to you. On the other hand, you probably share more genes with your sibling than you do with someone you are not related to, so in the case of competition with an outsider, siblings may have the same interests and therefore give each other strong support.

Parents of several children quite often allocate resources to each child on the basis of that child's need rather than evenly between the children. From the parent's evolutionary position, this is largely efficient; don't waste resources on a child who can survive without them if another child really needs the resources. Obviously it may not look quite like this to the siblings; a set of outcomes including sibling rivalry and cries of 'it's not fair' may well result. Younger children complain that the older ones are allowed more autonomy; older children complain that the younger ones are indulged and not made to stand on their own two feet. Human parents seem to find all this very difficult to manage; the psychological research suggests that good relationships between child and parent and lots of explicit discussion of everyone's feelings, needs, and rights may help. (There is some evidence of sibling competition in earwigs, though presumably not involving emotions or ideas about fairness.) Interestingly, if you make comparison with other species, we generally keep up relationships with our siblings for an unusually long time.

There are points in development when the parent's interest and the child's interest are not the same. For example during pregnancy, the fetus needs blood sugar which it gets from the mother's blood supply, via the placenta. But if the mother's blood sugar gets too high, that damages her, so her body produces more insulin which decreases the level of sugar in her blood. The placenta counteracts the mother's increased production of insulin by stimulating the production of enzymes that degrade insulin and leave blood sugar available to the fetus. The fetus may get some protection against the pregnant woman's stress hormones through changes in the neuroendocrine systems, but these changes may make the mother more at risk of postnatal depression.[36] And so it goes: a sort of war between the fetus and the mother which hopefully does not seriously damage either. In this case, a balance which allows the fetus all the resources it might demand might not actually be in its interest. Too high a blood sugar supply might allow the fetus to grow so big that its birth is extra dangerous and it might stress the mother's blood pressure system, which could reduce her capacity to complete pregnancy successfully.

Later, the child may have grown up enough to survive quite well without so much expense of effort and resources by the parent – for example the child may be ready to be weaned or to leave the parental nest – but might still quite fancy a bit of cosseting. There is often disagreement between parents and children about whether the child still needs parental investment. Parents may tend to switch their support from children who could be expected to fend for themselves to their younger, less independent children at a time when the older child would prefer still to draw on parental resources. A child may seek to retain investment from the parents even past the point when the child no longer really needs it and when it might be more in the parents' interest to invest in another, younger child who really does need the investment to survive. This tends to produce a period of parents refusing resources that they think the child can do without – mothers rejecting demands for attention, for example – and infants protesting. It is a common observation that toddlers often show more immature behaviour when a new baby joins the family, as if they were campaigning to show their mothers that they still need the investment that the baby is about to take away from them.[37]

The bit of parenting advice that I would derive from this is that your child's demands on you may, occasionally, be for attention or resources that would indeed benefit them but which they could cope without. If they could do without, and if the costs to you are high, then so far as your evolutionary duties are concerned, you can legitimately say no. And there are benefits to the child in being able to defer gratification or to say 'I did it all my own self', as I'll discuss later.

Some of the supporters of versions of evolutionary theory emphasise eliminating any sentimentality from their models. They suggest that there may be cost–benefit analyses of whether parental investment in a particular child is worth it. They see evidence that individuals who are less evolutionarily 'fit' or who are less crucial to their parents' chances of leaving descendants will receive less parental investment. In ancient civilisations, children who were handicapped might be killed at birth, and to this day, children who are handicapped, and stepchildren seem to be more at risk of being neglected or abused.[38]

Achieving reproductive success can require success in all sorts of other developmental areas, too, for example competition with peers and competition for status as well as competition for mates and having lots of babies. Parental investment may be made in care, education, networking, and dowries so that children are advantaged in these areas. This means each child costs the parents more, but the effects of the investment may spread beyond the individual child. Marrying your daughter to King Henry VIII improved the chances of her relatives rising up the power hierarchy at the Tudor court, though not the girl's own chances of having children (or keeping her head). Indirect parental investment can result in more social commitment to systems that can benefit all children – education and health services, for example. Part of what is happening is increased attention to the needs, and eventually the rights, of the child; this will involve the growth of new professions concerned with providing for children, such as teachers and paediatricians. Although these have to be paid for, the net result seems, historically and anthropologically, to be more prosperous societies.

There may also be more pressure on parents to provide for their children 'in the right way'. Interestingly, there have been books of advice for parents on how to bring up their children for many centuries. It appears that one very ancient Chinese one[39] included advice for pregnant women on the best sort of posture to adopt to enhance your fetus's chances of growing up to be successful in the fiendishly competitive system of exams which enabled the 2.5% who passed to become civil servants. So advice books for mothers – and, I suspect, blaming mothers – are not something new.

Humans have evolved to be social. This may be one of the reasons they have evolved big brains; Dunbar[40] indeed claims that there is 'a consensus' that the evolution of more complex ways of being social and more complex social networks were the prime movers of the evolution of the human brain. Species that have lasting social relationships (both pair bonds between partners and friendships) and live in larger social groups tend to have larger brains, especially larger frontal lobes.[41] Growing large brains (large anything, really) takes more time than growing smaller ones, so a longer period of immaturity and brain growth would be expected, bringing us back to neoteny and the uses of immaturity and of parents.

Living in a larger social group changes your ecology and your use of time. All animals can be thought of as having 'time budgets'. In order to survive and reproduce, they have to do whatever it takes to keep their bodies working properly; that is they have to get adequate food and shelter and rest, protect themselves from predators and dangers, relate as necessary to other animals. This means their time budgets have to include time for finding, preparing, consuming, and digesting food; time for resting and sleeping; avoiding, or at least managing, exposure to the harshest and most dangerous parts of the environment (e.g. predators, extremes of heat or cold); and time in activities which maintain the social group, such as grooming, talking, and joint activities and emotions. Each of these uses up time, and that time cannot then be used for other incompatible activities.

The amount of time you need for activities is affected by the ecology of your environment. For example, tropical high temperatures at midday mean that midday will be an uncomfortable time for foraging for food and probably needs to be a resting time. Beyond the tropics, seasonal changes make life challenging in new ways. Low light levels in winter and frequent days all through the year when it is dull or foggy would make hunting more difficult and dangerous. There's not much prospect of finding food during the hours of darkness, and you are at more risk of predators coming at you unseen out of the dark. (It looks as though adaptations to chronically low light levels evolved in similar ways in several species: nocturnal primates, Neanderthals, and modern humans living at high latitudes all tend to have larger eyeballs, retinas, and visual processing areas in their brains than those who operate more in bright light.)[42]

If you live several miles from the nearest food source, provisioning yourself takes more time and a different sort of planning than if you can just pop out to the nearest fruit tree or local shop. Some ecologies are easy for humans to live in and others are more hostile – a part of the difficulties of poverty and parenting that is often overlooked. Poorer parents tend to provide worse diets for their children and live further from shops with nutritious food (which is in any case often more expensive) rather than junk food. Not separate issues, obviously.

The amount of time you need for activities is also affected by your own characteristics. If you are very young, very old, or very weak, your digestive system may not be able to cope with your species' normal diet, and foraging for yourself could take an impossible amount of time. You need someone else to help. Human babies' very small stomachs and inabilities to digest anything except milk mean that they have to have small frequent meals of special food, provided by someone else, and they need to learn about what is good food – partly from what their mothers ate during their pregnancies, partly from what they are fed directly after weaning.

The time budget idea also makes interesting points about the size and functioning of the social group. Larger groups mean that the food resources of the immediate neighbourhood might not be sufficient for the number of people living there, so foraging means roaming over a larger area. Depending on your ecology, you may have to spend a longer time seeking food to provision yourself, you may have to carry food back to your social dependents left at base, you may have to use technological help (e.g. fishing nets, cooking, or online shopping and delivery systems), and you have to develop ways of sharing with others.

Larger groups improve the chances of there being enough people there to frighten off predators, or at least to decrease each individual's chance of being the one whom the lion catches. Larger groups also mean that there need to be new ways of maintaining social bonds. Where apes can do much of the bonding they need by grooming each other one on one, larger social groups mean you wouldn't have enough time to bond with every other individual by grooming them, so laughter, language, rituals, and mentalising[43] have been suggested as time-efficient ways of bonding and maintaining social bonds without needing to be quite so hands-on about it.[44] In humans, at least, some of these activities are compatible with other demands on the time budget; grooming while resting, for example, or sociable meals with conversation. Sharing and bonding may intensify the degree to which we feel related to others, thus contributing to the building up of long-lasting, rich relationships. Maybe there has been an evolutionary pressure for cooperation, not just for the competition ('survival of the fittest') that used to dominate in evolutionary theory.

Arguably, division of labour and territoriality are the core of social functioning. Humans have developed both these to a very high degree, but they have evolved in a number of other species; certain species of bees, spiders, and rodents may live in colonies where behaviour and status are differentiated. It may be helpful for individuals who interact with each other frequently to develop some specialisation within the group, perhaps in which social settings they engage in and what their repertoire of behaviour is. An individual who has specialised in foraging for edible roots is not so much in competition with another individual who has specialised in gathering fruits as they would be if both were looking out for the same food; and if they cooperate, then each has a better chance of a more varied diet. An individual who has specialised in dishing out grooming or in keeping the young clean is not so much in competition with an individual who expects to be groomed or to hunt for food as if they did the same job. Also, if individuals can be relied on to always do the same thing, they are more predictable to others, and that might make smooth interaction more likely than if there is a higher degree of uncertainty about what each person might do.

Feedback from others might strengthen specialisms in predictable behaviour. Ultimately, an individual's behaviour may become so consistent and predictable that it amounts to something like personality; this individual usually bosses others (is dominant), this one usually roams alone (is solitary), this one freezes in the company of others (is timid). Recent observations[45] of social spiders have shown that individual spiders learn a consistent way of behaving as a result of repeated interactions with other spiders that they meet often, so that there come to be stable individual differences in behaviour between different spiders. This suggests that living in a stable social group in which you in some sense 'know' who the others are allows you to develop differentiated personalities, and perhaps roles as well. Evolutionary pressures seem to have led to this in a wide range of different species, including, of course, humans.

So evolution has led to humans living in relatively large, long-lasting, and differentiated social groups and to having some relationships which are long-lasting and intense. To succeed at social life, it is useful to recognise other people, to give other people the right signals, to read other people's signals correctly, to remember what they have done in the past and pre-dict what they will do in the future, to trust them, and to care about other people's intentions, needs, wishes, and beliefs. With big brains that do a lot of learning, we have the brain space to do all of this – and probably some specialised mechanisms, which I will discuss later (mirror neurons and mentalising, for example). It seems to me that infancy and childhood (on the one side) and being a parent (on the other) will give a lot of opportuni-ties for learning and practising these skills, and it seems that these skills are rather necessary for succeeding at being a parent or a child.

Quite a lot of discussion of evolution has focussed on competition, and to be fair, the metaphor of natural *selection* does imply that some individu-als have failed to be selected, as if they were the teams knocked out in the early stages of the World Cup. But Darwin himself was clear that competi-tion does not rule out cooperation and sharing, as these are characteristics that might enhance your chances of success: '[Sympathy] will have been increased through natural selection: for those communities, which included the greatest number of the most sympathetic members, would flourish best, and rear the greatest number of offspring.'[46]

Thus, as well as being interested in other people and understanding them, we may have evolved tendencies to act in ways that benefit them – in other words to behave prosocially. These social rules will probably be expressed as moral rules and religious precepts, such as the 'golden rule' that you should treat others as you would like others to treat you and you should *not* treat others in ways that you would not like to be treated. The social group will probably put quite a lot of effort into teaching these rules and into sanctions against those who break them. Arguably, we have evolved a prosocial ner-vous system, and I will discuss its neuroscience and its endocrinology later, but my point for the moment is about children and their parents.

Prosocial behaviour benefits the social group, and altruistic behaviour benefits others in the group more than it benefits oneself. In terms of evo-lutionary fitness, altruism most clearly makes sense if it benefits your own genes. It can do this either via benefiting them in other people's bodies (thus altruism towards close family members makes more sense than altruism towards unrelated people) or if there are indirect benefits which outweigh the disadvantage it does to your own genes (for example a social contract of togetherness that means we all share resources according to need). Studies of altruism across species[47] do indeed suggest that kin are very frequently selected as the recipients of altruistic acts, and of course parents' behaviour towards children is a prime example. The parenting frames of mutuality, intersubjectivity, and modelling may all help to build up a tendency towards altruism. Parents have more responsibility than children for setting up the society's reward systems for altruism, too; they model it, discuss it, set up feedback and rewards for it, and issue rules about being kind or helpful or sharing or not hurting other people. They also support children's learning to understand other people (as I will discuss further). And they need to be reliable enough for the child to develop a sense that they can be trusted to help. Children's observation of the altruistic behaviour that their parents lavish on them must be a factor in their tendency to be altruistic themselves or to expect it from others.

All these social processes require memory for who an individual is and for who was or was not kind or helpful in the past, plus a long enough lifespan for there to be opportunities to reciprocate, plus a degree of social permanence and organisation. Human groups, both groups of children and groups of adults, do have these on the whole, even if they work imperfectly. Although there is a competing ethos of 'greed is good', which works against altruism, we value people who help others, we value sharing, and we value fairness.[48] And there is a substantial body of evidence that more altruism is associated with more equal societies, which tend to be healthier for all their members than unequal societies are.[49] We have a lot of evidence from studies of ourselves and other species that individuals who cannot protect themselves from unpleasant experiences, or are in a low-status positions in their social groups, tend to suffer more stress and more negative emotions.

These are some of the ways that understanding evolution helps with understanding children. We now know that genes are at the centre of the evolutionary process, so I am going to talk about them next. Differences in behaviour and differences at the level of neurotransmitters and hormones will follow in the chapters about endocrinology, epidemiology, and psychology.

4

---◆---

GENETICS AND EPIGENESIS

In which we look at why the 'language of the genome' needs interpretation

Our thinking about children and their development rather often gets into issues about nature and nurture. For the last seventy years or so, our ideas about nature have been dominated by what we know about genes. I hope that by discussing some of what we've learned from science, I can convince you that we have to be careful about equating nature and genes; but nevertheless, genes do have great importance in children's development. The story is turning out to be different, and more developmental, than the nature theorists would have supposed, and also different from what the nurture theorists used to say.

Colloquially, we say things like 'He's got the right genes,' 'It's all in the genes,' and 'We've discovered the genes for reading' as if the genes were little shiny bits of stuff which fixed the pattern of what we are. The metaphors of genes being blueprints or constituents on an assembly line are often used. Research enterprises such as the Human Genome Project were popularly understood as leading to identification of chunks of genetic material that inexorably produced brown eyes or high intelligence or heterosexuality or whatever. But development is not so inexorable as this, most of the time, and we need to revise our understanding. We do need to know about genes, but we also have to understand them within development.

So, let me describe some basics. In the nucleus of almost every cell of every human body (egg cells and sperm cells being exceptions) there are 46 chromosomes containing thread-like structures of *deoxyribonucleic acid* (DNA). DNA is the famous double helix which is made up of four bases arranged in pairs between the helical backbones like the rungs between the two sides of a twisting ladder. It is coiled around sets of proteins called *histones*, which support the helical structure; histones also turn out to have other functions, including helping with repair of damaged DNA and some controlling of what the DNA can do. We are used to seeing DNA drawn as an elegantly elongated spiral, but actually in addition to being twisted round the histones it may be twisted up on itself, with some of its parts inaccessible (see Figure 4.1).

Every human cell nucleus contains about 30 billion base pairs of DNA which are arranged in sequence on the chromosomes in an order that is largely consistent for all humans; indeed the order is very similar for related species. There are twenty-two matched pairs of chromosomes and one non-matched pair in the nucleus of every human cell (except the eggs and sperm). The classic picture is that within each chromosome, the DNA is organized as functioning units, *genes*, which are located at definite positions on the chromosomes and function together to control the development and functioning of the organism. The story of how cells use their DNA to make the proteins that they need in order to function and to develop is not settled enough for me to describe in fine detail, but fortunately it's also beyond the scope of this book, apart from a couple of examples.[50] Suffice it to say that it is a story of a complex sequence of events, with quite a lot of scope for minor variations which do not much disrupt the sequence. It is not so much of a rigid deterministic wham-bam leap from gene to characteristic as you might have thought.

Most genes are the same between individual humans, and indeed a very large number are also found in other species (about 98 per cent are the same in humans and chimpanzees, about 80 per cent are the same in humans and mice). Some genes found in humans are also found in the genomes of plants. In animals which are fairly close to us in the evolutionary family tree, the same gene appears to serve the same functions (which makes it possible to do research work on other species which helps us understand humans). Different species have different numbers of chromosomes and different quantities of genes: fruit flies have fewer genes than humans, for example, and flowering plants often have more.

There are 20,000 to 30,000 gene units in the human genome, most of them the same in all humans. The *genome* is the sequence of genes characteristic of a species, the *genotype* is the sequence of genes of an individual member of a species. My genotype may differ in its detail from the sequences of other individual humans because some genes come in different forms, or *alleles*. Our own individual genotypes, found in every cell nucleus of our bodies, will be extremely similar to every other member of our species, but

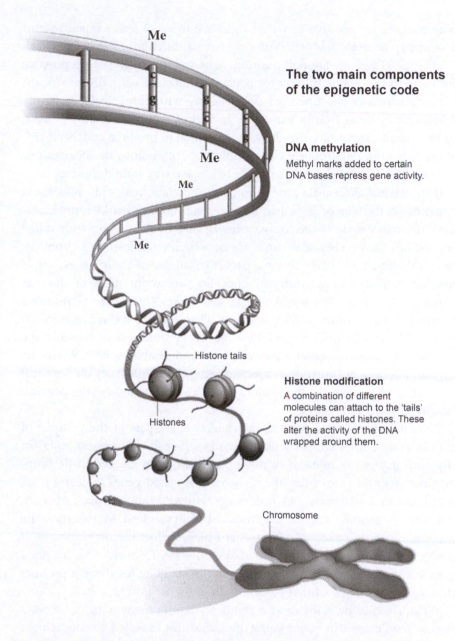

The two main components of the epigenetic code

DNA methylation
Methyl marks added to certain DNA bases repress gene activity.

Histone modification
A combination of different molecules can attach to the 'tails' of proteins called histones. These alter the activity of the DNA wrapped around them.

Me
Me
Me
Me

Histone tails

Histones

Chromosome

Figure 4.1 DNA and its support structures.

From Qiu, J. (2006) Epigenetics: Unfinished symphony. *Nature* 441: 143–145. Reprinted by permission from Macmillan Publishers Ltd.

where alleles are possible or where there are more or fewer repetitions of a sequence of DNA, my genotype may have a different allele or sequence from yours. There are enough positions where different alleles are possible for there to be genetic differences between almost all pairs of individuals; hence, analyses of specimens of DNA can say with considerable certainty whether they came from a particular individual.[51] Which allele you have, or how many repetitions, may have the potential to produce noticeable differences in your development or psychology or physiology or behaviour or life chances, or it may, so far as we can tell, make very little difference.

If an unusual allele makes for an unusual outcome, what this outcome is depends on the sort of organism it is in. One recently worked-out example[52] illustrates some of the complexities of this. Geneticists have identified around fifty genes where mutations are associated with deafness in humans; deaf individuals are likely to have particular alleles of these genes, while hearing individuals have different ones. So you might think of these as genes 'for deafness'. But this would be a mistake. What these genes do is at some distance from causing deafness. They encode for proteins called myosins. Myosins help form the little hairs in the inner ear of humans; the hair cells respond to sound waves and we are thus able to hear. When the myosin has been encoded by a defective gene, these little hairs do not form properly, and because the little hairs are not as they should be, the person's hearing is impaired.

The same genes, both normal and defective, are part of the genome of certain plants, for example wild mustard, where they similarly code for myosins. If they are mutated in these plants, myosins are not made properly. But does this mean that the plant with mutated genes is deaf, or has poorly formed inner ears? No, it does not. No wild mustard plant has ears, whatever its genome, and no wild mustard plant can hear. Mutations in the myosin-encoding genes in wild mustard plants affect the development of their roots, making them less able to absorb water from the soil. It's not a gene for deafness or for root development, it's a gene for myosin production, and myosin does different jobs in different organisms.

What a genotype leads to as a result of development is in some ways highly predictable: my own genotype could not have led to me being a fruit fly or a wild mustard plant or even a human male. However, there is a distinction to be made between the genotype, the inherited instructions for development and structure and functioning, and the phenotype, which is what you can actually observe in the individual's characteristics and behaviour. This, as we will see, is a result of the genes you have and of the environment and experience you have encountered and of a multitude of possible interactions between the two – and of some pretty much random variation. Two organisms with the same genotype stored in their cells may not look the same or act the same because the characteristics we see in their phenotype have been modified by nongenetic factors. Attempts to clone your favourite pet or your favourite child could result in the same genotype but would be very unlikely to result in the same phenotype, because we do not know how to control the nongenetic factors. Similarly, two organisms may look the same, or act the same, but not have the exact same genotype. My genotype now that I am an adult is virtually the same as it was when I was born, indeed as it was when I was conceived; the parts of it I got from my mother were organised before she was born. However, although my genes have changed not at all or very very little, the body and character that they contributed to, my phenotype, is substantially different from what it was when I was an infant: bigger, more able to walk, less able to bite my toes, possessed of a larger and more flexible vocabulary, etc.

DNA is passed on from parents to offspring. Humans reproduce sexually, remixing the genes of two parents each time. Each parent has two chromosomes carrying genes in the same sequence, so for most of their genes there is a corresponding position on the other chromosome and a paired gene. When egg cells are formed (and this happens while the mother herself is still a fetus), each egg contains at random one of each of the pairs of the mother's genes. When sperm cells are formed, each sperm contains at random one of each of the pairs of the father's genes. When an egg is fertilised by a sperm, the two half sets of genes combine to make a new set, of which 50 per cent overall comes from the father and 50 per cent from the mother. Each new individual has derived all its genes from its parents, but the exact combination of parental genes in the fertilised egg will be not quite the same as anyone else's.

There are two exceptions to this. One occurs naturally: if a single fertilised egg separated into two embryos during its early development, there will be monozygotic twins who came from the same egg and sperm and so have exactly the same genotype as each other. The other is a recent phenomenon, the result of intervention by scientists: clones have been made by inserting the complete set of a parent animal's genes into an egg whose own genetic material has been removed. Monozygotic twins or clones share the same genotype, but their phenotypes – the body and behaviour they develop – will develop to be very much the same rather than absolutely identical because genes affect development in conjunction with the environment, and the two twins or the clones will not have exactly the same environment. There is also in any case some chance or randomness in development, which would be a further reason why even clones or monozygotic twins will not be exactly identical in phenotype (though they would have the same genotype to pass on to their own children).

When unusual alleles are found, they may be associated with unusual outcomes, and when there are unusual outcomes, there may be unusual alleles behind them; we are beginning to have the technological capacity to identify these associations. All sorts of interesting information will come from both specific unusual alleles and from identifying regions of the genes that work together in different ways. The technology required to do this is developing rapidly, with the consequence that 'facts' may rapidly become out of date – a problem for those, like us, who are recipients and observers, but an exciting challenge for researchers at the cutting edge who can con-tribute to this advance. Meanwhile, it would be sensible to expect changes in theory. 'Junk DNA', for example, very likely has important functions, for example in the regulation of development, even though it does not code for proteins in the ordinary way.

Mapping the genes in the genome or the individual genotype will be an immense achievement with important practical implications, but genet-ics also needs to tell us about how the genes work. The simple model was of one or a very few genes 'for' some characteristic: genes which were programmed to produce blue eyes or curly hair or high intelligence. Cell biology corrects this view. Although I'm not going to go into the complexi-ties,[53] we need to remember that genes commonly interact with each other and also with the changes all the genes have previously produced. We have to understand that what a particular gene does in an individual is embedded in a biological system that is influenced by a multitude of other genetic and environmental influences, all operating together throughout all the years of the individual's development. And the environment, the individual's experi-ence, is also important. A gene can only rarely set the individual off on a pathway that then leads inexorably to a single endpoint, particularly if it is a complex endpoint, such as 'being highly intelligent'. Mostly the gene is one determinant amongst many others, and while some of these 'others' are other genes, some are not in any sense genetic.

Modern genetics has identified genes that control early development and are strongly similar across many species. Homeobox or 'Hox' genes[54] con-tain the same sequence of DNA in almost all animals. They do the same job: they specify proteins which promote or silence the transcription of other genes in the cells of the embryo, which may in turn promote or silence other genes in a cascade of influences. The net result is the timetabled build-ing of the embryo's body. The presence or absence of particular Hox genes, or differences in the timing of on and off, lead to development or the sup-pression of development. Snakes, which differ from animals such as mice in having more vertebrae and more associated nerves, seem to get that way through a shift in the clock controlling the formation of repeated segments along the head-to-tail axis. Consequently, they end up with many repeated segments and a very elongated spine. Giraffes have elongated necks, but they do not have more repetitions of their vertebrae, just the basic number of unusually large ones. The Hox genes did it differently for them. The Hox genes that start off brain development and that control the embryonic patterning of brain parts, the proliferation of neurons, and the formation of circuits in the brain are pretty much the same in most known animals, suggesting that a lot of the basic plan of the central nervous system goes back to a common ancestor 600 million years ago. This is another reason for thinking evolution is relevant.

But the basic genetic plan is just that, basic. It gets fiddled about with during development. The structure and function of the developing body (including the brain) are determined by how experiences shape the genetically programmed maturation of the nervous system. The social world and, especially for humans, the caregiver, will be crucial sources of experiences; these experiences trim or enable genetic potentials by subtle differences in neuronal growth and neurotransmitter production. Psycho-neuro-endocrinological fine-tuning affects the workings of the brain, and this fine-tuning may be particularly associated with the current interpersonal experiences of the infant and then with future interpersonal expectations, experiences, and emotions. Brains may be especially sensitive to experience in the early years; there may be 'critical periods' when they have to have a particular experience in order for development to go well. The genes you have may affect your susceptibility to outside influences.[55] What we need to do is to examine how all this happens, coordinating our levels of description as far as we can.

You may have come across estimates of heritability. Strictly, *heritability* is the proportion of population variation in a characteristic that is associated with characteristics inherited from the parents rather than with characteristics of the individual's experience of the environment. This looks like a way of estimating the relative importance of nature and nurture, but thinking of it like this can be seriously misleading.[56]

First, although heritability estimates can suggest that a particular characteristic is affected by genetic or environmental influences, the estimate does nothing to show *how* genes work (or how environments work either). Only if we know *how* something brings about effects do we have a guide to whether its effects can be changed and how we might change them. We have been used to thinking that the effects of genes can't be prevented, merely coped with afterwards, while environment and experience are easier to change, but I'm going to provide examples of why thinking like this is a mistake.

Second, a heritability estimate always depends on the particular population at the particular time with the particular measuring instruments, and it is not routinely generalisable to other populations, times, or measurements. The size of the heritability estimates will be different if environments or genes or measurement instruments change, or if the population studied turns out to be unusual.

Third, heritability can only be expressed as a percentage if there is variation in the population. Almost all human beings inherit a programme for having two legs from their parents, but as we have all inherited this programme, the population variance of leg number is effectively zero and the heritability is zero, too.

Finally, in most models, heritability estimates do not clarify effects that are obviously environmental as well as genetic. Sometimes writers inflate the apparent importance of heritability at the expense of the importance of the environment.

The best rule of thumb is that both genes and environment are *always* involved, and the heritability figure is not necessarily important for understanding the causal mechanisms (and thus to deciding policy). In particular, we don't know much about how genetic effects could be changed by changing the environment, but we should not suppose that the genetic effects can't be changed at all. Similarly, although we know more about the effects of changing environments (since history and policy do this visibly all the time), we don't know a lot about how this interacts with genetic effects.

Nevertheless, four intriguing points come out of this approach. First, these analyses suggest that there is a significant genetic contribution to the development of most normal and pathological psychological traits, with heritabilities around 20 to 60 per cent. The traits found to have fairly substantial heritability include people's likelihood of experiencing certain stressful life events and the sort of childrearing they do.

Second, studies of the heritability of individual differences in brain structure suggest that genes contribute more to differences in brain regions that evolved relatively recently, such as in the cortex involved in high-level thinking and language, than they do to evolutionarily old regions, such as the nucleus accumbens, which is involved in dopamine-mediated feelings of pleasure and in addiction.[57]

Third, the analyses suggest the possibility that heritability is lower in at-risk populations with tough environments than it is in populations whose environments are more benevolent. This suggests that the bad effects of a damaging environment may be so pervasive that they swamp the effects of most genetic differences. Genetic differences may have a more noticeable effect in an environment which is less challenging.

Fourth, there are some bits of evidence that heritability estimates rise as children move from childhood to adolescence and from adolescence to adulthood. The suggestion is that genetic differences may be swamped by environmental ones when the environment is controlled by the parents (and parent substitutes such as schools), but they become more visible as children develop more autonomy and are more able to select the environments that suit their genetic predisposition.

Thus, so far as the development of a child as a psychological and social person is concerned, there are no genes for differences in individual outcomes in the sense that having this particular allele completely predetermines this outcome. However people's genetic characteristics may make an outcome more likely or less likely. The genetic characteristics that make the outcome more or less likely are not randomly distributed in the population, and most of them may be genetically influenced. Because I am genetically female, it would be virtually impossible for me to be a guardsman or to visit the ancient monasteries on Mount Athos, for example. We need to examine the mechanisms by which characteristics, experiences, and outcomes are associated, recognising that some of these mechanisms may be genetic. This need not be a matter of blaming the victim for his or her genes, or of excusing him or her, either. Nor should we believe that we cannot change genetic influences. What we need to know is how characteristics are caused.

We already know about a number of genetic anomalies in single genes which are associated with very serious developmental problems. Examples would include cystic fibrosis, phenylketonuria (PKU), and Huntington's disease. These anomalies tend to be uncommon. Their effects are highly damaging, and if the damage occurs from early in life, those with the anomalous gene would be unlikely to survive to adulthood and have children; hence, the gene would turn up in fewer descendants than the gene that did not cause the problem.

For some disorders, the allele that causes it is also *recessive*, so that an individual is only noticeably affected if they have inherited it from both parents and are therefore *homozygous* for the gene. Individuals who are *heterozygous* have one copy of the abnormal allele, while the version inherited from the other parent is normal. They are *carriers* because although they do not show ill effects themselves (the one normal gene that they have being enough to allow them to function and develop normally), they are at risk of transmitting their anomalous gene to their children.

Recessive genetic disorders occur more frequently if the parents are themselves genetically closely related, as in cousin marriages, for example, because having a copy of the same recessive genes as your partner will be more common if your genetic material stems from close common ancestors. Some disorders are particularly prevalent in particular ethnic or cultural groups who traditionally intermarry a lot: Tay-Sachs disease and the Habsburg prominent lower jaw are examples. The pattern of which family members show the trait (or develop the disorder) can provide useful clues about whether a genetic process is involved. In some disorders there is evidence of a family tree of people affected and predictability to relatives; in others, the disorder appears unexpectedly but is then inherited. For example, something happened in the formation of Queen Victoria's genome which meant she had one defective gene for a blood clotting factor. Thus, she was a carrier for haemophilia, a new disease in the Royal Family. She passed it on to one of her sons and, via daughters, to several of her grand-sons and great-grandsons.[58]

In another Royal Family example, as a result of the generations of marriage between close relations preferred by the Habsburg family (uncles with nieces often, and cousins almost always otherwise), the last Habsburg king of Spain, Carlos II, had the family prominent jaw (mandibular prognathism) to such a degree that his bottom teeth were far in front of his top teeth. Thus, he could not make the top and bottom teeth meet, and so he could not chew at all. His mandibular prognathism and his abnormally large tongue also affected his speech, which was almost unintelligible. In addition to the extreme version of the Habsburg jaw, and again from inbreeding, he probably had epilepsy and probably was impotent; certainly he did not father any children. Medicine being what it was in seventeenth century Europe, his doctors attributed his problems largely to witchcraft, so he was the last of his line. Later kings of Spain (and of Austria, the other big Habsburg territory) were less likely to choose wives they were so closely related to, and they did not have such severe genetic problems as poor Carlos the Bewitched.

As I've said, every cell in the body contains all the individual's genes, but not all of those in a particular cell are expressed. In embryology, development begins with undifferentiated cells that take on differentiated forms and functions which they transmit to their daughter cells. Differentiated cells sit in particular places in the body and do particular jobs keeping it working: they have become specialised for some tasks and do not need to do others. *Gene expression* is specific to particular types of cells and regions of the body and also to particular periods of development. Genes necessary to hair growth are expressed in scalp cells but not in eye cells, and some of their genetic programming is expressed only at a particular time in the life of the individual, for example late in life and not early on, or early but not later. One example is seen in many cases of male baldness. You can't tell by looking at the little boy whether he is at risk of becoming bald later in life, but you can predict the risk if you look at older males who share his genes and have reached the age at which genetic baldness shows up in men. Bald fathers and bald uncles give clues to the pattern of hair loss when the child grows up.

In most of our pairs of chromosomes the two members of the pair are very similar, but for one pair they look very different. Males have a large X chromosome (from their mother) and a small Y one (from their father). Females have two X chromosomes, one from each parent. In each cell of the female, at a very early stage, one X chromosome is inactivated (and squashed up), and this inactivation is copied into all its descendant cells throughout the development of the embryo. The inactivation is random as to which X chromosome it happens to (though possibly if the chromosome has a defective gene, its descendant cells die off early on and are replaced by the cells with a normal genotype activated). X-chromosome inactivation is more or less complete and lasts for the life of the individual, but when egg or sperm cells are produced it is removed; the genetic material that is not expressed in the mother's body may be passed on in her eggs to her children.

Females have a bit of a genetic advantage here. If they have a defective gene on one X chromosome, there is a 50 per cent chance that it will be inactivated and therefore won't affect their functioning, and the cells which descend from the normal version of the gene on the other X chromosome may be enough to allow healthy development. Males, having only one X chromosome, are in trouble if it has a defective gene because they don't have a normal version to reduce its effects.

So, we have to consider development as involving adaptation between organism and environment and as absolutely crucial to the interplay between genes and environment, and we are talking about genes and their expression being affected by development. Thus, we are talking about *epigenesis*.[59] This is a term that has some ancient roots (in Aristotle, for example) but was most influentially used by the developmental biologist C.H. Waddington in the 1950s. Waddington used a metaphor that has become famous: the developing cell (or the developing individual) is like a ball rolling downhill through a landscape which is crumpled up into ridges and valleys. Its momentum carries it through the landscape, and it will roll into one or another valley as the land folds down in front of it. Once the ball has rolled down into a valley, extra energy will be needed to nudge it out again across a ridge, perhaps so much energy that it will never be able to escape. It is not predictable exactly which valley the ball will roll into, but which valley that happens to be will lead the rolling ball towards a particular endpoint, even though at the outset the ball might have rolled through the landscape on a different path and ended up at a different point.

This metaphor is a vivid picture of development happening. Some of the valleys are deep, and once you are in them, the endpoint is more or less inevitable. Other regions of the epigenetic landscape are more level, and the developing ball can roll across them much more freely so the endpoint is more variable. Valleys may start off separate and end up more separate, or start off separate but converge later. The landscape itself is capable of change during development, as if an earth tremor or a landslide cuts off some possible routes or opens up others or jolts development into an unexpected path. All of this implies that there may be different routes to any given endpoint (say between childhood disadvantage and adult difficulties). It also implies that there will rarely be only one cause of development; it is more likely that there have been many steps back and forth over a long period of time.

Epigenetic processes are thought not to change DNA, and hence they are not genetic. But they do bring about changes in *expression* of genes, changes which affect the development of the individual. How this happens is still being worked out. One of these better understood processes is *methylation*. At various positions on the chain of DNA in a cell, a tiny methyl group may be added. This addition is copied into any cells of the developing individual that descend from the cell with the methylated gene. The methylation causes an alteration in how the gene is expressed in the cell and in its daughter cells; for example the cells have a continuing signal that they have to be heart cells or lung cells or whatever. It may suppress the expression of any harmful bits of DNA that have accumulated in the genome, and it is one of the factors in X chromosome inactivation. When an egg cell or a sperm cell is formed, this new cell has typically kept its parents' DNA but lost its parents' methylation. It acquires its own methylation during its development as a new individual. Methyl groups also get attached to the histones that the DNA is coiled around, and this also affects how easily the DNA can be expressed.[60] Known factors affecting methylation include toxins, viral infections, aging, and, importantly, chance. Effects known to be influenced by methylation include various disorders such as diabetes, heart disease, cancer, and, recent evidence is beginning to show, brain development and, consequently, fine differences in behaviour. It is very likely that nutrition and rearing experiences – possibly including exposure to parental smoking and maternal depression – are other sources of methylation effects. I am going to say more about these later.

So as Waddington's epigenetic landscape implies, normally in individual development the early stages have rich potential which is not yet firmly specified, and there is progress towards differentiation, integration, and elaboration in development, with earlier stages influencing later ones because they have changed the starting point at which further development begins. We start off with the genotype that we have inherited from our parents, and this is the source of what we pass on to our children, but what we live with throughout our lives is a phenotype, which is derived from the original genotype and from the genotype's existence in the specific environmental contexts it has experienced. What environments we experience may be in part a result of factors well outside our individual control – history, luck – but it can also be a result of personal choices, choices made for us by others in reaction to how they see us, and by ourselves. And it seems increasingly likely that experience does affect the expression of the individual's DNA in his or her body and, presumably, his or her behaviour.

The importance of environmental effects and developmental approaches is one focus of work which tries to explain the development of diseases and disorders. Quite a lot of the illnesses that we develop as adults may have their origin in our very early development. One example is the association between early nutrition and later diseases, for example nutrition before birth and heart disease in adulthood. Undernutrition at crucial times before birth shows up as restricted growth and small size at birth; most such babies, given normal nutrition, then grow quickly (catch-up growth) and reach normal sizes. But as adults, these formerly small-for-dates individuals may be at increased risk of problems such as increased insulin resistance, heart disease, and obesity. It seems that during development, early environmental experiences such as nutrition levels may have 'programmed' the gene activity that will come during later stages. The result is that different sets of genes are activated or silenced in the cells of the body according to a sort of expectation that similar environmental experiences will happen late in life. The individual who has experienced undernutrition while a fetus may expect that food will be hard to come by throughout life, and therefore use the food it does get differently from someone who was well fed prenatally – fetal programming leading to a thrifty phenotype.[61]

In some cases, this sort of effect may also extend over more than one successive generation. We know this for sure in experimental studies of mice, but there may be some human evidence. Individuals in the remote Swedish region of Overkalix who had experienced undernutrition during a particular period of their development, but had survived and reproduced, had grandchildren who lived longer than the grandchildren of individuals who were well fed during these periods.[62] The timing of the sensitive periods of development (between the ages of 9 and 12 for the future grandfathers, and during this period but also during the fetal stage and infancy for the future grandmothers) suggests that the undernutrition was affecting the development of the individuals' eggs or sperm; thus, it may be that something was happening to the DNA that affected its expression and led to changes in the longevity of the next generation or the next few generations.

In another recent study, researchers investigated health over three generations. In the first generation, women suffered very severe undernutrition during pregnancy because of a famine in the Nazi-occupied Netherlands in 1944–5.[63] The level of food deprivation was extreme: for five or six months of the Hunger Winter, the daily food ration was between 400 and 800 calories, and even though efforts were made to protect women who were pregnant or breastfeeding, they had desperately inadequate diets. About 18,000 Dutch civilians died of starvation.

The babies who were in the last trimester (that is, at a time when the body is growing rapidly) when their mothers were starved were smaller than normal at birth, which is not especially surprising. As they grew up, they retained a tendency to be smaller than normal for Holland, and to be less at risk for obesity, heart disease, and diabetes. The children of the women in this group had normal birth weights when they came along. So this suggests that restricted food for your mother for the last few months before your birth stops the normal weight gain of the last few months, and there is some effect on your weight for the rest of your life but no effect on your children's birthweight. (We also know that the boys born after the Hunger Winter also had normal IQs as young adults, when they were recruited into the Dutch army.)

Things were more surprising if the fetus was exposed to a restricted food supply in the early stages (the first trimester) of its gestation. These Hunger Winter babies had normal birth weights, as the improvement in their mothers' diet once the war was over allowed them enough nutrients to do the normal rapid growth in the later parts of gestation. But later in life, they showed higher rates of diabetes, obesity, and cardiovascular disease than individuals born a year or two earlier or later, whose mothers were well fed throughout pregnancy. They were also more at risk of developing schizophrenia.

Another round of studies looked at the children of the women in the second generation group in Holland (grandchildren of the undernourished pregnancies of 1944–5). Where the child's grandmother had been starved during the last part of her pregnancy but her daughter was normally fed, the daughter's baby would be born at a normal birth weight and grow up to have normal rates of obesity and heart disease. But when the child's grandmother had been starved during the first trimester, the babies of her children were shorter and fatter than normal at birth and grew up to be at increased risk of obesity and heart disease. The grandchildren of the Hunger

Winter women were more likely to be rated by their parents as 'unhealthy', and in fact more of them did die relatively young than in the comparison group, where the grandmothers had not been starved in the famine. An increased risk of diabetes and of cardiovascular disease may be part of what is happening to worsen the health of these succeeding generations.

What was happening to bring about the increased risk? Between mother and child, it might be changes in the environment within the womb, for example in the efficiency of the placenta passing nutrients from the mother's body to the fetus, but how could mechanisms such as these work between grandmother and grandchild? The eggs that a woman will have as an adult are largely being formed while she is still an embryo, so there may have been changes in the cytoplasm that surrounds the nucleus of the eggs forming inside her that led to an abnormal growth pattern for the fetus of the next generation. Again, we don't know quite how this could work.

The possible causes of the apparent inherited impact of your ancestors' diet become a little clearer if you look at males. Males do not provide the intrauterine environment, so an effect of nutrition between fathers and sons and grandsons should not be due to changes in utero. The sperm cells that males provide to the next generation contain very little cytoplasm compared with the eggs that come from females, so famine causing changes in the cytoplasm might not be very relevant either. This leaves changes to gene expression as the most plausible route of influence. Back in Overkalix, the data about periods of undernutrition and the health and longevity of the population and its descendants included data on males. The data showed that diet during the periods of life when boys' bodies were making sperm and girls' bodies were making eggs was particularly important for the longevity of the later generations. So it is very possible that the restricted diet of the Hunger Winter or the Overkalix harvest failures produced subtle shifts in the way in which the genes that work in metabolism were expressed, and that this influenced the next generation's development, too, and possibly changes in the way they are methylated. There's very recent epidemiological evidence on gene methylation and nutrition in the ALSPAC study, which I will talk about later.

On the basis of these studies of Swedish and Dutch populations (and of other studies, including many on animals, and of other horrible historical events, for example the siege of Leningrad and the enormous Chinese famine of the late 1950s and early 1960s), it would appear that in times of low food supply, the expression of some genes in a developing fetus can be reversibly modified in a way that changes development or behaviour after birth so as to compensate for there being less food. Broadly, what seems to be happening is that the first generation experiences stress (undernutrition) at a particular stage of development, and as a consequence, the next generation or generations will develop in a way that would adapt them to this stress if they were to encounter it, too. The development of the expression of the genes in the grandparents involved a short-term response to the lack of nutritional resources they encountered (possibly through the methylation of the genes), which adjusted the ways the genes being copied into their sperm or eggs were programmed to develop, and this allowed subsequent generations to respond to the threats faced by their recent ancestors. This could be advantageous if they did indeed meet the same risks (which they might well have done, when historical change was slow), but it might be less helpful if they did not, as in the case of individuals who grow slowly during gestation because of these sorts of genetic programming, but after birth they are well fed (by the standards of their ancestors) and because they have more food than expected, they grow too fat and so are at risk of heart disease and diabetes.

It is really important to note that what happens after birth is also relevant. The Dutch babies, for example, were well fed after the famine, better than their early prenatal experience would have predicted. This meant that their growth could rapidly catch up to normal sizes, but later their tendency to store fat in their bodies was bad for their health. If they had had a restricted diet postnatally, they would probably have grown up smallish and thinnish but not at extra risk of diabetes or heart disease. We have to be very careful about panicking about a single indicator or thinking things are fixed and irretrievable.

Effects over the lifetime of the developing individual are less in debate than epigenetic effects lasting over several generations, where the best case involves extremes of nutrition. Another possible example of the early environment affecting the expression of genes is the effect of the mother's smoking on the development of the fetus she is carrying. It is well established that there is a statistical association between maternal smoking during pregnancy and the incidence of malformation of the testes and penis, infertility, and low levels of testosterone in males and of infertility in females. I will not begin to pretend to understand the complexity of the processes involved, but it has been demonstrated that chemicals from the cigarette smoke were getting into the fetus, and that there was lower expression of the desert hedgehog gene[64] (which is known to be involved in the formation of body parts and especially testis development) during the development of the fetuses of women who smoked. This might partly explain this pattern of association.

It has been known for a long time that mothers' smoking in pregnancy tends to produce restricted growth and lower birth weight in the babies (and also increases the risk of stillbirth and birth defects and lung problems).[65] The babies may then grow up to have a higher risk of asthma and of sudden infant death syndrome. This may be because the toxins that enter the mother's body when she smokes cross the placenta and impact on the fetus – potentially an increased dose of cyanide, arsenic, lead, tar, and carbon monoxide, as well as nicotine. Or it may be that smoking affects the blood flow to the fetus. Either way, the development of its lungs and consequently its ability to breath seem to be affected. More recent research suggests that these babies may also grow up to be at increased risk of obesity in childhood.

In other studies,[66] the researchers have looked at growth in the children of fathers who had started to smoke before the age of 11. The children of these men were likely to have a higher body mass index in middle childhood. It may therefore be the case that fathers' smoking affects their children and adds to the effect of mothers' smoking, though what the physiological mechanisms could be is not so clear.[67]

More controversially, there is a statistical association between maternal smoking in pregnancy and children's behaviour problems, for example attention-deficit hyperactivity disorder and severe antisocial behaviour. This is something that needs careful interpretation, in part because those mothers who continue to smoke in pregnancy, despite a lot of advice that it may damage their babies, may have needs or attitudes that make it difficult for them to give up smoking and also lead them to parent differently from people who obey the health advice. Measuring behaviour problems is also more complex than measuring BMI or testis development. I want to be very cautious about this, not least because I am a nonsmoker and the 'sins' you don't commit yourself often look particularly disgusting and stupid. But it is important to recognise that children are affected by their chemical environment, and this environment includes the chemicals that reach them before birth. There is evidence of harmful effects from prenatal exposure to lead,[68] and to PCBs, and to alcohol, and – quite conceivably – to other chemicals.

It looks as though early rearing conditions can affect gene expression. Being deprived of maternal care does not change the chemical/genetic content of your DNA, but it may affect how the DNA is expressed in the body. The structure of DNA in cells is folded in a complex way, and particular parts of the DNA sequence may be more or less accessible to do the work of building and maintaining the body and its functioning. This work involves the transcription of the original DNA laid down at conception, and it is the possibilities for transcription that may be affected by experience. In rats (who are born immature compared with primates), in the first postnatal week of life, more maternal licking and grooming reduces the methylation

of the genes which determine how many glucocorticoid receptors an animal will have in the hippocampus region of the brain. Methylated genes
are not expressed. More maternal licking leads to less methylation of these
genes which means that they can be expressed, which leads to the development of more receptors. Animals that develop more receptors are more able
to control stress levels efficiently, while animals with few receptors have
sluggish, inefficient responses to stress, more prolonged stress, and are at
more risk of overload of the stress-response system. In these animal studies,
the developmental effects of early maternal care seem to be irreversible, and
this might be because the expression of genes has been changed.

Research on the development of depression provides a very relevant
example of how genetic risk may meet environmental risk. If you have a
monozygotic twin who had depression (which suggests you might have a
bit of a genetic risk for depression) *and* a major life event such as bereavement, the combination of the two predicts that you are especially at risk of
becoming depressed, too. A longitudinal study in Dunedin, New Zealand,
suggested there was interaction between experience and a genetic variant
linked to how much serotonin transporter protein is produced, a protein
that is involved in the reuptake of serotonin from the synapse. Individuals
with a short allelic form of this variant showed an increased risk of depression compared to those who carried the long allele, but only when they had
been exposed to adverse life events. Thus, here there was no evidence of a
main genetic effect for this variant. But it may be that there is an *interaction*
between the variants of the serotonin transport genes and experience of life
events that are associated with major depression. This is still much debated.
The research findings are not consistent. The gene implicated here appears
to be linked to stress response and sensitivity to anxiety, so there may be
here some biological evidence of effects on the stress regulation system
both postnatally and prenatally.[69]

At present there is a lot of strong evidence for the effects of stress and
exposure on depression, and not so much strong evidence for differences
in the serotonin transporter gene 'causing' depression. But genetic differences could help us to explain why some individuals are not much affected
by environmental events which produce strong negative effects in most of
those who experience them. It is very unlikely that when we know the
complete picture it will suggest that the negative environment is not crucial
or that interventions to improve the environment are not worthwhile. It is
genetic vulnerability plus experience of risk that matters, not just genetic
vulnerability.

There has also been a significant number of studies which examine
the possibility of gene–environment interaction in the development of

attention disorders.[70] The main area of interest here is the number of repeats in the promoter region of the *MAOA* gene, in interaction with serious family adversity. A number of epidemiological studies have provided quite robust findings that males are at especially serious risk of attention-deficit hyperactivity disorder (ADHD) and other conduct disorders if they have both the genetic variation and also a lifetime history of parental maltreatment. It will be very interesting to see whether further studies can clarify whether the effect depends on the age of the boy when the abuse is experienced, on how long it continued, or whether other experiential factors moderate it, and thus give us a more exact understanding of the developmental mechanisms that contribute to development which is psychopathological or resilient.

For developmental disorders such as depression or ADHD, understanding gene effects is an interesting part of understanding the causes of these difficulties. Some individuals may be genetically at high risk, others genetically at low risk. But the effect of any single gene on risk is likely to be very small, and if we want to reduce the incidence of these disorders or help those who have developed them, we would do best to focus on preventing the environmental factors that are obviously relevant and well understood – maltreatment, neglect, abuse, lack of emotional support.

We can see genes and environment both contributing even when there is a disorder due to a single harmful genetic anomaly. One example is Phenylketonuria (PKU). This disease is associated with an identified abnormal gene on chromosome 12. We know a lot about effects at the level of protein encoding and cell biology. The defective gene leads to the absence of a particular enzyme, phenylalanine hydroxylase, from the body: the individual is unable to make it. Phenylalanine hydroxylase is needed in digestion to convert the phenylalanine from protein in the diet into another chemical, tyrosine. In the absence of the enzyme, phenylalanine cannot be metabolised and used in the body, and cannot be gotten rid of. High concentrations of phenylalanine in the body result in an excess of chemicals which are normally only present in minute quantities. In the person with PKU, they are present at toxic levels. These toxic chemicals interfere with the development and growth of the central nervous system. The baby's brain develops normally to birth, but once the baby starts a diet which contains phenylalanine, the phenylalanine cannot be metabolized, the toxic chemicals build up, and the baby's developing nerve cells are vulnerable. The connections between nerve cells begin to be damaged and broken down. Deteriorating brain development and irreversible mental retardation (with severe disturbance of emotions and behaviour) result. Thus, the genetic anomaly leads to marked anomalies in brain development and cognitive development.

However, it only does so in the normal environment, specifically if the PKU baby receives a normal diet. If a special dietary environment is provided during the period of brain development so the infant's diet does not contain phenylalanine, no such excess of deleterious chemicals is built up and the central nervous system can develop normally. The genetic defect is still there, but it has no effect in the special environment where there is little or no phenylalanine. PKU individuals still cannot produce phenylalanine hydroxylase, but if they do not need it to deal with phenylalanine because their diet contains no phenylalanine, they avoid the most serious consequences of their genetic abnormality. They have to stay on the diet which excludes phenylalanine as even small amounts of phenylalanine may produce brain damage and some cognitive impairment, even in late childhood. Some children and young people find it socially or emotionally difficult to stick to a different and restricted diet, and instead they eat normal foods. Where this involves eating foods that contain phenylalanine, they are likely to incur some brain damage.

Once brain development is complete, the individual with PKU is not harmed by a normal diet, as the mature nervous system appears to be resistant to the high levels of toxic chemicals which accumulate. However, if a woman with PKU whose own retardation has been prevented by a restricted diet during her infancy and childhood takes an unrestricted diet containing phenylalanine during her pregnancy, the baby may be born with severe mental retardation resulting from excess phenylalanine, even though it has inherited the normal gene for phenylalanine hydroxylase from its father. The build-up of phenylalanine in the pregnant woman does not affect her own brain because her mature nervous system is relatively resistant to it, but it swamps the circulation of the developing fetus and causes abnormal neurological development in utero. The child's prenatal environment gives it PKU mental retardation, even though it does not itself have the genetic abnormality that leads to PKU. Where the mother was at risk of a genetic defect, the child has been damaged by the environment. The mother has abnormal genes which function badly in a normal environment, and the child has normal genes which function badly in an abnormal environment, but the damage is the same.

I think the take-home messages from genetics in children's development are these. Whatever you are interested in, genes are likely to have affected it. Usually many different genes are involved, and they affect each other. It is not a simple pathway from gene (say FOXP2) to effect (say impaired language development). We know from genetics at the molecular level that the genome codes for the production of relatively simple substances. These – in cooperation with other substances produced because of other genes to a long timetable – cumulatively mean you end up with a very complex phenome. What the gene does may work better for you in some combinations of genes and worse in others. Thus, although sometimes by manipulating a few genes (by selective breeding or by gene replacement) you may get the characteristic you want, commonly you may also get things other than the effects you were aiming for. Further, always where there is a genetic influence this is unlikely to be all that matters. Environments and experience also have effects. Because of environmental effects, gene effects may be reduced or amplified, and also the genes you have will be helpful to you in the face of different environmental challenges. Similarly, gene effects may make different individuals more or less open to the influence of the same environment. The experience you have had may affect how your genes are expressed. It's not impossible to clarify all this interplay of multiple influences, but we certainly need to avoid being simplistic about it. What little kids are made of is partly what their genes say, but what is being said is complex and more like a long negotiation than an instruction book.

5

---◆---

NEUROSCIENCE

In which we look at the wiring and workings of children's brains

Another truism: brains are one of the most interesting factors in children's development. Brains are crucial in all the complex sequences of physical changes which keep our bodies working, and they deal with information from past and present. At all sorts of levels in the brain there are programmes for functions such as breathing, sleeping and waking, producing coherent language, perceiving particular shapes and orientations (including face recognition), remembering, evaluating, feeling angry, resisting temptation, and so on. Neuroscience is telling us more and more about how this all works, and about how it develops.

If you think that babies' brains are not ready to do complex thinking and remembering, you are, on the whole, underestimating them. It is true that their brains have a lot of development to do, as the need to have a head that can pass safely through the birth canal means that they are immature. But all the basic structures are there at birth,[71] and they can work well enough to cope with some surprisingly complex thinking and behaving. Very early on, babies can distinguish between the familiar voices and smells of their mothers and the less familiar voices and smells other women; they can distinguish between the languages their mothers speak and a foreign language; they may imitate simple facial gestures; they can see differences between light and dark and scan black and white patterns; they are especially interested in face-like patterns and in the results of their own actions; and they quickly come to do some organising of their experiences into categories with typical properties, for example expecting objects to be solid and only to move if something touches them and expecting people to want things and act on things intentionally. Some of this begins in predispositions in the brain at birth, some rapidly appears as babies learn from their experiences and the brain regions mature, and all of it develops as the children get older. Let's look at brains through the eyes of psychological neuroscience to see what's going on.

I'm going to begin by pointing out that the earlier specialists who supposed that babies and children didn't have brains that were good for thinking were wrong, but it was not their fault. One of the reasons we know more than them is we have better technology for looking at brains as they work. It is now possible to look at the structure of a living brain and see abnormalities, and it is possible to assess blood flow or the energy use of the brain and from that infer which regions become particularly active during different tasks. As techniques develop, it will be possible to get finer-grained information about brain activity in terms of both space and time (earlier methods tended to be acceptably accurate on either location or timing, but not both). Although earlier methods tended to be too demanding for use on children, there are now better and less invasive ways of gathering data on children's brains.

However, we are not anywhere near being able to identify precise neural networks, and possibly we never will be. There are several main reasons for this difficulty. The first is that we would need a minute scale of detail; the number of neurons you can get into a millimetre is enormous. The second is that there are billions of nerve cells in the brain (estimates vary, but say about 10^{12}), they consist of comparatively few different types, and the synapses where neurons connect look even more alike. This makes individual ones hard to tell apart from their neighbours. The brain is made up of branching, interlacing, tangles of fibres rather than anything like tidy colour-coded bundles of wires, let alone tidy circuit diagrams. The third reason is that all nerve cells have very many connections to other nerve cells, and a number of different chemical neurotransmitters are used. The fourth is that nerve cell firing is organised in time as well as in space, so what is an active and traceable network at one moment may be inactive and much less traceable at the next moment. A fifth is that although we think of brains as responding mainly to stimulation from outside themselves, actually there is a continual murmur of activity which is in response to other activity in the brain itself, a lot of endogenous activity. It is obviously going to be harder to see where this has come from, what started and stopped it, as it will be hard to match it up to anything the researchers are trying to scan. A sixth is that different individuals have brains of slightly different sizes and possibly slightly different configurations: two brain structures may be 2 mm apart in my brain, but 2.005 mm apart in yours, either because your whole brain is a bit bigger overall or because the different parts of it just grew slightly differently from mine. Finally, and very importantly for understanding development and learning, neural networks change over the lifespan. New ones build up and useless ones are dismantled. The network that was crucial to our being able to do arithmetic last year may not be involved so much in arithmetic or it may not be so important once we've learned to use a calculator.

All this means that we will probably never be able to trace exact pathways of electrical impulses at an individual level. But there is a good prospect of being able to understand how networks work. Researchers have reached a fairly advanced understanding of how comparatively simple neural circuits work (partly by studying invertebrate animals such as the sea slug). They have also made great advances in studying the connection patterns which underlie some of the simpler reflex actions of vertebrates and in the arrangement of brain cells into maps of the sensory information received from the eyes, the ears, and the skin. The functioning of the brain is known to be dependent on its structure: different nerve pathways lead to predictable outcomes, stimulation of particular parts of the brain leads to particular specific sensations or hallucinations, and damage to the brain, for example

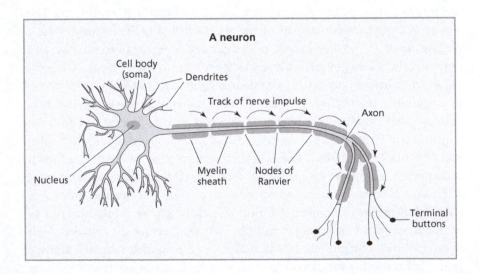

Figure 5.1 The structure of the neuron.

From Ward, J. (2015) The student's guide to cognitive neuroscience (3rd edition). Hove: Psychology Press. Reprinted by permission of the publisher, Taylor & Francis Group (http://www. informaworld.com).

from accidents or strokes, leads to changes in functioning which vary according to the area damaged. There are very orderly patterns of neural connections – of 'connectivity' – from one part of the nervous system to another that are similar across individual brains. The details of the circuits are the result of normal stimulation and functioning of the growing system during development. Abnormal stimulation will probably produce changes in the connection pattern and consequently in how it functions, and also in neurotransmitters.

The brain sometimes seems to have particular regions which are crucial to running particular functions, for example the reticular formation deep in the core of the brain is crucially involved in sleep–wake cycles, but input from and output to other parts of the brain are also involved in the minute-by-minute running of the programme. Increasingly, neuroscience is identifying both the individual regions which are crucially involved in serving a particular brain function *and* the democratic way in which they operate both internally and with other parts. We now know for sure that specific elementary cognitive functions are associated with specific regions of the brain, but beyond the simplest level, the picture is of several different regions of brain working together (as in reading, for example, which I will discuss later). Global distinctions, for example between a left hemisphere specialized for logical or sequential processing and a right hemisphere which is holistic and creative, turn out to be myths. There is an enormous amount of interconnectivity within the brain.

A lot of this connectivity builds up postnatally; it's one of the main ways that babies' brains are growing. This may mean that the way a very young brain is connected up to do a task may be different from the way a mature brain does it; I will discuss this for a couple of developmental tasks later. Many neural connections are a result of learning from experience, and this continues through childhood and adolescence and even into adulthood.

We know that the brain often does more processing than the minimum that you would think is required for success on a task; for example the visual system has distinct regions for colour, contrast, movement, texture, and so forth which are all used in recognising an object even when some of them are redundant. Sometimes there are different programmes for attaining a desirable result. Maintaining a stable body temperature is an example. As a warm-blooded species, we use our brains to respond to changes in the temperature of the environment and regulate body temperature. We have automatic responses to body temperature that are organised in the hypothalamus, for example shivering or sweating or panting. All land mammals use mechanisms such as these. But the cerebral hemispheres are also be involved in humans' feelings of being too hot or too cold. We can consciously assess the meaning of our feeling of heat and deliberately decide on a programme of behaviour which may involve a cerebrally mediated thoughtful response, such as choosing to walk down the shaded side of the street, instead of just relying on a hypothalamus response that induces sweating.

Human infants have the rudiments of hypothalamic temperature regulation but may need a bit of parental help. If they are healthy, they will do better at maintaining a fairly constant body temperature even when not being nursed than kittens, rabbits, or puppies can; these baby animals lose body heat to a dangerous degree when taken away from their mothers, while normally human babies can keep warm enough to survive for longer. Human babies who are not yet well developed, for example prematurely born babies, need a lot of help in keeping at the right temperature. Overheating in too many clothes or bedclothes is a risk for human babies, so we as parents need to make sure they don't get tangled up in bedclothes. Obviously babies are not going to be able to do conscious planning of how to keep themselves warm or how to cool down. And adults generally do not think that small children should be responsible for choices about crossing the street, even if it would help them avoid overheating.

There is very interesting evidence that if someone spends a lot of time learning to do some particular activity to an expert level, there are detectable changes in their brains, even in adulthood.[72] The earliest example came from studies of rats that had their bare and boring laboratory cages enhanced with a tightrope, which they rapidly learned to run across. Tightrope-walking rats had larger regions of their brain involved in balance than rats that just scurried round the bottom of featureless cages. Human evidence comes from an accumulating number of studies. In London, to be a taxi driver you have to get 'The Knowledge', an encyclopaedic learning of routes from all possible starting points to all destinations across the whole of the city. Men who had shown they had learned all this successfully and passed the entry exam to become a taxi driver tended to have overdevelopment in the regions of the brain thought to be involved in using maps. Professional violinists had overdevelopment in the regions of brain concerned with finely coordinated finger movements like the ones they had to do in order to play. In the regions where hearing children process speech sounds, children who were born deaf seemed to process visual information appropriate to understanding gestures and signing. Learning to juggle increases the amount of grey matter in some motor areas of the brain, learning to meditate did the same in other areas, and use of Facebook probably affects the brain regions involved in social memory. Brains continue to adapt to their environments way into later life.[73]

Not only do brains have more than one system for doing many things, but they also may do things slightly differently each time. We know that brain functioning is probabilistic, so not exactly the same combination of neurons may fire each time a task is done, and not exactly the same regions of brain will be involved for different individuals. There is variation between normal human brains just as there is variation between normal human hands or feet or teeth; the same basic patterns exist for almost all of us, but there are subtly different details of the brain or of finger length or of tooth spacing which may sometimes be relevant to functioning but often don't seem to make much difference.[74]

Knowledge of how the brain develops has developed at an accelerating pace over the last century. Until quite recently, it was supposed that the brain had a set of innately wired pathways which were modified to a relatively small extent by experience, probably by the history of use and disuse of nerve cell connections. And it was thought that the experience the brain got and the learning it did made only small differences to its wiring. This model underestimates the intercoordinations between nerve cells and their rich and complex developmental history.

The basic processes of brain development in an individual are: the birth of neurons, the proliferation of neurons and the glial cells that support them, cell migration from starting positions to different parts of the brain, cell death, cell differentiation into different types, the formation of synapses (connections between neurons), and the pruning of synapses. Beginning within the first month after conception, the embryo's cells differentiate into a three-layered wormlike structure, and the nervous system develops from a strip of just a few cells on the outermost layer. This strip thickens and then folds up to form a hollow tube. The cells in the front end of the neural tube develop into the brain. Neurons are born rapidly from approximately six to eighteen weeks after conception. They migrate to the position they will occupy in the mature brain, either by being pushed outwards by more recently developing cells or by finding their way past existing cells by clinging to the long glia cells that radiate from the inner to the outer surface of the developing brain. By the time neurons have reached the end of their migration, the embryo's brain has recognizable forms of the anatomical parts of the adult's brain.

All of this normally occurs in an orderly predictable and even 'programmed' way (though the development of particular brain structures will be affected by the development of other structures alongside them). The effects of information from outside the womb are not fully understood. The Victorian advice that pregnant women should 'think beautiful thoughts' or frequent art galleries so as to give their babies' brains an advantage was not well founded, though it might have been pleasant for the mothers-to-be, and their contentment could have affected their babies. It's becoming very clear that the mother's emotional state affects the fetus, as I discuss later. Diet, on the other hand, may be important; very low levels of folic acid, iron, iodine, and other substances can lead to problems. Mostly a normal healthy diet plus a bit of medical supervision with supplements, if necessary, will do. There are both traditional and modern suggestions that eating fish is good for the brain, and I discuss this later.

Once in their final position, neurons develop a branching pattern of dendrites, longer or shorter axons, and more or fewer synapses where messages pass from one neuron to the next. This happens at different times in different regions of the brain; most of it is complete before birth, but in some regions this sort of development continues to puberty or beyond. Most of postnatal brain development is due to changes in connectivity and neurons dying off, though it is possible that new neurons are sometimes formed. Connectivity is definitely fine-tuned by experience. The pattern of dendritic branches, axons, and synapses affects the quantity and quality of the signals that neurons receive and pass on to other neurons.

Throughout brain development, there are localized bursts of growth in which many more axons, dendrites, and synapses are formed, followed by a lot of them dying off. This 'pruning' reduces the number of connections and leads to stabilisation of the number and location of synapses and rearrangement of pathways between neurons; this stabilisation happens at different times in different brain regions. Some cells shrink and die off in the embryo even while other cells are proliferating and migrating, and programmed cell death continues throughout fetal development; this probably allows for correction of errors during cell division, the elimination of regions whose temporary usefulness is now past, and matching the number of nerve cell connections to the size of a target. Synapse formation and pruning begin prenatally and continue into childhood and adulthood, with particular connections surviving or being deleted depending (it is thought) on how useful they are. Neurotransmitters probably play a role in signalling to the immature brain which connections should be kept and which should be pruned out; a failure of neurotransmitters to function normally may possibly be a contributor to developmental disorders such as autism and Down syndrome.[75]

The neurons which integrate nerve impulses from different parts of the nervous system are developing patterns of connections and of activity even in the earliest months, before birth. They transmit substances which play a key role in the regulation of nerve cell growth and differentiation throughout the developing brain (and can play something of the same role if implanted into adult brains which have been damaged). By the time the embryo is eight weeks old and the cells which will develop into the neo-cortex are appearing, the lower parts of the brain have already developed an elaborate structure. The fetus's nerve cells interact with each other's genetically controlled messages, with the hormones and growth substances produced by cells, and with nerve impulses conducted through the network of nerve connections. They also, very importantly, interact with input from the wider environment provided by the mother's body. Her nutritional state, perhaps, but for sure her emotional state and in particular her experience of stress, will be part of this input.

Even before birth, the fetus will react to sounds in the outside world (and newborn babies have been shown to remember some of the sounds they heard before they were born, notably the characteristic sounds of the mother's voice).[76] To begin with, nerve cell interactions are generated by activity that is intrinsic to the brain, but the timing and patterning of exter-nal stimulation play a major role in determining the precise detail of neural networks, editing, sorting, and pruning connections. This creates the basis for the detailed perception, elaborated representation, and precise thinking which we need to apply to our experience. Development such as this goes on throughout childhood (and perhaps throughout life).

Different regions of the brain progress towards maturity at different rates. The cerebral cortex, which is what we think of as doing most of our think-ing, is a late developer. Its nerve cells are not distributed in the fully adult pattern until six months after birth, and connections are not fully mature until adolescence. Some of its features have developed before birth, but some psychological functions (vision is an example) have to be carried out in 'stop gap' ways prior to the maturation of the brain part which serves this function in the adult brain. Some regions may go through periods of reorganisation which disrupt how well the child can think; discontinuities in the workings of the prefrontal lobes in adolescence has been blamed for the rise in stroppiness and self-centredness that some adolescents stereo-typically display.[77]

The timing of brain development is important. Different regions of the brain have to develop in coordination with other regions. And outside influences may be more powerful at some times than at others. The idea of 'critical periods' of brain development implies that the brain must have particular experiences within a short time period of development if it is to be able to develop and function normally; experiences outside the 'critical period' are useless. There are some examples of this in the development of the visual cortex, largely documented from studies of visual deprivation of animals.[78] In classic experiments, kittens which were only allowed to see

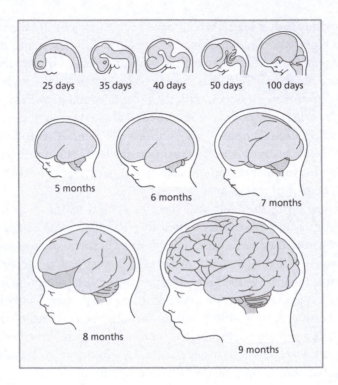

Figure 5.2 The embryonic and fetal development of the human brain.

vertically striped environments from the moment that their eyes opened developed many neurons sensitive to vertical lines and few that were sensitive to horizontal ones, while kittens which were only allowed to see horizontal stripes developed many more neurons sensitive to horizontal lines than to vertical ones. Human children who only get restricted visual experience may also develop visual cortex wiring that impairs their vision ever after; astigmatism and cataracts may cause these sorts of problems, and possibly myopia is affected by lack of exposure to enough bright outdoor light.[79] Getting the right experience may be especially important for the genetically vulnerable.

A lot of the evidence for 'critical periods' comes from studies of animals. Most of it comes from animals that have much shorter lives than humans do, and most of it is about relatively simple outcomes such as seeing stripes. I think we need to be cautious about using animals' critical periods as evidence for similar 'critical periods' in children, and especially as evidence for a need to give human children important experiences early, for example starting formal education very young. Undeniably, there are critical periods in human development, for example the very short time period when the tissues that will make up the mouth and lips grow together in the embryo; discrepancies in the speed of growth of parts of the face over this time lead to cleft palates and harelips. But in humans, it is probably better to think of 'sensitive' periods rather than 'critical' ones, since some learning is still possible even after deprivation in most cases. And some 'sensitive periods' are very long – from before birth up to adolescence in the case of learning about speech sounds, for example. On the whole, the animal studies use much more severe deprivation of stimulation than occurs in even 'impoverished' human environments; there may be a difference between the effects of 'nothing' and the effects of 'less than average'. Even in children rescued from a long period of almost total social deprivation and severe sensory deprivation in Romanian orphanages, the evidence of poorer brain development is as yet quite sparse.[80]

Findings in cognitive neuroscience also suggest that notions of the brain being 'ready' to learn some specific skill may be problematic; many brain regions appear to be fairly fully developed long before they come to be used for the functions they serve in a mature brain, and some cognitive functions are run by different brain regions in the immature and the mature individual without being seriously compromised. Similarly, while a child might not be 'ready' to learn some difficult skill (reading, for example), that child may well be perfectly ready to learn the precursors of the skill and may actually be busily doing this essential learning.

Another important area of brain development throughout infancy and childhood is the growth of an insulating sheath of myelin around nerve fibres. Myelin is a fatty sheath like a double-strength cell membrane wrapped repeatedly around the axon. This insulates nerve fibres from each other, allowing different axons to lie close to each other without their electrical impulses interfering with each other. It also vastly increases the speed at which messages pass along the axon. In different regions of the brain, myelination starts at different times and proceeds at different rates. Some regions have very little of it and function perfectly well. But regions which normally become myelinated tend to function much less well if their myelination fails; messages are conducted along axons more slowly and erratically, there is more interference from other nerve fibres, and there is a longer period of lack of response after each burst of activity in the nerve cell. Some of the same underfunctioning may be apparent in the immature neuron which has not yet been myelinated, which would have consequences for the behaviour of the very young.

Myelination is intrinsic to brain growth. It is most rapid during the first few years, but it continues into adolescence and adulthood. It is genetically programmed but also open to the effects of experience; a study of myelination in professional pianists found a significant positive correlation between myelin density and hours of piano practice, especially practice during childhood, in specific brain regions. Diet may also be important (iron and iodine deficiency pre- and postnatally may affect it).[81] Some regions are fully myelinated before birth. For example the regions of brain concerned with detection of posture and direction of movement are mature at birth, which would allow even newborns to quieten (as they do) when being gently rocked horizontally, and to become more alert when being held upright. Other regions need much more time for development. The very long nerve fibres that carry messages between the spine and the brain are gradually myelinated during the first year, enabling the dramatic change from a newborn with little control over his or her limbs and hands to the toddler with sophisticated grasping and movement skills. The myelination of the visual system begins just before birth and is completed rapidly over the first few months postnatally, allowing a rapid improvement in the baby's vision. Myelination of the auditory system also begins early, but connections to the cerebral cortex take longer to develop myelination, at least one year, probably two. Myelination in the limbic system may underlie changes in emotion regulation. The association areas in the cortex continue to myelinate well into adulthood.

There is speculation, and some emerging evidence, that disorders of psychological development such as autism and dyslexia may involve abnormalities in the connectivity of the brain.[82] As yet it's not clear whether this is the case and what the abnormalities would be. It seems very likely that there has been poorly regulated neuronal growth, possibly before birth, possibly after, and in various different brain regions. The research has picked up quite a range of small abnormalities, and it may be that not all of these are important in any given case. Diagnoses of autism and dyslexia tend to be based on a complex collection of symptoms, and the disorders may well have a complex set of causes. Good science can rule out some claims that something is the cause (for example the claims that the MMR inoculation 'caused autism' have been very thoroughly disproved[83]), which is useful progress; but identifying what is most important most of the time needs a very large number of cases with clear diagnoses, and a clear theory of how brain development happens.

Recent research on brain development suggests that there are significant changes in the brain during adolescence.[84] In many ways, the adolescent brain looks close to maturity: it has about 95 per cent of its adult weight, most regions are very close to adult size, and it has about as many synapses as an adult brain has. But there is a particularly pronounced spurt in brain development in adolescence which may perhaps bring about a radical improvement in how adolescents think and functioning socially, but after a period of possibly somewhat chaotic flexibility. Adolescents' increasing tendency to take risks might be associated with changes in the reward-seeking and emotional systems of the brain, while the decline in risk-taking that comes in adulthood might be associated with the maturation of cognitive control systems.

Rates of psychological disorders, such as anxiety and depression, and of antisocial behaviour increase rapidly at puberty. Adolescence is commonly thought of as a period of stress (*Sturm und Drang*) by theorists, parents, the media, and adolescents themselves. (I've been a fairly even-tempered person all of my life, but in adolescence I did my fair share of door-slamming, answering back, self-dramatising, and writing bad poetry.) We know that stress during childhood and adolescence can predict susceptibility to anxiety and depression in adulthood. Stressors in adulthood, and presumably earlier, can lead to the onset and exacerbation of psychological disorders and to changes in the structure and function of the brain. A combination of normal developmental change plus stress-induced alterations in the nervous system of the adolescent might contribute to vulnerability to the development of psychopathologies during adolescence.

Exactly what is happening in the brain during adolescence remains to be determined. However, it seems likely that several regions of the brain are affected. The prefrontal cortex and other neurological structures that contribute to decision-making, judgement, and behavioural inhibition are not yet mature, which may put adolescents at risk of making impulsive bad decisions. During adolescence, there is increased myelination of nerve fibres, and synaptic pruning in the prefrontal cortex increases, which ultimately improves the efficiency of information processing but may temporarily weaken it. Connections between the prefrontal cortex and other regions of the brain are strengthened, which may eventually make the adolescent better at planning ahead, assessing risks, and making decisions. This could lead to better evaluation of risks and rewards, as well as improved control over impulses.

The hippocampus, which is vitally important for learning, memory, and the regulation of emotional behaviours, continues to develop well into adolescence. Animal studies show that stress affects the volume of connections between hippocampal nerve cells, possibly with consequences for memory and emotion. Stress also affects the amygdala, which plays a central role in emotional memory and fear conditioning, and these changes are associated with high levels of anxious behaviour which do not reverse themselves over time. Stress damage from earlier in life may show up more clearly at adolescence than earlier;[85] stress in adolescence may produce long-lasting changes, and even permanent ones. If this is the case, we should probably think about the challenges that our society puts adolescents through, and whether this stress is going to be good for their later brain functioning. There's good reason to be very concerned when adolescents use drugs which affect the brain, such as cannabis, but externally inflicted trauma like having to get very high grades in examinations and facing high rates of youth unemployment are relevant, too.

There are a lot of hormonal changes in adolescence, and these would be likely to alter activity in the limbic system and its connections to the cortex and consequently have effects on the adolescent's emotional functioning. They might affect the fine-tuning of brain regions that are still immature at this point. The proportion of receptors for the excitatory neurotransmitter glutamate falls during adolescence, and levels of dopamine and serotonin go up. These changes may make adolescents more at risk of aggressiveness, boredom, and stress, and they make it more difficult for them to inhibit impulsive behaviours. There are individual differences in the size, connectivity, and activity of particular brain regions which may underlie differences in adolescent temperament, and some of the brain differences may be associated with differences in experience, notably in different behaviour by parents and different patterns of drug use. There is obviously a complex interplay of genetic and experiential influences here.

So adolescence is a time of profound changes in an individual's nervous system, physiology, and behaviour. Although this may make adolescents especially open to experience and vulnerable to harm, it may also allow for interventions to improve the brain functioning damaged by earlier emotional or physical stress. In one interesting study,[86] prepubertal male animals were operated on to produce a brain lesion that, if suffered by adults, would irreversibly damage their mating behaviour. Then some of the young animals were housed alone and some in groups; the latter showed no effect of the brain damage, suggesting that the quality of the social environment can diminish or even prevent the effects of brain damage. Other research suggests that animals suffer deficits in behaviour (high emotional reactivity, anxiety, and depression) associated with their mothers being stressed during their gestation, but that being raised in an enriched environment rather than the usual bare laboratory cage substantially reduces these problem behaviours.[87] This might all add up to the implication that good social relations might protect adolescents from vulnerability with regard to changes in their brains.

A human brain system does not work in isolation. Brains have social and emotional functions as well as cognitive ones. Because our evolutionary history has involved us being social, we would expect there to be things about brains that made it possible for us to act socially. Because we act socially on many different levels and in multitude of different ways throughout our lives, it's not going to be a simple task to map out exactly what we do and how the brain is involved. But I would suggest that some of the core areas are these: identifying the agent (identifying who is causing something); attributing mental states appropriately (we ourselves have them, other humans have them, other living creatures may have them, the nonliving don't) and identifying what the mental states are (thoughtful, cheerful, threatening, etc.); emotion processing (recognising emotional expression and regulating emotions); emotional empathy (not just knowing how someone else is feeling but also sharing that emotion and acting helpfully); knowing the history of interactions with individuals (who is this person relative to me, how have they behaved in the past, how are they likely to treat me); knowing oneself (self-awareness, self-concept, self-regulation); knowledge about in-group/out-group distinctions and social hierarchy mapping (are these people like me, where do I belong); and social policing (what's fair, what will be good for the social group, who's trustworthy, who's a threat).

These are all valuable skills that are very important for the normal processing of social information. Neuroscientists are clarifying what brain regions are involved,[88] and the current suggestion is that humans have several different overlapping systems. A network involving the amygdala and the orbitofrontal regions is involved in threat detection, emotional evaluation, and the regulation of emotions. A network in the medial prefrontal region and the superior temporal regions is involved in the automatic attribution of mental states. An empathy network in the insula and amygdala regions detects and responds to others' emotional states. And the parietal and prefrontal regions contain 'mirror neurons' which respond to both actions of others and to one's own actions. Some of these patterns of brain activity are shared with other species; most of them show activity from birth but change over infancy and childhood as the brain matures and especially as the individual learns how to behave.

Mirror neurons[89] respond to the sight (or sometimes sound) of someone else doing something with brain activity that strongly resembles what would happen if you were carrying out that action yourself. They were first discovered in macaque monkeys; activity in the monkey's brain when it observed another monkey grasping a banana or shelling a peanut, for example, corresponded to what its own brain activity was when it grasped a banana or shelled a peanut itself. Similar findings in humans have suggested that we have brain systems that respond to other people's actions and intentions and emotions as being similar to those we might have. These are partly wired-in, but they are also responsive to experience; the mirror neurons of professional dancers react more strongly to watching other dancers than the mirror neurons of individuals who have not been trained to dance. These systems would help us to recognise actions and goals, to imitate, to learn to do things ourselves, to predict others' behaviour, and to recognise others' emotions.

There is evidence of other brain systems which do 'mentalizing', that is systems which are active when people interpret what they see in terms of mental states. For example when you are playing 'scissors, paper, stone', you may think about what your opponent will do and how you can act to beat his or her expectations – 'he probably thinks I'll do scissors, so to beat him I have to do paper' (or, if you are a kind parent, 'he probably thinks I'll do scissors, so he'll do rock, so I need to do scissors for him to win'). Doing mentalizing seems to be a strong tendency from infancy onwards. If you show a child or adult a cartoon of two triangles where a large one is in contact with the back of a small one and they move together up a diagonal line, from a very young age this is seen as the large triangle 'helping' the small one get up a slope.

Babies are born with what amounts to a preference for looking at faces, which is one of the things that make them pleasing to adults. Exactly what attracts them to faces has been debated – symmetrical spots like eyes and a mouth in the right place, at a minimum, but quickly the whole moving, smiling, talking package. It's an impressive preference, and it can't be due to prenatal experience as babies obviously can't see faces when in utero (while they can hear familiar sounds such as their mother's voice while in the womb). There's a very early preference for human movements, too. Even newborns seem to look longer at displays where they can see lights moving as if attached to a moving body, rather than lights where the movements could not have been produced by real human movement. And newborns are quite likely to 'imitate' other people's exaggerated facial movements, for example sticking out their tongues or opening their mouths wide if an adult has done that. Real social smiles, part of interaction with another person, emerge six to eight weeks after birth, and so do different types of crying. Within the first three months, infants become distressed if an adult who has been interacting with them in a natural way stops and 'freezes', showing a completely unresponsive face. They get better and better at picking up other people's gazes and attending to the same things as another person. They get better and better at discriminating between emotions and using other people's emotions as clues to how they should feel themselves (for example being more likely to approach something if their mother shows she likes it and more likely to avoid it if she shows a negative emotion).

All these are things that parents can pick up and use in games – doing things responsively and feeling it all to be emotionally rewarding. This is among the beginnings of joint action and joint attention and of attachment. It's also worth considering how your own emotions might be picked up by even the very young child – anxiety about their eating or sleeping or separation from you, for example, can make the chid anxious about it and less able to do what you want.

In the right hemisphere of the brain, there are neurons specialised for responding to faces and to the emotions shown in faces. These learn from what they see – children are better at discriminating between faces that they are relatively familiar with than faces from a different ethnic group. Changes in brain activity in response to the sight of fearful faces develop over childhood, and so does children's ability to succeed on tasks involving understanding irony or understanding people's intentions. Differences in children's emotional relations with significant adults may be associated with differences in the balance of activity in the left and right hemispheres of the frontal cortex.[90]

Some parts of the brain are specialized for social behaviour. Parts of the frontal lobes, which mature comparatively late, are involved in attention to the feelings and emotions of other people. They are linked to regions of the brain concerned with emotion. In the famous case of Phineas Gage,[91] a railway worker who lost a lot of his frontal lobes in an explosives accident when an iron bar was shot through his forehead, he survived the injury with most of his thinking and his sensory and motor ability intact, but he no longer had a sense of the effect of his behaviour on other people, as if his social learning had been lost. A similar accident seems to have happened to a nineteen-year-old English surveyor, Thomas Colby,[92] when a pistol exploded in his hand and a fragment of the gun went through his forehead. Rather like Phineas Gage, he is said to have 'ricocheted between ascetic self-discipline and uncontrollable outbursts of passion', but Colby was able to have a distinguished career in surveying, becoming the superintendent of the ordnance survey mapping of Britain and a fellow of the Royal Society, and living for fifty years after the accident.

The crucial point is that the human nervous system develops in a social context and under the influence of a genetic endowment and in the course of an evolutionary history which expects and allows individuals to function as members of a social group. Other people's actions affect our brains. As I said, evolutionary theorists think that one of the reasons we evolved big brains is that they help with recognising the members of our social group and recognizing the complexities of their behaviours. We even seem to have nerve cells which respond to other people's actions in the same way as other nerve cells respond to our own actions, the 'mirror neurons' that I described earlier. Babies are born with what amounts to a preference for looking at faces, which is one of the things that makes them pleasing to adults. In the right hemisphere of the brain, there are neurons specialised for responding to faces. Changes in brain activity in response to the sight of fearful faces develop over childhood, and so does children's ability to succeed on tasks involving understanding irony or understanding people's intentions. Mirror neurons are a key factor here.

The speed and efficiency with which our brains get wired up is affected by the diet that is provided for us when we are very young. Evidence from laboratory studies of animals and from the epidemiological studies of children[93] that I will discuss later suggests that breastfeeding may be better for your brain than ordinary substitute milks, and that mothers who eat oily fish have babies whose vision development is subtly enhanced.[94] Not massive differences, but advantageous ones nonetheless.

Brains learn. We humans have evolved over millennia to be immature for a long time and to do lots of learning. We modern humans have set up educational systems which make learning a necessary condition of most types of success. Typically, learning is achieved through alterations in how excitable particular nerve cells are and alterations in connections between nerve cells, particularly through alterations in the strength of already-existing connections by changes in how much chemical neurotransmitter is released. As we encounter the same stimulus repeatedly, there are changes at the connections between neurons. If the repeated stimulation is not especially important, the strength of the connection will diminish, and the brain's reaction will die down. If it is a stimulation that is important – that signals danger, for example – the transmission of nerve impulses across the synapses and along the neurons will be enhanced, with more connections active, and each connection bigger and emitting more neurotransmitter. The chemistry of learning involves a complex sequence of chemicals resulting in more efficient neurotransmitter flow in the case of important events (we become *sensitized* to them) and less in the cases of ones that it is safe to ignore (we become *habituated* to them). As a long-term change, this may possibly include an alteration in the expression of genetic material and thus the subsequent synthesis of chemicals. This could last for long periods relative to the length of the life of the learner. For example as a child I lived in a village which looks out across the marshy estuary of the River Dee to the Welsh hills on the other side of the river. To this day, despite having lived in other places for much longer than I lived in Parkgate, if I see such a landscape I

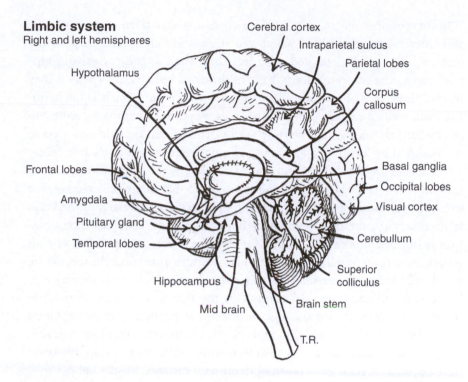

Limbic system
Right and left hemispheres

Hypothalamus

Cerebral cortex

Intraparietal sulcus

Parietal lobes

Corpus callosum

Frontal lobes

Amygdala

Pituitary gland

Temporal lobes

Hippocampus

Mid brain

Basal ganglia

Occipital lobes

Visual cortex

Cerebullum

Superior colliculus

Brain stem

T.R.

Figure 5.3 Some key areas of the brain.

Adapted from Figure 5.3 in Music, G. (2009) Neuroscience and child psychotherapy.
In M. Lanyado and A. Horne (Eds.) *The handbook and child and adolescent psychotherapy*. London:
Routledge, p. 65.

have a strong sense of being at home. The smell of salt marsh mud has the same effect, for much the same reason.

There is no single area in the brain which is the memory store. Although parts of the neocortex are probably involved in the storage of the results of complex learning, and the hippocampus may be involved in memory integration, it seems that memories are stored in the brain as multiple representations. Multiple memory representations might help to protect against loss of information. They might well show the little unevennesses that we may be aware of in ourselves, a good memory for faces and a poor memory for names for example, or a tendency to remember the actions needed to do something better than the ability to talk our way through it. If the different brain regions involved in memory mature at different times and late-maturing regions take over from early-maturing ones, that might be part of why so few of us remember anything specific from the earliest years of life.[95]

Brain regions concerned in learning contain a very large number of cells and interconnections, all of which are slightly different. The parts of the human brain most associated with learning, such as the cortex, the hippocampus, and the cerebellum, have millions of cells, each of which may receive thousands of synapses. This contrasts with regions such as the hypothalamus, which regulates all sorts of basic physical functions according to innate programmes which work so well normally that they do not need to be modified by learning, and so the hypothalamus has relatively few cells.

What cells are able to do is influenced not just by the stimulation that they individually receive but also by the stimulation that other cells receive. For example, simultaneous input from both eyes to the visual parts of the brain is necessary for the development of binocular vision cells. This coordination is important because it allows for the development of patterns of cells which record the regular combinations of events that occur in the world, and hence better representations of its regularities. Babies' brains have to learn to coordinate their visual input in the first few months after birth; their eye movements are also uncoordinated at birth, and these problems get in the way of efficient depth perception. I mentioned that diet, and specifically the mother's eating oily fish more often, may lead to a slightly faster development of good perception of depth and distance for the baby.

A lot of learning depends on experience that everyone developing under normal conditions will have. The learning brain 'expects' this normal environmental information and uses the input it actually gets to fine-tune the specifics of neural development. Almost always the environment is as expected, and the visual system develops normally. But if the environment that is experienced is not normal, the effects can include abnormal neurophysiological development and impaired behaviour. The kittens that did not see vertical stripes for a critical period literally could not see vertical stripes, and they never learned to do so.

It may seem odd that the evolutionary process has left development dependent on receiving the right sorts of experiences at the crucial moments, rather than 'wiring it in'. However, having the genes work to build up a general version of what the system should be like, and then taking advantage of expectable experience to get the system finely tuned to environmental details which actually occur, actually allows for a highly ordered and appropriate pattern to emerge. Sensory systems seem to start with a strong predisposition to function in a particular way, and if experience is near enough to normal, they will do so. If experience is very far from normal, the system will function in an unusual way, possibly effectively, but there may be some compensatory changes in other systems. Children who are born deaf may not develop speech perception in the usual regions of their brains, but instead these brain regions may be given over to perceiving signs and gestures. Myopic children with poor distance vision may not find it easy to be expert bird spotters or squash players, but often they become specialists at nearsighted or tactile tasks such as reading or needlework. Although there are still some who argue that excessive reading caused the myopia, and children should get lots of exposure to bright sunlight outdoors in the first few years of their lives, it seems certain that myopia has several different causes, and reading and playing outdoors add on to a programme of eye development significantly affected by genes and prenatal exposures.[96]

And it is not just learning very early in life that changes the brain. As I mentioned earlier, the experiences of taxi drivers, pianists, violinists, tightrope-walking rats, and blind people who read Braille changed their brains' activity and anatomy in the regions that were crucial to their skilled behaviour. Although it is possible to argue that people have only succeeded as violinists or taxi drivers because they happened to have brains which could cope with the need to use exceptionally detailed representations in the crucial regions, I don't think it is a big mistake to see brains as responding to exercise as other organs of the body do.

Individuals may perhaps differ in various ways, for example the amount of relevant experience they 'expect' or need for adequate functioning, or their resistance to adverse experience and their compensation for it, or their ability to evoke suitable experience, perhaps through social interaction. Future neuroscience investigations might help to explain the basics of differences in intellectual ability. So far as social and emotional differences are concerned, differences in neurotransmitters and stress hormones seem to be emerging as very important. I discuss this in the psychoneuroendocrinology chapter.

Understanding how brain growth proceeds is important as a corrective to simplistic models of cognitive growth. A staggered timetable of brain development for different functions would allow one system to act as a foundation for another. For example early visual and motor skills could be 'good enough' for what you have to do now and also act as the foundations for later understanding of spatial relations. It would also allow the activity of the individual in acquiring and organising experience to be important, and it could allow for some 'catch-up' growth rectifying earlier disadvantage. This sort of development would involve subtle variations between individuals who had slightly varying experiences. It is probably an advantage to have 'probabilistic epigenesis' rather than completely predetermined genetic blueprinting.

On the other hand, it can leave you open to bad effects from damaging environments. Epidemiological studies have supported neuroscience ones in showing that exposure to lead pollution has an adverse effect on development in the hippocampus, which might account for the worse learning and memory, and in particular the difficulties in concentrating, that are often found in children with high blood lead levels. Exposure to carbon monoxide and to other pollutants may also have adverse effects. This is why steps have been taken to reduce levels of lead in the environment. It is no longer added to paint or to petrol, for example.[97]

I've put forward a number of examples of an enriched environment producing better development in the person who experiences it: tightrope-walking rats, taxi drivers, musicians, and Braille users all seem to change their brains because they engage in more practice of particular skills. Is this an argument for trying to enrich people's environments in general? Will additional stimulation in the preschool years enhance people's development and later abilities? I think the evidence has to be looked at very carefully.

I feel confident that enriching a very, very unstimulating environment should have positive effects. If you live in the equivalent of a laboratory rat's cage – sterile but otherwise almost devoid of stimulation – then having access to the equivalent of a tightrope or toys or other rats will probably help your brain and your abilities.[98] But that does not at all mean that if you start with a greater-than-normal stimulation this will produce greater-than-normal brain development. You have to think about two massive issues. The first is, what do you mean by *stimulation*? We bring a lot of value judgments to this definition when we think about helping 'understimulated' children. They are very unlikely to be in an environment that is shorn of stimulation in the way that a lab rat's cage is, when compared with a rat living wild. Epidemiological data on families' activities suggests that Western children in poverty may get more exposure to television, to talk between many adults not addressed to the child, to shopping centres, and to amusement parks than middle-class children do. This is not being understimulated in the sense that rats in plain lab cages are. We need to be more specific. It is likely that what they get less of is the particular sorts of stimulation and skill practice that are highly valued in schools and later by employers. If the problem is that they may not have developed middle class skills because they have not had as much *educationally relevant* stimulation, the sort of 'stimulation' that is valued by the middle classes, then that is clearly a different sort of diagnosis from a diagnosis of 'brains that have been starved of stimulation'.

The second big issue is that stimulation occurs over a limited period of time. I don't mean this just in the sense of critical periods, outside which stimulation is less powerful. I mean simply that we all have only twenty-four hours per day, and time we spend on one activity cannot be spent on another. If you have to spend a lot of time digesting your food, you may have less time for exploring your world. If you use your time to practice your football skills, you have less time for practicing your skills as a pianist, and vice versa. If you spend lots of time watching soap operas or following the details of the lives of celebrities, you have less time to learn mathematics or be politically active, and vice versa. Given that there is a rather plausible rule of thumb that people are almost never experts in their fields until they have practiced in them for at least 10,000 hours, normally under the supervision of older experts, this will matter for anything we want our child to become an expert in. Even at the highly intensive level of forty-hour weeks for fifty weeks of the year, 10,000 hours takes at least five years to build up. Dissipating your time commitment with multiple activities means getting that much practice takes longer still, but on the other hand, full-time engagement in one skill means that you are not getting practice in others. The danger of engaging with many activities may be that you don't spend enough time on any one activity to become an expert, and the danger of concentrating on few areas may be that you are an expert in those areas but hopelessly unpractised in another. I was a very bookish adolescent, and there were points in my life when I had little idea how to get along with my male peers, who were not (so far as I could see) at all like Mr Darcy or Mr Rochester. This was a bit of a disappointment, as I had given myself a lot of mental practice at how to be Elizabeth Bennet or Jane Eyre.

If we summarise what recent neuroscience studies are suggesting to us about how the brain learns and remembers, it seems that such processes depend on the possibility of alterations of the connections between neurons and alterations in their sensitivity, efficacy, number, mapping of interconnections, and so forth, and that such alterations, both temporary and permanent, occur throughout life. A number of brain centres operate together as a complex system so that signals from the outside world and signals from other parts of the body indicate whether (and in what way) an action has been rewarding, and so should be learned and repeated or not. Advantageous programmes are more likely to be repeatedly used and smoothly learned and remembered; less rewarding ones tend to fall out of use. Patterns of connections are set up by a combination of inheritance of general structures and tendencies with fine-tuning of specific details through environmental experience. These patterns represent the organism's knowledge of the environment and allow it to produce the behaviour appropriate to the environmental situation and the organism's evolutionary goals. Normally brains operate as a united system comprising the knowledge and life patterns of the individual. In these brain workings lie the subjective unity of his or her mind and personality.

Recent work in cognitive neuroscience is using the techniques I have described to identify the brain regions that are most active in a range of cognitive tasks, allowing links to be made with models derived from experimental psychology. I will very briefly mention neuroscience on attention, memory, reading, and mathematics, and I'll return to what psychology says about these later.

Attending to something means noticing it, becoming alert, losing a focus on other things, and maintaining it in the centre of our mental gaze and our activity. These are not simple behaviours, and many of them have developed during childhood because, in part, of brain development. Babies' visual attention is a good example. Newborns' brains make much less use of the visual cortex than adults do; instead, they mainly rely on subcortical pathways from the retina at the back of the eye to a region in the midbrain (the superior colliculus), which controls reflex actions like flinching away from an object that looks as though it is looming in on them, and is also involved in the jumpy eye movements called 'saccades'. As the cortex matures, it becomes enormously more important for visual attention. Messages from the eye go to the visual cortex (which is far away at the back of the head, one of the arguments against brains having been 'designed' for effective functioning), and the visual cortex initially disrupts the functioning that was under the control of the superior colliculus. Until the balance of power gets sorted out, babies can only track moving objects in jerky saccadic movements, and their attention can get 'captured' by a visual event so that they seem unable to look away. Concentric patterns of light and dark rings seem to be particularly attention-grabbing. Mostly, as the brain matures, such attention problems diminish. I would think that the exposure to the world that normally occurs contributes to this; there is no evidence that small differences in exposure make much difference to the outcome, but extremes do.

For other parts of attention, we know about the different regions involved but not so much about how they contribute to development. The ascending reticular activating system and the prefrontal cortex seem to be involved in the alerting and interrupting functions, the parietal lobes in disengaging attention, the midbrain in moving attention to a new focus. Children will be better off if they develop some control over their attention – 'learn to concentrate', 'learn to ignore'. Individuals with impaired functioning in these brain regions may have attention difficulties. Because we put children in environments such as classrooms where they need to focus their attention on the task at hand despite a lot of competing attention-grabbers around them – other children, other things to do, a lot of ambient noise – lack of control over attention may be a serious problem.

Neuroscience helps us understand attention-deficit hyperactivity disorder. This is usually diagnosed when a child has very serious difficulties in fitting in with adults' demands for controlled attention. There is some neuroscience evidence for differences in the brains of children with ADHD. Normal brain activity tends to be rhythmic, with a characteristic slow rhythm when you are doing nothing in particular (for example sitting relaxed and with your eyes closed) and faster rhythms when you are concentrating. Brain rhythms in children diagnosed with ADHD tend more towards the former, even when they are trying to apply themselves to a task. They may have a bit less white matter insulating their nerve fibres in some regions of the brain, for example in the basal ganglia, which are involved in the switching of attention from one thing to another. They may need larger amounts of the neurotransmitter dopamine to react as needed. All this could be reducing their capacity to control their attention and could contribute to their being more impulsive and inattentive. Possibly there is slower brain development, which means that their attention control stays like that of very young children for longer than normal and makes it difficult for them to cope with schooling, but their brains' natural maturation should eventually allow them to improve. The problem may be not so much the brain as the fit between the brain and the environment, and the problems (such as anxiety and a poor self-concept due to an unhappy experience of school) which persist even after brain development has caught up to normal.

My deliberate effortful control goes on largely in my prefrontal cortex, which shapes my behaviour to fit my goals by inhibiting inappropriate impulses and actions and by encouraging more useful ones, and in my anterior cingulate cortex, which monitors performance, regulates emotions, decides between alternatives, and corrects errors. These are brain regions that mature relatively late (and continue to develop into adulthood). The state of the brain has a lot to do with our abilities to function in self-controlled and effective ways.

We do not expect the very young to plan or to control their impulses, and I hope we do not blame them when they cannot. A lot of brain maturation is needed. There may be some genetic differences behind individual children's rates of developing self-control, with the genes that are involved in the regulation of serotonin and dopamine being important. But such influences seem to be small compared with the impact of experience with your parents. I introduced parental framing earlier, and there will be more in the psychology chapter.

Remembering information is another set of skills we have to master both for education and for cognitive development in general. Research in experimental cognitive psychology suggests that memory is multifaceted.

Psychologists distinguish between memory for facts (such as who is prime minister) and memory for enacting procedures (such as reciting the alphabet in order); between short-term and long-term memory (seen as analogous to what is on the desktop and what is in the archive, respectively); and between different stores of information in different parts of the brain. Cognitive neuroscience confirms this. Human memory is distributed across many different brain regions which work together. Even the simplest stimuli can be encoded in different ways, and different brain regions are involved in the different codings; for example visual coding and visual presentation of a word activate regions in the occipital lobe, auditory presentation and encoding activate the primary auditory cortex and language processing regions in the left temporal-parietal cortex, and regions in the frontal lobe are involved in semantic processing and memory. Frontal cortical regions are involved when subjects are asked to think about their own personal history.

Given we have multiple memory systems in the brain, being able to use multiple ways of remembering could be an asset. We can scan a visual picture, we can construct lists and categorise, we can embed information in a narrative, and we may construct an autobiographical memory which does lots of these things. How our culture does it will influence how we remember things and it will define what we are expected to remember. Our education will provide us with 'cultural amplifiers' that make it easier to remember what we have to – being able to read and write, for example. Games involving remembering things look like a worthwhile activity which can contribute to learning how to remember (and be fun in themselves).

We know from experimental cognitive psychology with adults and children that reading involves coordinated processing of orthographic, phonological, syntactic, and semantic information. Not surprisingly, cognitive neuroscience studies show that a lot of different regions of the brain are involved. There is activity in the occipital-temporal regions when subjects are processing visual features such as letter shapes or distinguishing between words and nonwords. Regions in the left temporal-parietal junction are involved in processing speech sounds. Regions in the frontal lobes are activated when real words have to be defined. Dyslexic children sometimes show reduced activity in these regions, and targeted reading remediation has been shown to increase brain activity in them as well as to improve reading performance. There is evidence that learning to read can itself change the functioning of brains. For example, in a study of literate and illiterate women in Portugal, the women were asked to repeat both words and nonwords. Different brain regions were activated in the brains of the literate and the illiterate women as they repeated the nonwords. Dyslexic individuals may have brains that were always set up in not quite the optimum way for learning to read, or they may have developed brain differences as a result of their different experience of reading, or both.

Neuroscience studies show that there are brain sites that are particularly active in the complex processes of understanding numbers and doing arithmetic. Comparing experimental tasks, the left parietal lobe seems to be a critical area in arithmetical calculation, the right parietal lobe in rapid enumeration, and word problems and arithmetical reasoning involve the prefrontal cortex. There seem to be similar brain networks active in monkeys and humans. But several of these regions will probably be active together in most real-life arithmetic tasks, partly because several different strategies may be brought to bear on the problem, and partly because the different regions are connected.[99]

It looks as though there is an evolutionarily old system for processing very small numbers (seeing the difference between two objects and three, for example). Rather a diverse range of other species (nonhuman primates, dolphins, lions, and salamanders, for example) seem to be able to do this sort of discrimination, which suggests that the roots for this basic human number sense come from far back in evolutionary history. It is probably a basic, evolved capacity of the human brain.[100] It seems to be associated with brain activity on both sides of the brain around the intraparietal regions.

The first thing this innate number system can do is discriminate between sets of different sizes instantly if the sets are very small. Adults can produce the correct number for small sets (up to four) and very well-learned larger sets (such as the configurations on playing cards and dominoes) very quickly and without observable counting. Young children can also assess the number in small sets of two or three items, possibly even as newborns, though babies' abilities here remain controversial.[101] A baby who has sat in a lab and watched a single object disappear behind a screen will look longer, as if surprised, when two come out; if the baby has watched three disappear, he or she will look longer if only one or two come out. So it looks as though we may have an evolved brain capacity to construct a numerically accurate representation of small sets; up to about two or three for babies and chimpanzees, perhaps slightly larger for human adults. Anthropological evidence has come up with several languages where the number word system consists of words for *one, two, a few,* and *many,* which would fit this basic discrimination.

Interestingly, we seem to be able to do this sort of quantification on sets we can see (such as pictures of a cloud of spots or organized objects) and on sets we can hear (such as ringing tones or taps or even rhythms) and to link what we hear and what we see. Young children who hear two taps were more likely to look at a set of two objects than a set of three, for example. This sort of matching across different senses can be demonstrated in babies in the second half of their first year.

We also seem to be quite good at noticing relative sizes in larger numbers. It seems to be quite easy to tell which of two large sets has more in it (for example seeing that a set of fifty objects has more in it than a set of twenty), even if you cannot actually count accurately. The discrimination here would be something like *many* versus *even more*. This assessment of relative size may be another evolutionary given. Obviously it fails if the difference between the sets is small compared with their absolute size – we don't easily see the difference between a set of 100 and a set of 120, let alone between 1,000 and 1,200. But even in babies, there are signs of a bigger than/smaller than representation of some larger sets, provided the ratio of the two sets is roughly 1:2; for example babies show awareness that a set with six in it is different from a set with twelve.

So neuroscience and anthropology and developmental psychology all suggest that we may have two core systems of number, which are largely operational within a few months of birth and are similar to those found in other species. One represents the exact number of very small sets. The other represents the approximate numerical magnitude of large sets and can discriminate between large number sets in terms of the ratio between them. Numerical reasoning is easy if it can use these systems. If they can run almost automatically, they are probably useful much of the time we have to deal with simple number tasks. Interestingly, they seem to be operational very early and to be linked to regions in the brain that control eye movements, perhaps as if a 'mental eye' is scanning along a number line or some similar concrete representation of numerosity.

However, if we want to count accurately or do any other reasoning about number or do abstract mathematics, we have to build on the evolutionarily given foundations for number. If we have to get the exact number in a larger set, or work fluently with number representations of, for example, fractions, square roots, or negative numbers, we have to invest time in learning the number systems our cultures have developed (or use its technology to do the work for us). Once learned, a lot of this other number knowledge is represented in different ways in different brain regions. Counting on the fingers activates an area of the parietal-premotor brain which may also be active during more sophisticated calculation; calculation may also involve visuo-spatial regions, as if the subject was using a mental image of the number line. Many number facts are stored in the brain's language system along with overlearned verbal sequences and memorized poetry – the many hours of chanting multiplication tables that I did in my primary school classroom still come up as a sort of poem if I have to do a multiplication calculation today. Learning new arithmetical facts primarily involves the frontal lobes and the intraparietal sulcus, but using previously learned facts involves the left angular gyrus, which is also used in retrieving facts from memory. The organization of neural networks is not static, but changes as the process of learning changes into a process of remembering. These changes allow the brain to process numbers more efficiently and more automatically. It no longer has to work everything out; some things it just knows.

There are some individuals who struggle with even very simple arithmetic, despite being well able to read, do geometry, and use computer packages to do statistics. These people struggle to count small arrays of dots, or to say which of two sets has more in it, or to map between counting on their fingers and counting objects, tasks that a normal child can deal with at the beginning of schooling. Current research[102] seems to be showing that when adults and children with dyscalculia are doing arithmetical tasks their interparietal sulcus is less active, and that there are fewer connections between these regions and the other brain areas involved in processing numbers. This different pattern of activity might make arithmetic much more difficult for them. However, we have to be careful about timing here. If the brain difference exists very early, when children have had almost no experience of doing any arithmetic, then the brain difference might be causing the dyscalculia. But if the brain difference can only be demonstrated at later ages, then it might be a consequence of spending less time on arithmetic. The arguments that applied to dyslexia apply here, too. A child who gets the hang of numbers may choose to spend time in number games – such as voluntarily counting up to a million, however many playtimes that takes – which could augment the brain's development. A child who is becoming frightened of numbers because they mean nothing to the child except humiliation probably won't engage in number games that could enhance his or her brain development. We know that the children who play lots of number games with their parents, or whose parents involve them in counting, one-to-one correspondence, and so forth, seem to have an advantage in early understanding of arithmetic, though I don't think there have been studies of whether they have more advanced patterns of brain development in the relevant regions.

As with dyslexia, brain differences are best shown to be a source of performance differences in arithmetic if we have complementary studies: studies which show a difference in brain structures in good arithmeticians and poor ones of the same age, studies which show differences in the very young associated with them turning out to be good or poor arithmeticians years later, studies of brain damage which show acquired deficits in arithmetic performance, and studies of interventions which show both improved performance and changes in brain activity. So far, we only have a few patches of this evidence.

I have to make the important point that assessing whether young children have mastered a particular cognitive skill is often complicated by task demands that are in principle separable from the skill of interest. Neuro-imaging can reveal what is going on by using and comparing tasks with little extraneous demand, for example by measuring and picturing the brain activity of people simply looking at displays rather than requiring them to make a verbal report. Perhaps even more exciting, a collaboration between neuroscience and education might eventually identify the ways in which educational processes and programmes affect brains, and how brains influence people's responses to educational processes and programmes, something which could vastly improve formal education and reduce our vulnerability to suggestions that all children need for their cognitive development is a particular food supplement or activity.

I called this chapter 'neuroscience', and in fact all I have talked about is the brain. This is partly because we tend to think of brains as more special than the rest of the nervous system. But actually there is a lot more to be discussed than what is inside our heads; we have neurons running in from and out to every part of our bodies, systematically forwarding or gathering information everywhere from the skin of our toes to the tops of our heads, and we have neurotransmitters washing about between neurons. Research on some of these systems is showing that subtle differences in how they develop make for pervasive differences in how we handle stress and manage our emotions. This is the topic of the next chapter.

6

•

PSYCHONEURO-ENDOCRINOLOGY

In which we consider hormones, feel good factors, and other contributors to coping with stress and challenge

There are currently some very exciting areas of science aiming to establish how everyday experience might 'get under the skin' and affect how we function. This work is looking at the production and 'flow' of biological substances which are fine-tuned by daily experiences as we develop, such that differences in everyday experience are associated with differences in the functioning of the systems that give us our characteristic emotional patterns, our reactions to stress and challenge, and our sense of well-being. If these biological systems are dysfunctional, then this may affect our chances of being healthy and happy. As persons and as parents, we feel that our childhoods have a lot to do with our personalities and how well we cope with life. If we're anxious, or optimistic, or patient, or sociable, we're likely to think that this came from very early roots. The troubles we encountered as children, the ones we were protected from, the ways in which we learned to cope with them, seem to us to carry forward to later challenges. 'As the twig is bent, so grows the tree', we think, and we are largely right to think this.

The science I'm going to discuss in this chapter is about what we understand about what's flowing along under the skin. For convenience, I'll call it *endocrinology*, though more exactly I should be calling it *psychoneuroendocrinology and neuroscience and immunology*. At the centre of it are physiological systems for stress management and learning. I think the emerging findings support our intuition that early experiences of challenge and support may have lifelong consequences, they may nudge us a little way into sugar and spice rather than puppy dog tails. This means that how we help our children learn to deal with stress may be enormously important all their lives.

Stress reactions occur when there are unexpected events which may have important implications for our health or survival. We become more alert and vigilant, we focus our attention and our thoughts on the event, and we react to it emotionally; our bodies reduce the amount of work on functions that are less relevant to the present challenge and prepare themselves for fight or flight, if that should be necessary. Life is full of such events, and always has been, and so we have evolved (and we have invented) a range of responses to it, some of them automatic, some part of our culture. When we meet a stress – an infection, a predator, a challenge to our social status or our sense of success – we have a set of interlocking systems to adapt the functioning of our bodies (brains included) to stressful challenges.

Stress is not necessarily bad in itself. Challenges that are brief and met successfully are potentially good for us, as they energise us in the short term and allow us opportunities to practice coping with challenge – practice that we can use in later stressful situations. Challenges and stress that we face with support from others – for example brothers and sisters comforting each other when one of them dies – may also have their positive aspects. But we do need to avoid sustained or chronic stress faced without adequate support, which tends to be debilitating or even dangerous. Challenges increase arousal, but high arousal needs to be followed by a period of recovery. Too much arousal, or arousal for too long, tends to be damaging – chronic 'allostatic load' can lead to disease and to changes in patterns of physiological regulation.

A host of hormones, neurotransmitters, and brain regions are involved in our systems for managing stress and challenge. Neurotransmitters such as dopamine, serotonin, glutamate, and acetylcholine provide widely spreading systems over many parts of the nervous system. They carry the nerve impulse across the synapses between neurons and modulate activity. They are important not just for the thinking that the brain does, but also for many regulatory functions including stress management and meeting challenges. Neurotransmitters tend to have many functions and many effects, and the working of each one is linked to the workings of other neurotransmitters. Because coping with stress has been needed throughout evolution, there are similar systems at work in many other animals, and so studies of other species allow a detailed look at what is going on in development to produce calmer, more resilient individuals.

Thinking about what is happening in children's development that affects their emotional well-being and their development of ways of coping with stress, important hormones and neurotransmitters include oxytocin, vasopressin, norepinephrine, serotonin, and dopamine.[103] Oxytocin was first identified as the hormone that influences contractions in the uterus during childbirth, but it is also involved in the emotional processing areas of the brain, promoting feelings of belonging and closeness, attachment, and generosity. It is known to be important in calming and soothing, in empathy, in mother–infant bonding, in father–infant bonding, and in romantic partner bonding. Levels of oxytocin predict more affectionate touching, a more sympathetic understanding of other people's feelings, more behaviour which is in synchrony with another person's, and more prosocial behaviour. Vasopressin is structurally similar to oxytocin and does similar jobs, including involvement in coping with stress and pain. Testosterone is also relevant here.

Norepinephrine is involved in (amongst other functions) attention, arousal, sleep–wake cycles, learning, memory, anxiety, pain, mood, and brain metabolism. It is involved in maintaining vigilant attention, especially to very stressful events which require a strong response or events that mean what you previously knew has to be updated. Its levels may control the balance between exploring for something possibly new and working towards a known goal and determining what is felt to be rewarding.

Serotonin is involved in the digestive system, in sleep–wake cycles and sleep stages, in aggression and mood, and in depression. It is found in the nervous systems of a very wide range of different species, often being involved in reactions to the availability of food or to social threat. In humans, if there are very low serotonin levels in the brain, people act less cooperatively and more impulsively; they judge unfairness more harshly; and they are less likely to restrain their aggression. Experiments with mice and rats have shown that their emotional reactions to adverse events and their willingness to explore were affected by their exposure to different levels of serotonin in the first week or two after birth.

Dopamine is crucial for, amongst other things, voluntary movement (it is heavily implicated in Parkinson's, where individuals' movements are progressively disrupted and uncontrollable), appetite, temperature regulation, sexual behaviour, learning, and memory. It is also active in the brain circuits that are involved when prosocial behaviour is rewarded. This may increase people's reward from acting altruistically, refraining from overreacting to threat, and acting cooperatively. Social learning may affect dopamine levels in the brain, and they are implicated in depression.

For all these hormones and neurotransmitters, there are differences between individuals in several ways. There may be differences in how much is chemically present in the brain. There may be differences in the numbers of receptors on neurons. And there may be differences in how quickly the hormone or neurotransmitter is produced, does its work, and is cleared up. Each of these could matter for the functioning of stress management and emotional stability.

Emerging evidence suggests that early experience may affect stress-response systems, and it is likely that you get some of the most relevant and powerful experience via other people. For example problems with heart rate variability and sleep organisation in children are linked to maternal high anxiety in the second trimester of pregnancy and to interparental conflict (worse if these are experienced), and also to skin-to-skin contact ('kangaroo care') and more reciprocal mother–infant communication patterns (more of these being associated with better development, more mature sleep cycles in babies, and with the baby spending more time in quiet sleep or alert wakefulness).[104] There may be early experience risk factors for the functioning of the nervous system later in life, and consequently for heart disease and metabolic disorders as well as for emotional stability.

There are major similarities in physical and psychological responses to challenge across mammals. Our bodies have several ways of reacting to and reducing stress levels. There are complex cascades of events in each of these systems as we react to stressful events. I am going to do a little bit of describing this with regard to the following: the autonomic nervous system (ANS) and especially its control of heart function; the hypothalamic-pituitary-adrenal (HPA) axis and its secretion of cortisol; the immune system; the brain systems concerned with social information processing and social affiliation and belonging; and the frontal cortex and systems for memory, attention, and executive control.

The aspect of the autonomic nervous system that I want to describe, briefly, is a control system for functions such as heart rate, digestion, and breathing. Mostly this system is automatic and not under our conscious control, and much of it is below brain level in the spinal cord. Some research findings that are exciting for understanding children's development are coming out of studies of the control of heart rate by the vagus nerve. Under normal conditions, heart rate is kept to a moderate level by high 'vagal tone' – as if the ANS acted as a brake on heart rate becoming too fast. When a challenge comes along, the brake is lifted so that heart rate can increase and the body is ready to deal with the challenge, by fight or flight if necessary. Once the challenge is over, the ANS restores a higher vagal tone, which keeps the heart rate down. It's thought that a baseline of high vagal tone, which quickly falls in response to stress and then is quickly reestablished once the stress is over, is optimal for health. Children who have been exposed to a lot of stress themselves or via their mothers; have been exposed to their mothers' use of substances such as alcohol, nicotine, or cocaine; or have had poor quality parenting may be at risk of having a weaker brake and poorer recovery from challenging situations.[105]

When signals of stress reach the brain, especially the amygdala, the hippocampus, and the prefrontal cortex, neurons in the hypothalamus secrete corticotropin-releasing hormone into the pituitary gland, where corticotropin is synthesised. Corticotropin promotes the release of the hormone cortisol from the adrenal gland, and cortisol releases blood glucose to energise fight and flight. Higher levels of cortisol circulate throughout the bloodstream, including into the brain. So the HPA axis helps us build up a powerful stress response. But the HPA axis also helps to modulate stress responses and close them down if that is appropriate. We know that it is fine-tuned by early experience, and this gives it great importance in the development of the individual.

In the short term a fight or flight reaction may be adaptive, but chronic HPA activity may overload the system and lead to worse functioning. If it becomes overactive or hyper-responsive, then this influences the development of hypertension, cardiovascular disease, immune system suppression, and insulin resistance, hence susceptibility to diabetes. A hyper-responsive HPA axis may also be associated with anxiety disorders, depression, memory problems, developmental delay, and growth retardation. If the HPA axis becomes underactive or hyporesponsive, this is associated with autoimmune diseases such as rheumatoid arthritis and asthma.

It appears that early life stress may lead to short-term hyper-response and long-term lack of resilience – rather like the changes I mentioned in how the ANS works. These may show up in behaviour as short-term tendency to anxiety and longer-term psychic numbing. An individual who had too much stress early in life may seem to overreact to threat and to become aggressive or defensive even to events that would not look like challenges to most other people and then to be unreactive and callous and lacking in empathy for others' stress.

Cortisol production and processing seem to be a crucial part of the body's response to stress. Cortisol (a hormone produced by the adrenal gland, remember) tends to increase blood pressure and blood sugar and reduces immune responses. At birth, cortisol levels are not very organised, but from infancy onwards, levels vary during the day. The highest levels are on waking; levels then fall gradually over the day, rise again in late afternoon, and gradually fall through the evening, to be lowest a few hours after sleep begins at night. An individual person's daily rhythms of cortisol secretion tend to be consistent, but there is significant variation between individuals, and changes in cortisol levels have been seen in connection with illness, trauma, fear, pain, depression, and stress. Caffeine, sleep deprivation, and intense physical exercise are among the factors which tend to increase

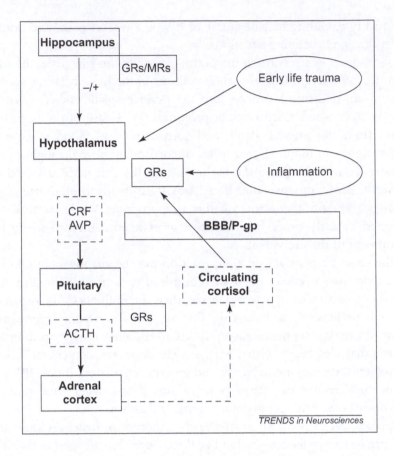

Figure 6.1 The hypothalamic-pituitary-adrenal (HPA) axis.

From Pariante, C., and Lightman, S. (2008) The HPA axis in major depression: Classical theories and new developments. *Trends in Neurosciences* 31(9): 464–468. Reprinted with permission from Elsevier.
CRF adrenocorticotrophic hormone releasing factor; AVP vasopressin;
ACTH adrenocorticotrophic hormone; GRs glucocorticoid receptors;
MR mineralocorticoid receptors; BBB Blood-brain barrier; P-gp P-glycoprotein

cortisol levels: omega-3 fatty acids, massage, meditation, laughing, and crying may be amongst factors which reduce it.

It seems that babies and young children who spend the day in group care, for example in nurseries, tend to have higher levels of cortisol than babies and children who are in one-to-one care. There is emerging evidence[106] that children who are often excluded from group activities by other children tend to have higher cortisol levels than nonexcluded children. For some individuals, this may indicate an elevated level of stress (though we know from social psychology studies that this may not be a problem; some individuals are quite happy to spend a lot of their time alone).

All in all, then, it looks as though the HPA axis and cortisol in particular may be shaped by experience of stress, and the effects may be long-lasting. Not necessarily permanently and unchangeably for everyone, but enough to be worth thinking about. We can't avoid every stress challenge to the HPA system, but we might be able to reduce the danger of chronic stress, especially for children at their most vulnerable.

All organisms sometimes encounter pathogens that might infect and damage them. They therefore have evolved ways of protecting themselves. Some of these can be seen even in simple animals, for example stopping pathogens getting inside the body by having a tough outer skin, or having what yoghurt advertisers call 'friendly bacteria' inside the body to compete with the 'unfriendly' ones, or producing a fast but generic response such as inflammation. There are also (in more complex animals such as humans) more specific reactions involving recognising a particular infection that you have been infected with earlier and using the defences you developed the previous time. This learning process means you can react to these infections more effectively: you have acquired immunity to them, and sometimes immunity to other closely related infectious agents as well. This is why inoculation with cowpox, a mild disease, gave immunity to smallpox, which was often fatal. This infection–resistance–immunity sequence builds up into a multilayered immune system over time.

Before birth, the baby is largely protected from pathogens by the mother, as her antibodies can be transmitted to the baby across the placenta. This means that if the mother had an infection such as measles earlier in her life, her antibodies to the measles virus have been passed on to the fetus, and they protect the newborn for a few weeks against infection if the measles virus turns up again. After birth, the mother's antibodies are present in her breast milk and give the breast-fed baby some protection against the infections that she has been exposed to. The baby's own immunity to infection builds up gradually, which is why pathogens that cause little trouble in adults may be more serious for the baby, and they need to be protected from them. Generally, young babies need to be kept away from pathogens, or dirt that might contain them, until their own resistance has developed. Clean water is especially crucial. Inoculation against diseases like measles, which used to kill babies and young children, and still could if they were not protected, is another important part of public health measures.

Viruses like measles and smallpox work by getting into a body and multiplying inside it at a speed which allows a lot of copies of the virus to be made and also keeps the infected person alive for long enough that new copies of the virus can spread to other people. In someone who is inoculated, the virus will not be able to take hold and copy itself. The person will not be a good host for the virus, will not get the illness themselves, and also will not be infectious to others. If you can inoculate almost all of a population against an infection, then everyone in it will be protected, either because their own bodies can resist it due to their own inoculation or because they never meet an infected person – what is called herd immunity. This is what has been done worldwide against smallpox. Inoculation against smallpox meant that the virus could not find bodies that would support it while it multiplied and could spread to other people, and so it died off all over the world. Now it only exists as heavily protected samples closed off from every possible host where it could grow again. The campaign to eradicate polio in the same way has made a lot of progress, though resistance to inoculation by people who believe it is a threat to their communities rather than a benefit has meant that the disease is still present in the real world, and could spread again.

If the number of nonimmunised people in the population goes up, there is an increased risk that the virus will find a good host and be able to spread to others. This happened for measles when parents in the UK believed that inoculation with the MMR vaccine could cause autism and they took their children out of the immunisation programme. The 'evidence' used to suggest that MMR caused autism has been comprehensively discredited, with data being taken from more than 2 million children.[107] However, the fall in the proportion of the UK child population who had their MMR jabs has meant that currently enough young people are still vulnerable to measles that the infection can spread and cause serious illness, and even death. This risk is why it really is important for people to be immunised if possible, and why we ought to accept the very small risk to us as individuals of being inoculated, because of the much greater benefit that herd immunity has for us all.

Some exposure to minor infections, chickenpox and colds being examples, gives the immature immune system the exposure it needs in order to develop acquired immunities. A little bit of challenge to damage-limiting systems seems, on the whole, to benefit them. I will talk later about epidemiological studies that have shown that children who have several older brothers show more resistance to infections than those who don't, presumably because they are more exposed to their siblings' introduction of grubbiness into the home, and their immune systems got a little more practice.[108] There might be similar advantages from spending time with other children in day care settings.

But the importance of other people in the development of a well-functioning immune system goes beyond resistance to infections. We know from studies of rodents, primates, and humans that the separation of the infant from its mother suppresses its immune system and affects immune system development (though separation from mother may also involve a loss of breastfeeding,[109] which could be expected to affect the immune system and possibly the context of the separation also needs to be considered, e.g. what alternative social attachments are present, what are the effects of prior mother-child relations). So stressful separations can potentially have bad consequences for your immune system as well as for your HPA axis.[110]

The social brain is involved in stress management. There have been many studies which show that people who have good social support networks are more able to cope with stress. This may be because such people tend to be healthier overall and so are less at risk when things get stressful. Their emotional states may be more positive, their lives more predictable and stable, and they may be able to draw on more resources. All this may help them to appraise threat as being actually less threatening, so that their response to it is less extreme. The reassurance that a child received – that actually there are no bears under the bed, that you really can get better at scoring goals, that a broken friendship can be mended – is one of the important social functions of a parent or friend. (Although sometimes, the social setting may make stress even worse. Failure may be more painful if it is very public – one of the problems once you are in school and your peer group is constantly ranking everyone's performance, or if you have very pushy parents. It may also be paralysing if your public depends on you to do well – as witness the Brazilian football team whose whole country was willing it to win the World Cup of 2014 when their opponents relentlessly scored five goals in ten minutes. Every physiological sign of falling apart under stress was visible for the rest of the game and after – players who couldn't run anymore and visibly trembled, spectators were in tears, the president of the country boot-faced and booed.)

Just as the neurons in the brain are fine-tuned by being used in reaction to events (and to what is going on in neighbouring brain regions), experience guides the functioning and development of stress systems and may result in differences in development, feelings, and behaviour. We are getting to know more and more about how experiences early in life – including exposure as a fetus to the mother's stress – may nudge the development of basic physiological systems in more or less favourable directions, with consequences for the individual which may be lifelong. They may even affect future generations if they influence the sort of experience that parents provide for their offspring.

Developmentally, it is important that we all learn to manage to get reduced stress levels and to regulate our emotions. From infancy onwards, a number of physiological and behavioural systems are available, some operated by the child (such as averting the gaze and peeping only briefly if something is too close or too intrusive or too frightening). Some of these systems appear to be fine-tuned after birth by parenting behaviour.

A long sequence of experimental studies of rats has found a cascade of effects following on from giving the baby animals a brief period of handling by humans during a short period of their lives. In one series of studies,[111] the baby rats spent most of their time in a simple laboratory cage with their mother and their littermates. Daily, during weeks three to nine after birth, they were gently removed from their cage for half an hour and gently rocked about a little on a sheet. This experience at this time was associated with the handled rats later having a lower base level of corticosterone, with a sharp peak in corticosterone in response to stress and a rapid return to base levels. Nonhandled animals had a higher base level of cortisol and a more blunted response to stress. There seemed to be a lifelong effect for the handled animals of differences in the expression of genes, reduced levels of cortisol, a smaller loss of neurons in the hippocampus, and less deterioration of their memory and learning as they aged. Handled animals coped better with later stressful situations, such as the smell of a cat.

But it was not just the handling by humans that had done it. When the rat pups were returned to their mothers after the handling, the mothers engaged in extra licking, grooming, and nursing that they did not offer to the pups who had not been taken away. Further research showed that this maternal behaviour was important in changing the corticosteroid levels, and it affected the expression of genes that were involved in the development of the HPA and of certain cognitive functions. The rats who were not (as it were) cuddled by their mothers ended up with an HPA system chronically geared for stress reaction, which would be useful if they were constantly under threat, but was not so good if they had favourable circumstances and opportunities to learn and remember over time.

Experiences of maternal deprivation, social isolation, the mother's licking or grooming of the young animal, and handling of the young laboratory animals by humans are known to affect the development of these regulatory systems. Such experiences probably affect gene methylation, the expression of proteins which help with the establishment of brain connectivity and neuron development. There are short-term changes in the efficiency of synaptic connections and long-term changes which affect the building-up of connections. The mother animal's reaction to infants who have been taken away from her briefly and handled is important. She reacts to the separation by providing more maternal licking and grooming when they are reunited, and this is what mediates the effects of human handling on the baby animal. Rats, mice, and monkeys who are low on maternal contact for a critical period soon after birth tend to be more fearful and to show physiological stress for the rest of their lives. Additionally, rodents and monkeys who have had little licking and grooming tend to parent their own litters in the same way, leading to similar patterns of stress in the next generation.

Evidence from studies of rodents shows that even if overall contact is the same, fine differences in the quality of contact with the mother lead to a reduction in stress responses in the young animals and better learning of longer term stress management strategies. One example involves the maternal behaviour of rodents. Different genetic strains of laboratory rats and mice show different amounts of licking, grooming, and arched-back nursing (LG/ABN) during the first week after birth, and given the genetic differences between strains, this might be a genetically programmed behaviour difference. Females raised by their genetic mothers who do lots of LG/ABN treat their own offspring to lots of LG/ABN; those raised with little LG/ABN provide little of it for their own pups. However, there is a possibility that rates of LG/ABN were affected by experience. Researchers[112] cross-fostered infant females with mothers of the other genetic strain so that animals born of mothers from the genetic strain that was high in LG/ABN were fostered by low LG/ABN mothers, and vice versa. When these fostered animals grew up and had litters of their own, they treated their litters to the same amount of LG/ABN that they had experienced themselves, acting like their foster mothers. Whatever the genetic background was, the amount that the mother rat had been licked, groomed, and nursed by her own 'mother' was what predicted how she nursed her own litters, and her and their stress reactions. It looks, therefore, as if postnatal maternal care programmed later maternal behaviour and vulnerability to stress. The experiences of young females in generation 1 led them to behave in particular ways when they became mothers to the pups of generation 2; this parenting shaped the development of generation 2 and their parenting of generation 3; and so on, over succeeding generations.

A lack of LG/ABN is worse for rats' stress management throughout their lifetimes, though there can be some recovery if the young animal is exposed to interesting environments and social stimulation. In primates, too, conditions which impair or exclude maternal care are associated with attachment problems and changes in the neurobiology of stress hormone production. Very possibly there are similar effects in humans who lack cuddles, especially for those who are at risk, for example infants who have a fearful or irritable temperament. If the infant lacks reliable and affectionate parenting, there may be a chronic activation of basic stress-response mechanisms, leading to a cascade of risk and cumulative effects. This 'risky families' model centres on change in chronic stress load and a lifelong reduction in ability to cope with challenge and stress.

This could all be adaptive if environmental challenges encountered early in development are likely to persist through life, in which case programming stress systems to expect stress might improve survival. A stressful environment, for example where there are dangers such as an unreliable supply of food, would reduce the amount of LG/ABN that the mother can provide to her infants, as she will be busy coping with the challenges of the environment. The infants receiving lower levels of LG/ABN would tend to be fearful and responsive to stress. It might be advantageous for those infants to expect the environment to be full of challenges and so to be fearful as they grow up and not waste their energy on superfluous LG/ABN towards their own offspring when the burning issue is survival itself. It might also be advantageous in a risky environment for human infants to be easily distressed, as distressed infants will do more to attract the care and attention of their parents. In a classic study[113] of temperament in Kenyan infants during a time of food shortage, it was the infants previously identified as having a difficult demanding temperament who survived the food shortage best, because they made more demands on their caretakers and consequently were less likely to be left short of food than the quieter, more compliant babies. I've seen children quietly fall badly behind in the classroom because the teacher was having to work with extremely challenging classmates. With her attention and energy concentrated on stopping Little Samson from causing grievous bodily harm, the teacher genuinely thought that Little Mouse, though quiet and slow, was doing all right for her age, but also that Mouse was one of the youngest in the class when she was actually one of the oldest.

Clearly, the parenting that the young receive may contribute significantly and in many different ways to the development of stress regulation systems. What is developmentally important is warm and responsive parenting. Probably this specifically means that breastfeeding is ideal. Breastfeeding is interesting scientifically because there are extensive benefits for human infants and analogous findings in other species.[114] Obviously, it provides nourishment including key fatty acids, vitamins, and so forth which are so strongly implicated in favourable cognitive development that baby food manufacturers are now adding them to formula milk. Breast milk also strengthens the immune system, giving better resistance to all sorts of infections at a time when the baby's own immune system is immature. It means that mothers do not have to risk infection to their babies from water that is not perfectly clean. And breastfeeding involves closer physical skin-to-skin contact and perhaps more mutual gazing with the mother than other ways of feeding. The science shows that the human infant's experience of skin-to-skin contact is associated short term with reduction in stress and long term with more rapid maturation of vagal tone (implicated in digestion, heart rate, facial expression) and more settled sleep cycles, maybe with better growth and behavioural development. Gentle touch affects hormone levels, especially oxytocin, throughout life.

In the last paragraph, I used the phrase 'warm and responsive parenting'. I should clarify this. There is strong evidence that if there is very little warm and responsive parenting, then things are less likely to go well for the child. But high quality parental care does not have to be provided every minute of every day of every year of the child's life. When Mary Ainsworth looked at attachment years ago, she defined a 'responsive' parent as one who responded to about 30 per cent of the young child's behaviours. There is a lot to be said for some experience of 'benign neglect'; children who have enough support to be able to learn to support themselves may well be better able to cope by themselves when they are stressed and their other support systems are not available. The evidence on psychological resilience and the evidence on separations from the caregiver suggest that developing a good range of coping strategies is better than always relying on one.

On the other hand, 'neglectful neglect' and 'malign neglect' are very well known to be bad for the child. Children who suffer neglect at the hands of their parents are highly likely to have higher cortisol levels and a risk of poorer mental health outcomes in later life. Family poverty, which is associated with stress in the parents that makes responsive parenting more difficult, is associated with abnormal cortisol patterns in the child.[115] State benefits given to the parents but targeted on the child, and nurse support, lead to lower cortisol levels in the child and the mother. Ending neglect, whether by the parents or by others, seems to improve cortisol levels. And with lower stress levels there probably come better self-regulation, more positive emotional states, better concentration on school tasks, and a whole host of benefits for the children, their families, and for the wider social world.

Babies develop a buffering system against the disruptive effects of stress.[116] This may be detectable in brain differences. For example, babies who have a secure attachment to their caregiver have more left frontal lobe activity compared to right, an asymmetry which is associated with positive emotions, while insecurely attached babies have more right frontal lobe activity, which is associated with negative emotions and inhibition. EEG studies of humans show that infants with depressed mothers are less likely to show left-hemisphere activation. What mothering the baby gets seems to be mediating between depression and EEG. It appears that there may be differences between brain responses to stress of infants with withdrawn, normal, or intrusive mothers. There may be differences in gene methylation, too.

Stress reactions develop over the lifespan. In humans, newborns react to pain or stress, such as medical examinations, with fussing and crying and the secretion of adrenocorticotrophic hormone and cortisol. Neonates do not have the adult daytime-related pattern of high cortisol levels in the morning getting lower throughout day, but this is beginning to be established by three months. By one year, there tend to be diminished neurobiological reactions to stress, though infants produce the behavioural reactions of crying and fussing; perhaps less distress and more protest is involved? Evident distress does not necessarily mean high levels of stress hormones; for example some babies may cry to elicit care, but they have low cortisol levels. Usually when their signal has been responded to, these babies calm down quite easily. Inevitably, if parents respond to crying with stress-reducing care, babies will learn to cry for care, which is excellent except when the parents can't supply it. In this case, babies need to have learned alternative ways to cope, and these alternatives may have had more chance to develop if babies have had opportunities to calm themselves and haven't always had parental care straight off.[117] I remember my mother saying I was 'making a rod for my own back' by being, she thought, too attentive to my baby. The baby went to sleep fine if I was cuddling her, but much less well if I left her to settle herself. I therefore did lots of go-to-sleep cuddles, which was as it turned out rather selfish of me; it was in fact my childminder who was inconvenienced and who had to talk me into letting my daughter learn to calm herself rather than doing it for her.

Sensitive and responsive parenting seems to influence regulatory processes in infants' immature regulatory systems and to facilitate the long-term development of stress response systems. The processes involved may affect neurodevelopment and the expression of genes. A lack of sensitive parenting and the experience of maternal separation will stress the infant and simultaneously remove the person who normally destresses him or her. Early experience of parenting may have long-term effects on social and emotional development and also on cognitive development via affecting the child's ability to marshal cognitive resources to task, to sustain attention despite stress, and to lay down and access memory effectively. We might also expect risk-taking behaviour to be associated with early experience of stress and stress reduction. I will come back to this later.

Recent research on humans provides exciting evidence about the developmental impact of certain patterns of human parental behaviour. It looks as though there may be interaction between what genetic alleles you have and your rearing conditions. Meaney and his colleagues[118] describe studies which found that the expression of genes was affected by early life differences in being parented. In work by Caspi and Moffitt and their colleagues,[119] the researchers found interactions between genes and experience. Individu-als who both had an unusual gene for an enzyme called *monoamine oxidase A* (MAOA) and were abused as children were highly likely to suffer the adverse outcomes of depression and antisocial behaviour as adolescents or young adults. Individuals with the gene but with no experience of abuse were fine. Individuals without the unusual version of the gene were still damaged by parental abuse, but they were less likely to develop antisocial behaviour.

There is evidence about the effects of abusive parenting from animal stud-ies.[120] Some macaque mothers tend to abuse their young infants, typically by dragging, throwing, sitting on, or biting them; the behaviour sometimes results in superficial injury and sometimes serious injury or death. These abusive mothers are not just being clumsy with their babies (as first-time macaque mothers sometimes are), and they usually get on well enough with other adult macaques; abusive mothering seems to be a specific set of maladaptive behaviours, limited socially to how the mothers treat their babies. This behaviour seems to run in families (daughters resemble moth-ers, sisters resemble sisters) and to recur across an individual mother's different pregnancies.

So why are these monkeys behaving in this damaging way? Are they in some way born to be bad mothers, genetically destined to abuse their babies? The evidence (from cross-fostering studies) is rather that it was the mothers' own experiences of abuse which predicted whether they would abuse an infant, and it was the females who had suffered most abuse in their own infancies who were most likely to abuse their babies. The females might have learned their mothering techniques from observing their own abusive mothers mistreating their siblings, but it is also highly possible that their own suffering from maternal abuse resulted in long-term changes in neural circuits or neuroendocrine processes that affected their own parent-ing behaviour. There is no evidence in these studies of a genetic tendency to abuse the infant; the macaque mother's own experience appeared to be a much stronger predictor of risk (just as it was rat mothers' experience of LG/ABN from their own mothers that predicted their care of their litters).

The big psychological theory that is relevant here is attachment theory, which I will discuss later. Secure attachments seem to be the best founda-tion for dealing with stress positively, insecure but consistent attachments are less helpful, and insecure disorganised and unpredictable attachments are the most stressful in themselves and the least satisfactory foundation for development.

Stress levels in young children are affected by other children as well as parents. Peer effects are evident in preschool day care: normally, secretion of cortisol shows a morning peak followed by a drop off, but for young children in day care whose peer social skills are still developing, there can be increases in cortisol levels throughout the daytime spent with peers unless there is good supportive care from adults. In social settings later in childhood, peer-rejected children have higher levels of cortisol and poor control of their aggression and negative behaviour. Peer-neglected children start to show higher levels of cortisol in early adolescence, maybe because they have accumulated more aversive social experiences, or maybe because of the different social demands of the period.

Buffering seems to become less effective in smoothing out stress in adolescence. Some endocrinological studies show a peak in basal glucocorticoids and reactivity around puberty and some show a more gradual increase, so the evidence is inconsistent as yet. If there is a peak in the base level of cortisol and other stress hormones at puberty, this may be associated with the increased moodiness, impulsive behaviour, and disorder that we tend to expect at adolescence.

Another system for getting environmental influences inside the skin involves the brain systems concerned with social information processing and social affiliation and belonging – the 'social brain'. I talked about brain regions and about mirror neurons in the neuroscience chapter, and I mentioned how different neurotransmitters and hormones are involved earlier in this chapter, so I won't repeat myself here. But there are links between social functioning and stress. People sharing the same stress – student exams, teenager worries about being too fat – may 'co-ruminate', endlessly discussing the awfulness of it all, and so exacerbate their feelings of helplessness.[121] Depressed mothers have more difficulty responding to their infants' social signals, and the infants' behaviours change in response to this.[122] Nine-year-olds who are excluded from activities at school and rarely chosen by their classmates to be partners in activities tend to have higher cortisol levels and worse stress reactions. People who are depressed, anxious, or isolated have similar problems. People who are stressed tend to make more mistakes 'reading' other people's social signals. People who are stressed are less often invited to everyday social activities and get to spend less time in relaxed social interactions, and they may find them less rewarding if they do get involved. They may also be less attractive to others, so they do not get invited to the positive social experiences that might cheer them up.

The final area I listed at the beginning of this chapter is the systems for memory, attention, and executive control that we need in order to learn, to remember, to focus attention, to switch attention, to choose between actions, and to inhibit inappropriate action. Some of these, especially focussing on a task but being able to switch focus between relevant aspects of the task, and being able to suppress one's immediate reaction in favour of a more considered action, are difficult. We have to manage our attention, however, in order to cope with the complexities of the world (and perhaps especially of the social world). These skills have to be practised.

In neuroscience studies,[123] the prefrontal cortex emerges as key to this effortful attention control and to the related concept of deferred gratification (postponing a small immediate reward in order to get a bigger one later). Research is showing that stress hormones, notably cortisol, affect how synapses are formed in the prefrontal cortex and how active they can be. High cortisol levels mean poorer executive control and more difficulties in concentrating, in focussing on what's important, in recalling relevant information, and in choosing the best course of action. There might also be underlying genetic differences, but if there are, they probably combine with experiences from infancy onwards, especially in interaction within the family. A combination of mutually responsive orientation between mother and small child and lower levels of parental power assertion, for example, is associated with better self-regulation by the child and more positive development of interpersonal and moral behaviour. There is relevant psychological theory, which I will discuss later.

I hope I have produced a convincing argument that there are very important physiological processes involved in emotion regulation, and that early experience in general, and experience of parenting in particular, may have profound effects on the fine-tuning of these systems. Self-regulation of emotions, cognitions, motivations, and psychological processes in general is one of the most important areas of the development of competence. All societies expect their members to regulate themselves so as to fit reasonably well with social expectations as to feelings, thoughtfulness, goals, and social functioning, and socialisation therefore invests a great deal of effort in these. Measures of how children regulate their psychological processes to learn or to cope with strong emotions or stress predict their mental health. Undoubtedly there are many definitional questions about how general, how pervasive, and how constant self-regulation is, or whether it might not often be specific to a limited range of settings. An individual might be able to be highly self-regulated in one setting or at one time or with one partner, but be very precariously self-regulating in another. Similarly, it is likely that a wide range of complex mechanisms are involved in such behaviour and in its development, and a large number of apparently different pathways might lead to indistinguishable outcomes.

I think there is reason to believe that difficulties with self-regulation of emotion may underlie a whole range of psychosocial disorders. If a child fails to develop ways to moderate feelings of anger and anxiety, such as shifting attention away from provoking events or inhibiting emotional impulses, he or she may be prone to aggressive or anxious behaviour, which may in turn damage relations with parents, peers, and teachers. Children who have better emotional self-regulation may be able to inhibit an immediate aggressive or anxious response, giving themselves time to find more constructive and positive ways of coping with the problem and making it less likely that they'll react in ways that provoke others. Differences in emotion regulation and capacity for 'effortful control' can become deeply entrenched and difficult to change, in part because they are expressions of basic biological mechanisms, and in part because they may be grounded in relationships and interactions which pervade the child's development. It seems highly possible that aggressive and anxious children have experienced many family interactions where both parent and child are 'stuck' in emotional exchanges which may bear little relation to the actual situation. Well-functioning children may have more experience of parent–child interactions that shift flexibly according to the immediate context. People seem to get stuck in chronic negative appraisals of the situation, such that they see everything that happens as negative, even when a neutral observer would judge that the action or expression in question was truly neutral or even positive. This experience could have consequences for control at the cortical level, and neuroscience studies of brain functioning may be beginning to show what these are.

It is worth briefly noting here that there is an extensive research literature on the effects on children's self-regulation of their emotions. Exposure to events such as conflict and violence between parents or bullying at school can have damaging effects. For example, children who have been exposed to higher levels of domestic violence have more problems with regulating their behaviour and emotions, which is in turn associated with more negative interactions with other children; more social problems, such as being teased or excluded; and higher levels of problems such as depression and antisocial behaviour. They may also show less awareness of people's emotions, which could make it difficult for them to build and sustain intimate relationships, either with friends or with romantic partners, and to work out positive resolutions to conflicts when these occur. This is not just a problem for Western middle-class children. Beijing children who had received particularly authoritarian parenting were more likely to show externalising behaviour problems if they also experienced negative school events and had low coping skills and low efficacy in emotional control.

I briefly mentioned testosterone earlier. This hormone is familiar in some ways – males have higher levels than females, high levels of testosterone are associated with more aggressive behaviour, males who are without testosterone because they have been castrated develop unusually feminine body shapes and singing voices and behave in less masculine ways. But there may be more subtle effects, too. Simon Baron-Cohen[124] argues that the testosterone that the male fetus's adrenal glands and testes produce (at very high levels in the middle of their gestation) diffuses through the fetus's skin into the amniotic fluid and can thus wash around other areas of the developing body and brain. Female fetuses produce very little testosterone and so their bodies and brains get much less exposure to it prenatally – unless they are in the womb with a male twin, in which case they will have prenatal exposure to the same high testosterone levels in the amniotic fluid. Baron-Cohen believes that this prenatal exposure masculinises the developing brain and organises its neural circuitry so that males' brains are, thereafter, subtly different from females'.

He also believes that differences in male and female behaviour are largely down to differences in neural circuits in the brain. In his studies, differences in behaviour linked to prenatal testosterone levels include: the amount of eye contact babies make with familiar partners; vocabulary size in the second year of life; poorer social relationships and less talk about people's feelings and mental states during the preschool years; sex-stereotyped behaviour and play; and symptoms of autism from infancy to age 10. He does not rule out nonhormonal influences, and we would all have to agree that social pressures do act in ways that could cause sex differences, but for Baron-Cohen, the brain as shaped prenatally is massively important.

Postnatal differences in testosterone are small until puberty, when the level in boys increases; this is behind the familiar adolescent increase in body size, deepening of the voice, and secondary sex characteristics. Late developments in brain regions with receptors sensitive to androgens might also be fine-tuned according to testosterone levels. Baron-Cohen mentions evidence that giving adults extra testosterone led to lower scores on recognising social threat, on recognition of others' emotional states, and on generosity and collaboration; these were short-term changes in response to unnaturally large doses of the hormone, and fortunately they wore off, but if more evidence builds up to confirm such results, this too would suggest a big effect of hormones, neurotransmitters, and the brain on people's behaviour.

I think research in psychoneuroendocrinology is emerging as coherent in its picture of the effects of early experience of parenting on the long-term development of the young individual. I must nevertheless emphasise that more work needs to be done, and there are possible problems of interpretation and detail. There are always problems with cross-species comparisons. Comparing humans and animals gets us beyond correlational studies into experimental ones which can clarify causal patterns, but we cannot make uncritical extrapolations from one species to another. For example there are questions about the timing of possible 'critical periods' for development, with changes in different sorts of early experience seeming to have more powerful effects if they come at one short period of time compared with earlier or later, but there are differences in the precise timing between species, and humans develop over a much longer period of time than rats or even other primates. Similarly, some animals in research studies experience a laboratory cage environment which may not be comparable with a normal human one (or with the normal environment of that sort of animal). We have evolved to be a very social species, so we might expect the wider social environment to be involved at many levels. We have evolved to have very long and detailed autobiographical memories, so we may tell ourselves about our history of difficulties or triumphs much more than other species do, dwelling on the stress and possibly recreating it.

I should identify some gaps in the evidence for my case. There has been a considerable amount of work on infants and their mothers. But there is not enough work yet on infants' stress and other partners – little even on fathers and little on other sorts of social settings such as groups of children. There are issues about brief stresses and chronic ones, and about different types of stress and adversity. How far are our stress management systems general and how far are they specific to particular sorts of stress? Are there lifetime changes? Can we recover as adults from the effects of childhood stress? If there are therapies that successfully change behaviour, what are they doing at the most physiological levels? Are there systematic individual differences, such as gender effects or temperament-based effects? Are there shared genetic factors as well as or instead of parenting effects? Are there differences between individuals growing up in different socioeconomic or sociocultural environments? Can we generalise models of 'normality' to children in conditions of higher or lower risk?

At present we have an increasing body of very interesting findings, and the beginnings of a precise understanding of how certain sorts of early experiences may have lifelong effects on emotion regulation and stress management systems. I think that there may be rapid progress in this area, and we will soon have a more secure grasp on how certain physiological systems come to operate in ways which amount to different personality types. Subtle differences in psychoneuroendocrinology, modulated by experiences during development, may turn out to be rather important. While we wait for knowledge to progress, it certainly looks like a good idea to provide both lots of cuddles and lots of practice at different ways of maintaining a degree of calm; and to avoid stressing out pregnant women, breastfeeding mothers, and the very young. They have a lot to get on with, and we should be helpful.

7

◆

EPIDEMIOLOGY

In which we look at what affects development (along with everything else)

A lot of the science I have talked about so far is lab based, uses experiments, involves biochemical analysis or high-tech brain scans, and so forth. The next section is a bit different. The science here is epidemiology, which seeks to find the relationships between exposure to risks (such as infection) and undesired outcomes (such as disease). The typical questions would be on the lines of: 'Is exposure to lead pollution in infancy associated with lower achievement in school?' 'Is breastfeeding associated with higher achievement in school?' And it can discover relationships between patterns of exposures and outcomes; if the answer to the second question was that there is an association between breastfeeding and school achievement, it may be useful to know if the association is still important if you allow for confounding variables, such as the tendency for mothers who are better educated to breastfeed their babies for longer than less educated mothers, as well as providing a different educational environment to the school-age child.[125] And you would want to trace the causal pathway: what set of events and influences mediated between the starting point and the outcome.

I think this is a very important contribution. An association between A and B is very interesting, but surely the real issue is this: what is the step-by-step pathway between the possible 'cause' and the outcome you would want to avoid or to bring about? You need to examine the confounding variables and mediating variables which may be involved before you can determine anything about the causal relationship between A and B. If there are many such confounding variables, and if individual people's pathways can also differ slightly, in order to sort out what is going on you may need evidence from more cases than you can recruit for an experiment. Epidemiology complements case studies and experiments to clarify causes and pathways. The studies I am going to talk about use data which are biological and medical, data which are psychological, and data which are demographic or economic or social; and it uses a range of statistical techniques to examine causes, to test models, to assess interventions, to develop theory, to test hypotheses, and so to inform policy. I'm going to talk about methods before I get on to findings, because epidemiological methods are somewhat different from the sciences I have looked at so far.

In children's development there is rarely one cause leading inexorably to one effect. Most outcomes are caused by a chain or web of factors accumulating over time. One factor makes things a little better in these ways; another factor makes things a bit worse in these other ways; a third factor only influences things if a fourth is present, but the combination is then very powerful. Generally, epidemiology is a great tool for examining the complex interplay of causal factors. Effectively, it tells you not just which 'causes' are important, but which causes are, *other things being equal*, still important. For example, neuroscience suggests that eating fish in pregnancy is good for you and your baby on the basis of studies of the nervous systems of animals fed on different experimental diets.[126] Epidemiology looks for the association between mother's diet and child's vision in humans and examines whether the association is still there when you've allowed for all sorts of other factors – maybe mothers who eat fish are better educated, richer, or healthier; or some other factor other than the amount of fish eaten could have affected the child; or the fish might be good for you in one way but bad for you in another. Effectively, the strategy is: find an association and then patiently investigate whether you can get rid of it by considering other factors. A complementary strategy is to check whether there is an association but only in part of the population, or only in partnership with some other cause.

Effective epidemiology is a business of measuring various factors as carefully as possible over a possibly prolonged period of time. To do this, you typically need good ideas of what to look for (ideas that may come from experimental science), good measurements (with an intelligent balance between what you can get from hands-on precise science and what you can get from simply asking people), and a large number of cases (both so that you can pick up rare events and so that you can use sophisticated statistical techniques in the process of allowing for patterns of factors). Theory and policy will guide the choice of what to look at, and different disciplines will contribute appropriate measures. Studies will probably be big, take time, and consequently be expensive – but if you think epidemiological knowledge is expensive, try ignorance!

John Snow's investigation of the Broad Street cholera epidemic is a foundational study in epidemiology, and a heroic bit of science. It started with a sick baby. In the summer of 1854, there were outbreaks of cholera in London which spread rapidly and killed most of the people who were infected through a horrible combination of diarrhoea and vomiting leading to dehydration and organ failure. At that time, doctors did not know what caused the epidemics of cholera that came around every few years, though one favourite theory about London outbreaks was that the foul airs – 'miasmas' – rolling off the heavily polluted and stinking River Thames were to blame. When the 1854 epidemic started in Soho, this was the dominant theory. But Dr Snow, doubting the theory, drew up a map of where the patients lived. This map showed that the majority of them lived in or near Broad Street in Soho, and they got their water supply from the Broad Street pump. This water came from a well sunk into the rocks below London. The water tasted fine, and some individuals felt it tasted so good and so pure that they arranged for supplies of it to be sent to them in their homes elsewhere. But, typically for the time, it was not treated in any way. The water was used straight from the pump.

This turned out to be a disaster. Many households got rid of their waste, including their faeces, into cesspits in their backyards or their cellars, where it might lie in stinking heaps for months or years. In some cases, the wells supplying water were old, and waste from the cesspits of houses near to them could seep in. This is what had happened in the case of the Broad Street pump. The faeces and soiled clothes of a sick baby had been dumped in the cesspit which was in the cellar of the tenement house that the baby's family lived in. The waste in the cesspit contaminated the nearby well, from which the Broad Street pump pumped up drinking water and washing water for the locals. Unfortunately, the well water became infected with the cholera bacilli excreted by the sick baby, and the people who drank it died in their hundreds.

One of those who drank it and died was a rich widow who had moved to Hampstead, but she was having the delicious water from the Broad Street pump sent to her house. Hampstead is much further away from any deadly airs from the Thames than Soho is, so her infection was obviously less likely to be due to a miasma than to the water sent daily from the pump. People from neighbouring streets who used other wells were very much less likely to fall ill – another bit of evidence that it was the not general miasmic pollution. People who lived and worked on Broad Street but did not drink from the well – the inmates of the workhouse which had its own water supply, and the workers at the brewery who drank beer rather than water did not fall ill. This is a pattern which suggested this specific well was the problem, not foul city air or the general unhealthiness of the poor crowded into squalid accommodation.

Rather against the wishes of the locals, Dr Snow arranged for the Broad Street pump to be closed down. Quickly the number of new cases of cholera started to fall, and soon the epidemic was over. Examination of the water from the well under a microscope showed that it contained a lot of minute squirming white creatures such as had been found in cholera victims' excrement and vomit. Examination of the well walls and the local basements showed where cracks had allowed these bacilli to seep into the water. The cholera victims had swallowed the bacilli when they drank water from the Broad Street well, and the bacilli they excreted in their illness had carried the cycle of infection on. Stopping drinking from the infected well had broken the cycle of infection (though it might not have been the only break, as local people had taken flight from the outbreak if they had somewhere else to go, and those infected died so fast it reduced the chance of the bacteria being passed on to others).

Not so quickly as you would hope after this demonstration of the dangers of an unclean water supply, laws were passed about the supply of water and the building of sewer systems to remove excrement and other dangerous waste. These public works transformed the health of London, the identification of the bacillus showed what was causing the disease, and recognition of the importance of dealing with patients' dehydration revolutionised treatment. John Snow's epidemiological work led to advances in scientific understanding, medical treatment, and preventive public health which have made cholera a rarer and more survivable disease. Dr Snow's map is now one of the treasures of the British Library in London, a mile or so from the site of the Broad Street pump, and there is a pub in Soho named after him – two nicely varying memorials.

As my second introductory example, I want to talk a little about the British Doctors' Study. This was a study of nearly 41,000 British doctors who from 1951 onwards were asked about their general health and their smoking habits; data were also collected about what they died of and when they died. Over time, this study has showed that smokers died earlier and were more at risk of a range of serious diseases than nonsmokers were. More than half of smokers die of a disease which is related to smoking – lung cancer, bladder cancer, heart attacks, respiratory disease, and many others.

Various people had disapproved of smoking much earlier (including the not very appealing pair of James I and Adolf Hitler), and some of the increased risks of these illnesses for smokers were known about before the Second World War, but in the 1950s, the tobacco companies were still claiming that smoking had health benefits (curing sore throats, for example). The Doctors' Study has produced such clear data on the ill effects (including throat cancer), and the absence of positive physical effects, that it has demolished the tobacco companies' claims. This research has been an important component of the change in social attitudes to smoking. If smoking was dangerous even in a sample of doctors, much more privileged than the norm for society, then perhaps it would better for public health to discourage it.

Debate continues about some other effects, especially effects on children if their parents smoke. When I was talking about genes, I mentioned studies of the effects of smoking on the fetus – increased risk of low birth weight, stillbirth, congenital defects, poor lung development, and sudden infant death syndrome or 'cot death'.[127] To add some effects later in children's development when they are exposed to smoking postnatally, living in a smoking household increases risk of ear infections, increases risk of asthma, may compromise the immune system, and increases the risk that the child will become a smoker. The evidence on other, wider effects is inconsistent.

John Snow's research on a cholera outbreak was a reaction to a crisis and looked at the current pattern of outcomes to see what the risk factors had been just a little bit earlier. Its focus was mainly on the people who did get cholera and what they had in common (which turned out to be using the water from the Broad Street pump). It was what we would now call a short-term *retrospective* study; it started with the cholera patients, and looked at their housing and their local water supplies and established the perils of the pump. The experiment of stopping the use of the pump confirmed that using it was the central risk for cholera in the area. Checking on other water sources, plus bacteriological work on samples from cholera victims, showed that the disease was caused by an infectious organism, not by impure air, and showed how to prevent further infections. Once the politicians had overcome a squeamish unwillingness to consider sordid things like faeces and how they might get into drinking water, they legislated for measures that reduced the risk of future cholera epidemics. London still relies on the Victorian sewers that were put in as a result of Dr Snow's epidemiology.

The Doctors' Study is an example of a *prospective* epidemiological design; you collect information long before the outcome you are interested in begins, knowing that an outcome (like lung cancer) will happen for some members of your sample but others will escape it, or if (like death) it happens to them all, it happens sooner for some than for others. This reduces bias due to the way in which you have selected your sample; for example if you select on the basis of the adverse outcome having been diagnosed earlier, you might miss cases where it happened but more mildly, so that the diagnosis was never made. It also reduces the risk that cases will occur, but the evidence of what they were like earlier may be missing – for example the patients' medical records might be incomplete. In a prospective study, you will have thought about what might turn out to be a risk and have measured it before it is needed. Thus, you have generally got information on the people in your sample before they got near to having the adverse outcome that you are interested in, and you can use this to identify both things that were important close to the outcome (*proximal* factors) and things that came earlier but were still part of the causal chain (*distal* factors). A prospective design helps you to identify more early risk factors, and this is important because even when you know about a proximal risk factor, there are other questions to be asked. For example, what are the reasons why some people smoke more than others? Might the reasons why someone smoked in the first place be what caused the poor health, irrespective of the smoking?

Investigation of why people suffer from cardiovascular disease is a useful example of how different sorts of study build up into a rich picture. Heart attacks are a major cause of death from middle age onwards, especially in men, so there has been interest in risk factors for a long time. Initially, many studies sampled middle-aged men and identified current or recent risks, such as obesity, diet, smoking, and lack of exercise. So far so good, and certainly very important to know this, but why were there differences in obesity, diet, smoking, and lack of exercise? Subsequently, researchers looked at more distal causes. It was apparent in demographic studies that the geographical areas that had high rates of heart disease in adults also tended to have high rates of infant mortality: could the two be linked? In prospective epidemiological studies it turned out that evidence of poor growth early in life, as shown by low birth weight, for example, predicted an increased risk of adult heart disease.[128] Putting these together, it was suggested that children who were born after their mothers had had an inadequate diet during the pregnancy were in effect biologically programmed to 'expect' food scarcity to occur after their births. If instead they grew up with a more plentiful supply of food than their bodies expected, they might be more at risk of obesity, raised cholesterol levels, and eventual heart disease. You may remember this as the thrifty phenotype or biological programming hypotheses which I discussed earlier. When we looked at the later lives of the individuals who were born during and after the Dutch Hunger Winter, we saw what might be the same pattern. We are improving our understanding of the epigenetic mechanisms by which this happens.

Prospective long-term epidemiological studies have additionally provided evidence that biological functioning was affected by other sorts of

experience, especially being exposed to stressful psychological circumstances in early life. I talked about the effects of parenting and separation
from the parent on the development of the HPA axis earlier, effects which
have now been seen at every level down to the expression of the genes. And
socioeconomic circumstances such as poverty, parental unemployment, and
social inequality may have the same sort of effect, even indirectly for those
at the top of the heap.[129]

Initially, the biological programming hypothesis implied that there was
an early critical period when experience determined later outcomes, with
later experience being absolutely ineffective in changing them. Some theo-
rising put this down to the wrong genes: 'Biology is destiny' was how Freud
put it. I've described in earlier sections why it is wrong to be as deterministic as this for most outcomes in the processes of children's development. The
epidemiological evidence also shows that determinism needs to be modified. More precisely, if an epidemiological study has fine-grained data from
a succession of time points, it can show how early events shift an individual
towards a developmental trajectory that leads to a particular outcome. For
example, the association between low birth weight and later heart disease
is much stronger in individuals who had become obese, and there may be
little association in individuals who did not develop a lot of fatty tissue or
become overweight.[130]

Another strength of epidemiological studies is the possibility of dealing
with the regrettable fact that risks tend to co-occur. (Sadly for the individual
who suffers them, and maddeningly for the researcher.) This means that
the path from initial risk A to outcome B may be routed through any of difficulties C, D, or E, which are packaged in with A or tend to follow it. The
link between maternal drug use and poor outcomes for the child may be
there because of a prenatal programming effect on the embryo; or because
there is also postnatal exposure to parental drug use; or because of parental
modelling of drug use as a normal and acceptable behaviour; or because
of access to the parent's drugs and contact with drug dealers; or because
of parental poverty, partly as a result of resources being spent on drugs; or
because of stress due to a drug-using parent having difficulty in comforting
the baby appropriately; or because of stress due to separation from the parent who is imprisoned for drug use; or because of several of these factors,
and undoubtedly others, too.

Epidemiological studies can also give opportunities for looking at interactions between different risks. Gene–environment interactions are one
example, gender differences another. When I was looking at endocrinological studies, I mentioned that it looks[131] as though variations in the form of a
serotonin transporter gene may influence liability to depression in the face

of the environmental challenges – bereavement, isolation, poverty – that are risks of depression for almost all of us. To continue with depression, women report it more, seek treatment more, and possibly suffer it more than men, and it is strongly associated with pregnancy and parenthood if there is not enough social support. Epidemiological studies can be a good way of teasing out these issues.

I discussed earlier how there is a lot of interest in everyday biological systems which get experience under the skin in children's development. Genes, hormones, neurotransmitters, and neuronal networks are all biological systems which seem to be fine-tuned by early experience and somewhat modifiable by later experience, too; they support healthy development if they work properly, but may lead to adverse outcomes if they do not; and they are normally subject to daily wobbles or stability along their developmental pathways. (Catastrophic derailments do sometimes happen, but we have mainly been concerned with variations within the normal range.) What does the evidence about 'how to get under the skin' that comes from epidemiology look like?

Just to remind you, the HPA axis is part of our system for perceiving and reacting to stressful circumstances. If it is stimulated, levels of cortisol go up, and the levels of cortisol affect the activity of many of the organs of our bodies (suppressing digestive activity, for example, and enhancing the components of our fight or flight systems). This may be what we need short term in order to cope with the stress, but chronic high HPA activation and high levels of cortisol may be damaging.

We know a lot about the HPA axis from studies of animals, as I discussed in the section on endocrinology. Epidemiological studies add to this in humans.[132] Early infancy differences in cortisol levels are associated with differences in attachment and in social behaviours. The quality of the young child's attachment relations affects the HPA axis and also affects behaviour; poorly attached toddlers have more reactive HPA systems and more difficulties in coping with socially demanding situations. Young children with chronically high cortisol levels may have more difficulty in picking up, using, and remembering social cues than children whose basal cortisol is lower and whose reactions to stress do not involve such a prolonged rise in cortisol.

Children who have suffered chronic stressful experiences – the Romanian children brought up in desolate orphanages, the children brought up in families with the stresses of poverty and social exclusion or parental mental illness, children who do not think that much was possible for their lives – may have chronically higher cortisol levels right into adulthood. Adults living under chronic social stress may too. For example, in a comparison

Figure 7.1 Child refugee in Kabul. Children who have suffered chronic stressful experiences may have chronically higher cortisol levels right into adulthood.

of Eastern Europe and Sweden in the 1990s, healthy adult men had higher cortisol levels in Lithuania than in Sweden and a range of psychological indices of lower happiness, and mortality from heart disease was much lower in Sweden.[133]

So looking at children can help us understand adults' health and well-being, and obviously it can help us understand children's health and well-being, too. There has been a succession of epidemiological studies of children's development. Typically, these have selected children at birth, or earlier, on the basis of being born at the same time. So far as possible, the participants in the study have formed a *birth cohort* – a representative sample of all those born during the period in question. The intention is to recruit a very large sample – thousands of individuals – in order to have the statistical power to find rare outcomes and small effects and to detect the probably multiple factors that led to them. The participants are followed up at intervals for a long period and information is collected about physical and mental health, family and parenting, education and employment, environmental exposures, social attitudes, and achievements on various cognitive tests at various ages. With such large numbers, the main data collection is through questionnaire surveys, plus links to other sources such as school records or sometimes to hands-on measurements. Some studies have included physical samples (the study I know best, ALSPAC, has collected placentas, blood samples, and baby teeth donated to ALSPAC rather than to the Tooth Fairy), which makes it possible to do genetic analyses. These studies explore the antecedents of a wide range of outcomes and the effects of a wide range of factors that affect development – to answer questions such as if the mother smokes during her pregnancy how does that affect the child, or why do some individuals develop autism, or fail at school, or what outcomes are associated with what sorts of diets. In particular, they can examine how complex histories of health, wealth, and experience are woven together in the lives of individuals to lead to better and worse outcomes and achievements for those concerned.

The study I have worked with is ALSPAC – the Avon Longitudinal Study of Parents and Children. Every family expecting a child in the health districts in and around Bristol was eligible to be a member and was invited before the birth. This area contains a big city (glorious Bristol), suburbs, seaside resorts, small towns, and some remote rural areas. The local population has fewer ethnic minority families than the UK as a whole, and the average educational level is a bit higher, but we know that in most ways it is a reasonable representation of the UK.

The local focus undoubtedly contributed to the very successful retention of a large proportion of the original sample for twenty years (and counting). ALSPAC news figured frequently in the local media; access to special clinics where children were weighed, measured, tested and interviewed was possible with relatively short journeys; and local schools had a majority of their pupils taking part and telling their friends about it. This is important, because there is real difficulty in retaining study participants over a long period, and typically the loss of participants (the *attrition*) is biased. Participants who have time and resources and appreciation of the study are more likely to persist with returning questionnaires, accepting interviewers, and turning up for research clinics. Participants whose lives are full of stress are much more likely to drop out, and it can be hard to retrieve them later. The result is that all longitudinal studies lose cases, and the lost cases may be the ones most likely to suffer risk factors and have adverse outcomes.

ALSPAC recruited about 14,000 babies and their families in 1991–2. The participants – mothers and their partners, initially, and teachers and the children themselves later – have filled in questionnaires several times a year ever since. The children and the parents have been invited to research clinics where hands-on tests were done. There are medical data, psychological data, demographic data, genetic data, and links to government data sets such as school records and records of contacts with the criminal justice system. Research reports are pouring out at an accelerating rate.[134] Working with this has been like living in a sweetshop – whatever hypothesis you feel like chewing over, ALSPAC has had data which can be brought to bear on it, and other data to check whether the result is really what it looks like at first glance.

I can only select a few topics to illustrate the ways in which an epidemiological study can clarify the processes of children's development – for more, see ALSPAC's online sites, which have both friendly summaries and access to papers in learned journals.

Our bodies need to respond to the substances that our environments provide; humans, like other animals, have many-layered immune systems to cope with those that could threaten our health. Sometimes, our immune systems react very strongly to substances which are not normally harmful, and we have an allergic reaction which, at the extreme, may itself be life-threatening. Eczema, asthma, and hay fever are examples of allergic disorders that are relatively common.

Having an allergy has a genetic component; for example monozygotic twins (genetically identical) are more similar in their allergies than dizygotic (only 50 per cent identical) twins. However, there has been a big rise in cases of allergy over the last few years, which strongly suggests that environmental changes must be relevant. Epidemiological studies provide very useful evidence on what is going on.

One set of ALSPAC evidence is relevant to the hypothesis that allergies may develop because the immune system has had too little exposure to mildly threatening substances.[135] ALSPAC children were more likely to develop allergies if their homes were cleaner than if the homes were slightly grubby. Parents' use of a lot of cleaning substances was associated with more allergies. The presence of several older siblings, particularly brothers, was associated with fewer allergies. Experiencing a lot of brothers' grubbiness not too resolutely cleaned away may give the immune system useful practice with manageable challenges. We may have evolved immune systems geared to protect us from environments with lots of natural challenges – nettles, pollen, insect bites – that are irritating but not serious. If we don't encounter such things, and good honest dirt, and maybe organisms we think of as parasites, while we are young, our immune systems may overreact to whatever challenges we do meet and cause an allergic reaction.

(Just to mention: I may be a bit biased about this. I decided very early in my time as a mother that I would reduce my standards in some areas. Meticulous housework and having clothes that were vulnerable to sticky fingers and infant mess went, in favour of having more time to relax and enjoy being with my child. Given that my low involvement in housework and in clothes that need dry cleaning hasn't changed back since she left home, this may have a big component of sheer laziness. But the ALSPAC data on use of cleaning materials is independent of me, so I do think you could rely on it.)

A second ALSPAC set of studies looked specifically at asthma. Air pollution outdoors and household cleaners indoors were shown to play their part, but there's evidence that the prenatal environment also has a strong influence on the development of asthma. Mothers reporting more anxiety during pregnancy and mothers taking paracetamol were both associated with risk of asthma in the child. Whooping cough vaccination, which had been a suspect as a cause of asthma, was not associated with any increase in any sort of wheezing.

A third set of ALSPAC evidence accounts more precisely for a particular allergy. Increasing numbers of children are allergic to peanuts, and this particular allergic reaction can be so severe that it stops breathing. A number of individuals die from this anaphylactic shock every year, and therefore food manufacturers take precautions now to make sure that there are no traces of nuts in the foods they make. ALSPAC checked which children had peanut allergies and examined their early exposure.[136] It was found that the children with peanut allergies were five times as likely to have had serious oozing crusted rashes early in infancy, compared with children who showed no sign of peanut allergy later on. The more serious the rashes, the greater the increased risk of later allergy. If the baby's rash had been treated with oils or creams containing peanut oil, the risk was up almost seven-fold. The children may have been extra sensitive in some way, causing the early rashes and also the peanut allergy, or they may have become sensitised to peanuts by having lotions containing peanut oil administered to soothe their broken skin. The specific use of creams based on peanut oil does look like a possible culprit, so it could be worth avoiding them.

ALSPAC has done several studies of the effects of mothers' mental wellbeing on the child. There is a lot of evidence about the effect of postnatal depression on the child. ALSPAC was one of the first studies to document the fact that, in general, mothers had more signs of depression and anxiety during pregnancy than they do postnatally. (This is a problem because obviously it would be unwise to treat pregnant women with the drugs that might otherwise be used to treat anxiety or depression.) A series of studies led by Tom O'Connor and Vivette Glover and their colleagues[137] has shown that prenatal anxiety and mood disturbance appear to have a relationship with child outcomes such as hyperactive behaviour, disturbed sleep in childhood, and cortisol levels in the child. Mothers' level of anxiety late in pregnancy was positively correlated with children's daily cortisol levels, even when postnatal mood disorders and all sorts of social and demographic variables were allowed for. Mothers' anxiety prenatally appears to have lasting effects – probably up to adolescence – on the child's risk of behaviour problems and emotional problems. If the mother's anxiety was very high prenatally, the child's risk of mental disorder nearly doubled (from 6.8 per cent for low maternal anxiety to 12.3 per cent for high). There may be an effect through the developing child's HPA system for reacting to stress. While you would also need to explore why the pregnant women were feeling so anxious and depressed, I think this corroborates the suggestion from endocrinological studies that stress in mothers is bad for their babies, and that it is essential that everyone should be extremely nice to pregnant women and mothers.

I've described the famine studies which suggest that the pregnant woman's diet may affect her baby's development at certain periods of pregnancy and set up a lifetime increased risk of obesity and related diseases. But there might be other effects of prenatal diet.[138] ALSPAC found an association between the amount of oily fish that pregnant women ate and their children's development. Mothers who ate more oily fish during pregnancy and breastfeeding gave their babies access to more omega-3 fatty acids, which are known (from animal studies) to be beneficial for the development of the brain and in particular the visual system. (I pointed this out in the neuroscience chapter.) There are risks of contamination by mercury and other pollutants in seafood, particularly in fish like tuna, which are at the top of the food chain, so a diet high in oily fish might be problematic. Studies in the United States in the 1980s showed that children who had been exposed prenatally to a high level of polychlorinated biphenyls (PCBs) (because their mothers had eaten fish contaminated with PCBs during pregnancy) had worse scores as neonates and more errors in short-term memory at the age of four. ALSPAC's data showed that mothers who ate very little oily fish were at substantially higher risk of having children with worse social development, prosocial behaviour, communication, and fine motor scores, and with a slower development of stereoscopic vision, even allowing for all sorts of other variables. There is some support here for the old wives' tale that eating fish – or in this case your mother eating fish – makes you cleverer (provided it is not contaminated fish)!

ALSPAC's data on the effects of environmental pollutants adds on to results from previous epidemiological studies. High dosages of certain substances, for example mercury and lead, are known to poison the nervous system. Some of the substances are, at a low level, common environmental pollutants. It may be the case that they cause brain damage even at low levels, particularly to the rapidly developing brains of children prenatally and postnatally. Lead is one of the best known of these pollutants. In the first place, we have learned from physiological studies that lead in the body interferes with enzymes, competes with calcium (so that it can be found in the teeth and the bones), and affects neurotransmitter release in the brain. Clinically, we've learned that high levels of lead in the body (measured in the blood or the teeth) are associated with intellectual impairment, behaviour problems such as hyperactivity, and, at the highest levels, gross neuropathology. Exactly when the child ingests the lead may influence the effects on behaviour through different stages of brain development, perhaps; there is some ingestion before birth through the mother's exposure to lead pollution.

A series of epidemiological studies[139] of school children clarify what effects lead at low levels may have on cognition. An Australian epidemiological study examined children's blood lead levels in the lead smelting town of Port Pirie, South Australia. There was a fairly high degree of pollution throughout the town, but the risk of having a high blood lead level was increased fourfold by having a household member working with lead at the smelter, six-fold by having flaking paint outside the house, threefold by being a nail-biter, fourfold by having dirty hands, and fivefold by having dirty clothes, dirtiness of hands and clothes being rated by the child's teachers. Ambient lead dust ingested orally would seem to be the source here.

Studies of children in New Zealand and Scotland assessed IQ and reading; behaviour problems as seen by teachers and parents; and various background variables such as frequent changes of residence or of school, poor family relations, or mental health, and some characteristics of the mother. These variables made it possible to take social, environmental, and background factors into account. Social disadvantage plays a major part in poorer child development, and socially disadvantaged children tended to have higher lead levels. The research has showed that raised blood lead level was associated with a small but significant increase in children's behaviour problems, inattention, reading difficulty, and hyperactivity.

A study of newborn babies[140] suggested that lead pollution before birth does cause some brain damage. Samples of blood were taken from the umbilical cords of newborn babies, and lead levels from those samples were statistically significantly correlated with later scores on baby intelligence tests. So although social disadvantage variables unarguably affect children's development later in childhood, an 'intelligence' deficit in very young babies does look like a lead effect.

ALSPAC's evidence, more recent than these studies, shows association between even lower levels of lead and developmental damage. After adjustment for a good range of other variables, children's blood lead levels measured at age two and a half predicted educational attainment, antisocial behaviour, and hyperactivity at ages seven to eight.

A recent review[141] suggests that the effects of lead on development begin at very low levels and extend through life. They show up in lower intelligence, concentration, and ability to resist distraction, and hence worse academic achievement, on the one hand; and also show up in difficulties with social behaviour, such as conduct disorder, aggression, and delinquency, on the other hand. Probably even low levels of exposure to lead in the environment (and conceivably to other pollutants, which have not yet been so thoroughly researched) is associated with a tendency to attention deficits, emotional reactivity, and hyperactivity and to worse performance in school. The effects of lead interact with the effects of other socioeconomic variables, probably being more severe for socially disadvantaged children than for middle class ones who have more resources that might compensate. The association shows up best in large samples which are carefully measured. Lead does not all by itself cause inattentiveness or educational retardation or delinquency or hyperactivity, but it does contribute to such pervasive problems.

This research justifies public concern about the effects of lead pollution, and consequently, steps have been taken to reduce environmental lead levels. It is used less in paints, cosmetics, and canning food than in earlier years; petrol is now mainly unleaded; and lead water pipes are no longer installed in domestic water systems, though many remain in older housing. However, lead remains a common potential danger to the developing brain, and children may ingest a considerable amount of lead from the air near roads with heavy traffic, from soft water supplied by lead pipes, from plants grown in contaminated soil, from painted objects which they lick or chew, and from dust licked off dirty fingers, dropped sweets, and so forth. Preventing lead poisoning, provided the substitutes for lead have fewer adverse effects, will have small but not insignificant benefits.

These have been some examples of epidemiology clarifying how risks work at many different levels. Some rare ones are catastrophic all by themselves, but most just tend to nudge development a little in a less optimal direction. Many we can avoid or reduce or make sure they only happen occasionally, and we can do this personally or through general policy. What makes things harder is the coincidence of different risk factors, especially when they become chronic and last for long periods of time. Even here we are not necessarily doomed to a poor outcome – even with a substantial increase in risk we might escape it and we may be able to do something to ameliorate the effects. But we do need to recognise what makes things a little harder or a little easier and take action accordingly. Epidemiology helps show us what to consider and, related to the other basic sciences, explains how risks get under the skin and produce the slugs and snails of development, rather than the sugar and spice.

8

♦

PSYCHOLOGY

In which we look especially at parenting behaviour

I've spent my working life, and some of my personal life, too, thinking about, talking about, reading about, writing about, researching, and teaching developmental psychology. This last science chapter is about this discipline and some of its most important contributions to how we might think about parenting.

Psychology, just to warn you, has two traditional definitions: 'the science of behaviour', what people (or other animals) can be observed to do, and 'the science of mental life', which implies more attention to unobservable events such as thoughts. There is an uneasy tension between these traditions, and both of them have an uneasy relation with the biological level I have been talking about so far.

Way back at the beginning of writing this book I talked about parent figures' frames for children. This talk is going to reappear here. But nearer the front of our attention will be the idea of developmental tasks. 'Developing' children is analogous to developing a photograph; there's what the picture is doing as it gains detail and clarity ('tasks'), and there's what the photographer is doing to bring about that change ('frames'). Tasks and frames are interrelated, so they're both on the agenda of this chapter.

We all need to learn to love and learn through loving. Only the stony-hearted would deny that loving and being loved by other people is important for the happiness of the child (and the parent). The theory about what love does for you has developed in ways that involve contributions from many scientific disciplines – evolutionary theory, brain development, endocrinology, ethology, anthropology – and it is one of the star areas of developmental psychology. There are enormous implications for child development and parenting.

At the core of the psychology of this is John Bowlby's work on attachment, which was influenced by a wide range of factors – his own personal history, his observation of deeply troubled children in a school where he taught, his training in and use of psychoanalysis, his scientific interest in evolution and animal behaviour. The place that love plays in the child's life has both biological and social bases. Babies and young children have a strong need for protection, nurturance, care, and comforting. Being able to get other people to look after your interests preserved the safety and well-being of generations of ancestors, so it's not a surprise that babies are born with an evolved capacity to relate to significant others; to seek to be close to them; to rely on them for the fulfilment of their needs for nurture, protection, and relief from distress; to feel happier and more confident when they are within reach. Behaviours such as smiling, watching, seeking to hold the gaze of the other, crying, following, clinging to, snuggling up to, and using your attachment figure as a base and reference point are all biologically programmed to develop and maintain attachment relationships, and staying near to your attachment figure should help to keep the very young out of danger.

We see these behaviours in many other species. Attachment is something that is universal in normal children and in a lot of other young animals. Chicks, lambs, calves, foals, and many other animals seek to be near their mothers; they have special distress calls which attract her attention and she has special calls to summon them back to her. Many birds who are able to walk soon after they hatch quickly develop a preference for following their mother, though they can be tricked into 'imprinting' on someone else if they see the someone else moving in the right way at the critical period of time. Konrad Lorenz easily taught the geese he bred to follow him like they would naturally follow their mother. Birds who have been induced to imprint on the wrong sort of object (a bird of a different species, for example – or a human ethologist) may look for creatures like it to mate with when they are adults. In *King Solomon's Ring*, Lorenz tells a number of anecdotes about imprinted animals 'falling in love' with an inappropriate partner from a different species.[142] One is about how a jackdaw that had imprinted on him when very young later tried to court him, for example by trying to get the ethologist to squeeze into the cavity (only a few centimetres wide) that the bird had chosen to nest in, and by assiduously feeding him chewed-up worms. Sometimes scientists really do suffer for science.

Brain studies of birds suggest that the process of imprinting affects how synapses are pruned away and changes neurotransmitters, which could be the mechanisms for the long-term memory of what sort of person to get attached to. Classic experiments with monkeys showed that warmth and cuddliness are a more important component of attachment than providing food. The licking and arched-back nursing that rodent mothers supply to their pups is an example of what seems to be important for getting the stress system modulated so that the young creature can cope with difficult situations. The amount of licking and grooming that infant rodents and primates receive comes out in many studies as affecting the balance of neurotransmitters, the myelination of nerve fibres in the brain, the expression of genes, and how resilient the animals are able to be in the face of challenge, as I discussed earlier.

There is a lively interaction here between the biological, the psychological, and the social levels of evidence. It is biologically adaptive to form lasting emotional ties, to seek proximity and contact with loved people at times of stress and danger, and to feel increased comfort and security in their presence, with benefits also for the psychological well-being of the individuals concerned and for the functioning of the social group. Seeing the other people that you know as willing sources of reassurance and support, and as recipients, too, should make the social group warmer and more cohesive. Seeing that people believe you are worthy to be loved and protected could be very good for your self-esteem. All of this affects your basic physiology and (probably) the expression of your genes.

Like Lorenz's baby birds, human babies are not born 'attached' to specific adults (even though they may have learned before birth about the sounds of their mother's voice and about her smell, and they have been affected by her emotional states, too). Up to about six months old, they will interact quite happily with pretty much any adult they meet, but gradually the caregiver who provides love and soothing and social interaction becomes the preferred source of reassurance in distress. Familiarity, consistency, responsiveness, and warmth seem to be the crucial factors. By the end of the first year, children will normally have at least one person to whom they are strongly attached. As the mother is usually the main caregiver, she is highly likely to be one of them, but children become attached to either parent, to their childminder or nursery worker, to siblings, and even to nonhumans – a favourite toy, pet animal, or a piece of cloth that smells of mum.

This developing preference for the familiar person intensifies over the second half of the first year, and now for several years most young children strongly prefer to be within reach of their attachment figure. They will seek to get close to this person when they are distressed, they will be less confident when alone, and they may protest about the absence of the attachment figure and the presence of strangers or if the attachment figure becomes preoccupied with something other than the child. They will probably enjoy games which play with separation, such as peek-a-boo or hide and seek, provided that they are not left to be frightened for too long and the attachment figure reappears reliably.

As they get older, children develop language skills, memory, better emotion regulation, and more mobility, and they become better able to tolerate being separated from their attachment figures. But in situations of great stress, it may be their attachment figure that they want to turn to, even years and years after the attachment first developed. My mother told a poignant story of how when she was twenty-six and giving birth to her first child, she cried out for her own mother, poignant because my grandmother had died the year before.

We saw that there is evidence of what is going on at the level of brain activity. Babies develop a buffering system against the disruptive effects of stress. The processes involved may affect neurodevelopment, the immune system, and the expression of genes. Parenting influences regulatory processes in infants' immature stress regulation systems. Many brain regions are still maturing during the middle of the first year, and this may change how stress regulation can function. For example although the HPA axis is active from birth, from around six months of age it also comes under the control of the amygdala and the hippocampus. Myelination of nerve fibres, especially in the limbic system, and sensitivity to the hormone oxytocin and to naturally occurring opiates are probably important here. The timing of brain development may be at the root of the timing of attachment development.

Individual differences in brain development may be part of what underlies the individual differences in attachment relations. For example, some babies have more left frontal lobe activity compared to right, an asymmetry which is associated with positive emotions, while other babies have more right frontal lobe activity, which is associated with negative emotions and inhibition. When we look at their attachment behaviour, babies in the former set tend to be in the category of 'securely attached', and those in the latter tend to be 'insecurely attached'. It appears that there may be differences between brain responses to the stress of infants with withdrawn, normal, or intrusive mothers. EEG studies show that infants with depressed mothers are less likely to show left hemisphere activation. Insensitive mothering seems to be mediating between depression and EEG. A lack of sensitive parenting and a lack of maternal contact stress the infant and simultaneously remove the person who normally destresses the child.

How does a child develop a secure attachment, as most do? It helps to have warm, sensitive, responsive, and consistent treatment with cuddles and joint activity and mutual enjoyment and communication. If there is little of this, and especially if the parenting is very inconsistent and even frightening, the child's feelings of attachment will fall into a different pattern. Differences in attachment show up especially clearly when the child is in a slightly stressful situation, for example being in a strange place without its attachment figure. Clinicians and researchers use the 'strange situation', where a baby and its attachment figure are observed in a playroom new to the child, and there is a sequence of social situations which involve the attachment figure temporarily leaving the child in the room with a stranger. Most babies between six months and two years find this somewhat distressing: they stop playing, try to follow their attachment figure, cry, and seek contact and reassurance when the attachment figure returns. For securely attached babies, the majority in most studies, the distress is real but not overwhelming, and the child is relatively easily reassured when the attachment figure returns.

Avoidant babies act as if they feel they cannot rely on the attachment figure. They are not responsive to parental attempts to interact with them, and they may even turn away to avoid them. They seem to deliberately divert their attention from anything that would evoke attachment behaviour and avoid relying on the attachment figure. If they are distressed by the strange situation, they cannot use the attachment figure to recover from their distress; their behaviour is tense and irritable and rejecting. They seem not to be comfortable in turning to the parent when they are under stress, as if they are not confident that the parent will be a reliable source of warmth and comfort. Typically, their interaction with their significant others has often been tense and irritable, with the adults being rejecting or intrusive and overstimulating. It looks as if the baby's attachment behaviour is deactivated because it has not been a useful resource.

Anxious or resistant babies also act as if the attachment figure is not a source of security. They are not reassured by parental attention and comforting behaviour, and they have great difficulty reducing their distress, so it is hard for them to regain an emotional equilibrium. Often they are extremely dependent, clingy, demanding, and angry. They may make excessive demands on the attachment figure and have great difficulty in playing autonomously. They seem to not have faith in themselves or in their caregiver, and they are continually checking that everything is all right rather than getting on with exploring new possibilities. It seems that their attachment figures may have been inept or inconsistent rather than rejecting; hard to reach and insensitive rather than too much in opposition to the baby's needs. It is as if the baby's attachment system has become overactivated because he or she has not had a feeling of being reliably supported.

Disorganised or disoriented babies have not settled into a consistent attachment strategy. They do not behave coherently, showing signs of both avoiding the parent and resisting the parent, as if they had confused expectations or were depressed or afraid. They cling and avoid and resist incoherently, as if they felt both confused and fearful, angry and anxious, frightened and unresponsive. In some cases, their attachment figure has perhaps maltreated them or suffered from mental illness – really serious depression, for example, can be associated with disorganised attachment in the baby.

Long term, there is strong evidence that having a disorganised attachment predicts a high increase in risk of problems for the child later on. The relationship between anxious and avoidant attachment and later problems is less strong.[143] It's worth noting that there seem to be cultural differences in how frequent such attachments are that fit in with cultural expectations, for example North German babies show a high rate of avoidance (or is it independence?) and Japanese babies show a high rate of anxious attachment (fitting in with the culture of *amae* or constant closeness between mother and child). But while being avoidantly attached or anxiously attached may have only a moderate link to later problems, it does seem to be clear that a secure attachment tends to be protective and a disorganised one often put the child at risk of problems.

So secure attachments seem to be facilitated by responsive, warm interactions between baby and caregiver, by an emotional environment that is positive and responsive in quality. If the caregiver is reliably sensitive to the baby's needs, reliably anticipates what they will be, reliably provides for the baby, and reliably shows pleasure in the interaction between the baby and the carer (and by 'reliably' the researchers mean upwards of 30 per cent of the time, not 100 per cent), a strong positive attachment is likely to develop between them such that each will feel and show pleasure in each other's company, have confidence that the partner is available and supportive and nice to be with, and have an ability to cope when stressful circumstances arise. Part of what is crucial here is ease of emotional communication, and I mean communication over negative as well as positive feelings. In a healthy relationship based on a secure attachment, the partners can express both positive and negative emotions safely, and do not have to censor or distort their emotions lest they put the relationship at risk. Some people talk of this as 'unconditional affection', but it also, I think, involves tactful honesty.

Many parenting frames are relevant to this, for example if you enjoy someone's company there are more opportunities for joint attention, shared jokes, and supportive feedback. But a key part is learning how to regulate emotions and to stop arousal leading to loss of control. Babies have little ability to control their arousal, and caregivers need to look after them in ways that reduce distress and eventually provide the baby with ways to self-comfort. The experiences involved in developing a secure attachment can modulate arousal systems in positive ways, which may be embedded in brain functioning and patterns of stress hormones such as cortisol as well as visible in behaviour. The knowledge that one has reliable ways of reducing distress endures throughout subsequent experience. Later experience, however, can modify this certainty such that enough misfortune may reduce even the person with a history of secure attachment to anger or despair. But such a person will typically show more resilience than someone whose early attachment experiences were less than good.

For babies and very little children, this attachment is based on feelings, the pattern of interaction, facial expressions, tone of voice, touch, warmth, and so forth. As children develop language and reflect on themselves, cognitive and narrative levels of attachment come into play, but they do not displace the nonverbal constituents. Even as adults, we may find it hard to like the colleague who does not smile at us, does not make eye contact, ignores our actions, speaks in a harsh tone, appears to cross the street to avoid us; and a working model of such a person as disagreeable and untrustworthy can be hard to change. Similarly, although we may cope better with separations from the person we are attached to once we understand the reasons for the separation and that their absence is temporary and does not have to be interpreted as a final and irrevocable rejection, such experiences still put us at risk of distress, anxiety, anger, and depression.

Of course children's characteristics, including characteristics derived from genes, affect the behaviour of their parents. For example, highly irritable and hard to soothe infants tend to receive less sensitive care and then have insecure relationships. Even sensitive parents may find that infant negativity makes attachment processes work less well. Attachment is enhanced when the child stimulates the mother and responds positively to her bids for interaction, and thus elicits more sensitive, warm caring and attention.

Bowlby himself pointed out that the attachment between a child and a parent "turns at each and every stage of the journey on an interaction between the organism as it has developed up to that moment and the environment in which it then finds itself".[144] More recent researchers point out that we should not assume that the antecedents, meaning, and consequences of attachments are the same across all cultures (and indeed all historical periods).[145] The parent–child relationship exists within a nervous system, a family, a community, and a culture, and it will be profoundly affected by factors at these levels. I want to mention, briefly, two aspects of this: first, working mothers, child care, and the possibility of multiple attachments, and second, cultural differences in attachment.

Throughout evolutionary history, animals that parent have had to provide child care as well as getting on with their other activities. Nest-building animals leave their young in the nest to forage for food for themselves and their offspring; in some species the parents take turns, in some it is the work of only one parent. Human parents may carry their infants with them as they work to support themselves, or delegate infant care to particular individuals – sometimes just one parent, sometimes another family member who may or may not be of the parents' generation, sometimes to profes-sional carers. Despite what I said about the importance of parental frames, total undivided focussed parental attention has been something that chil-dren have been able to expect, let alone to enjoy, only some of the time. Children have evolved to be able to cope with a certain amount of 'benign neglect', as my mother's doctor told her when she was fretting about her first child. The 'highly responsive' mothers of securely attached babies were only responding about 30 per cent of the time, and getting it right presum-ably only some of that 30 per cent.

Historically, most care has kept the child in the normal social community, which allowed plentiful opportunities for keeping an eye on the child but may often have meant that attention to the child's needs was intermittent because of the demands of the workplace or of domesticity – I am thinking of farm women's babies stashed in the long grass at the edge of the field while the mothers worked to bring in the harvest, or the swaddled infant in a cradle which the mother rocked while she attended to her cooking. Rich families have used surrogate, part professional child care for centuries; English royal children, for example, were generally brought up by whole households of unrelated adults with grandiose titles and visited by their parents only once or twice a year. In traditional societies, an older child would often be a caretaker for a younger brother or sister. Most such child care will have involved fairly small numbers of children at the same age and, in most cases, carers with a relatively strong commitment to the individual child. Increasingly, twenty-first century infants and young children may spend time in groups with age mates in settings such as nurseries or play groups where carers are in loco parentis but on a less individualised basis and are trained professionals rather than family members. In our evolutionary and cultural history, this is rather a new thing.

There has been a substantial amount of research on what effect modern out-of-home care has on young children. There are consistent answers in some areas, less consistent ones in others.[146] In almost all the large-scale epidemiological research, there is consistent evidence of preschool group experience having a favourable effect on children's language and their development of the skills needed to work in school classrooms ('school readiness'); the benefits are larger where children have encountered better quality group care. This is gratifying, but not very surprising. In most preschool groups, some attention is paid to school-like activities such as sitting in a group listening to a story, painting, taking turns, lining up to go and play outside, and so forth. The staff in such groups may behave like teachers, be called teachers, even be qualified as teachers, and may have an explicit curriculum of school-like skills and routines for the children to engage with.

There is a body of rather less consistent evidence[147] that group care may sometimes have an adverse effect on social skills; children with experience of preschool group care are reported to show higher cortisol levels, more aggression or assertiveness, more anxiety, and poorer relationships with other children, possibly lasting for some years. This may perhaps be grounds for concern about the effects of preschool group care for very young children. However, it appears from the large-scale epidemiological studies such as ALSPAC that this negative effect seems to be detected mainly with vulnerable children, particularly those with poor family relationships and insecure attachments to their mothers. Group care can work well provided the child does also have an opportunity to develop personal attachment relationships.

It is clear that environments which are chaotic, inconsistent, understimulating, or emotionally cold are bad for attachment formation, whether they occur at homes or in group care. Over recent years, evidence has built up from studies of children reared in orphanages in the former Eastern bloc, including Romania and Russia.[148] Care in these institutions typically involved little or no warmth and interaction between the staff and the babies, and the babies did not build up attachments to the staff. They were often retarded in their physical growth and their language development, and they seemed not to have learned to relate positively to other people.

The Ceausescu dictatorship in Romania, anxious to raise the birth rate, discouraged contraception and made abortion illegal but presided over high unemployment and increasing poverty. The result was that many parents could not take care of their children, and they were abandoned in bleak orphanages where they were not cuddled, played with, or talked to. When the regime was overthrown, a substantial number of the orphanage children came to the UK or Canada for adoption by Western families. Researchers have kept in contact with them and published a succession of reports.[149] These children showed rapid physical and cognitive development, catching up to something like the UK and Canadian norms within a couple of years. Although there was enormous improvement in social and emotional skills, the children still showed a higher rate of problems than nonadopted children. Most of these adopted children developed more secure attachment relationships with their adoptive parents than they had been able to develop while in institutional care, but they still seemed to be more at risk of insecure attachments than nonadopted children.

The rate of behaviour problems, such as anxiety and aggression, is a little higher amongst adopted children than nonadopted ones, and the rate of referral to mental health services is markedly higher, but they were much lower than for children left to be reared in institutions or than for those children living with dysfunctional families of origin. The worse their preadoption experiences were, and the longer the poor experiences lasted, the more all adopted children appear to be at risk of worse outcomes after adoption.[150]

Cultural differences in attachment patterns are an interesting possibility, and there is some evidence that they may exist. As I mentioned, studies of children from infancy to late childhood carried out in Germany used the strange situation assessment and found a higher-than-expected rate of independence of the infant from the mother, which under the conventional interpretation would be considered to show an insecure attachment. The German mothers, however, valued emotional self-sufficiency in their children, and the children had frequent experiences of brief separation in which they had learned not to be too distressed by their mother's absence. On the other hand, Japanese mothers valued *amae*, a continuing emotional dependence of the child on the mother, and separations between mother and child were much rarer in their culture (it would be common for the child to sleep in the same bed as the mother up to age five, for example), and they approved of a degree of child dependence on the mother that Anglo-American raters would regard as problematic. Japanese children were expected to be very distressed when their mother left them in the strange situation and very clingy when she returned, even at the age of five, and far more Japanese five-year-olds than American five-year-olds behaved like this. Arguably, the strange situation was much stranger for the Japanese children, who would rarely have experienced anything like it, than for the German children, whose families were training them to be independent.

It is important to recognise that there might be cultural differences in the parental behaviours that underlie attachment. In particular, if mother and child are normally in close proximity, even in physical contact, the mothers may have more cues that the child is about to do something or need something than if they are physically further apart. Thus, mothers may have opportunities to anticipate behaviour sensitively as well as respond to it sensitively. Most of the research on ways of promoting secure attachments has been done in cultures where sensitive mothers engage their babies in a lot of face-to-face synchronised interchanges, games or conversations, or emotional soothing. Mothers who carry their infants on their backs will not be able to engage in this sort of face-to-face interaction so often; instead, these mothers frequently touch the infants, for example patting them or jiggling a protruding foot or hand. Recent small-scale studies[151] of babies' reactions to sitting in a buggy facing their mothers or facing away towards the outside world found that facing outwards went with somewhat higher cortisol levels, so perhaps it is more stressful; on the other hand, the mother-facing baby may make strenuous efforts to turn away from her and see the fascinating street beyond. Some further research would be useful here.

The early attachment relationships between child and parent seem to have some influence on later peer relationships and friendships. Children who have had secure attachments tend to show more positive behaviour towards other children, while those with insecure or disorganized attachments show more negative behaviour – more frustration and inhibition for those with early insecure-ambivalent attachments, and more aggression and anger for those whose attachments were insecure-avoidant or disorganized. The suggested linkage between early attachment and later peer relations is complex. Research suggests that the child's early experience of parental warmth, sensitivity, and responsivity induces a sense of trust in relationships and trust in oneself as worthy of a positive response from others; this leads to a secure, confident interaction style and active confident exploration of the world, which facilitates positive play with peers. The next step involves the positive exploration of ideas, perspectives, roles, and actions, and thus the development of positive social skills. 'Mind mindedness' – attention to other people's cues about their internal mental and emotional states – might also be a key part of the sequence. Children who have had a poorer attachment experience, on the other hand, might feel and express less trust, more hostility, and more avoidance in their approaches to the world.

Looking at it the other way round, the parents of unpopular or peer-rejected children tend to use more inept, intrusive, and harsh discipline and socialisation techniques. Parents of popular children display more reasoning about feelings, more responsivity, more authoritative control, more child-centred behaviour, more warmth. Children who are aggressive towards peers tend to have parents who model and reinforce aggression and show high levels of impulsive behaviour, inconsistent discipline, and rejection.

While this pattern feels credible, the evidence base is limited, the size of the association is weak to moderate rather than strong, and the degree to which the attachment pattern and the peer relationships fit into wider social structures and experiences has not been thoroughly explored.[152] What is more, the developmental influences of parents, peers, and others interact and modify each other. People can recover from attachment problems; I have known biographers infer that their subjects were spurred to out-standing achievement by an unsatisfactory relationship with parents.[153] No researcher has found worse outcomes from a secure attachment, however, and the pleasures of loving your child (or your parent) and being loved back are undeniable.

Almost all children learn to talk without difficulty. It's one of the big, exciting, and essential achievements of childhood. The first word comes (on average) a little while after the first birthday, and by the second birth-day, the child will normally be rattling away, producing upwards of fifty words, combining words into sentences with grammar, and using language to convey and request information, to express feelings, and to control other people. By five or so, the child will have almost as much mastery of lan-guage as adults do. Although there are differences in how fast this happens, and of course in the details of the language, it's rare for the process to be seriously problematic. This learning is also apparently spontaneous, near enough universal, and generally fast and free of effort. There is very relevant and well-grounded science on how this happens.

One relevant line of scientific inquiry involves comparing language in humans and in other species. Although there's a long historical tradition of seeing language as unique to humans, or at least as vastly different from other animals' languages, careful observation of what other animals do has reduced this uniqueness. Many other species communicate with each other to exchange information and to operate the social hierarchy – for example bees do a wiggle dance to tell other bees where there is a food source, other social insects use pheromones to send messages about sexual availability. Many species use vocal noises ('speech') to do this – for example birdsong, whale song, and alarm calls in birds and monkeys. Many species can com-bine their different vocal signals in rule-governed or topic-specific ways: vervet monkeys and prairie dogs give different alarm calls depending on whether the threat is from a land-based predator or one in the air, and the other animals respond accordingly. Some species can use their language to talk about things that are distant in time and space; for example monkeys or birds may continue to make alarm calls well after the threatening preda-tor has left. Primates have been seen to deceive others,[154] possibly through vocal communications, and certainly by omitting vocal communications. So most things that humans do with language are not completely exclusive to humans.

However, humans have languages that include much larger vocabularies and more intricate grammar than any other species, and we use language in more complicated ways (so far as we are aware). The sharing of language with other species suggests that human language has its roots way back in evolution, that it will have evolved because it is useful, and that there are probably genes and brain structures that support it.[155] Human hyper-development of language must be built on these foundations, but it goes far beyond them.

What do we know about the evolutionary history of language? Not a lot is certain. There are debates about evidence for brain lateralisation (which could be relevant as modern humans have language areas located in the left hemisphere, which also tends to be a bit larger than the right hemisphere) but there could be other reasons for lateralisation (as it is there to some degree in the fossil skulls of much earlier creatures, for example prehistoric sharks). The earliest date when there is evidence of human symbolic activity – art, religion – is relevant because it's difficult to see how early humans could have gone in for these activities unless they had language to talk about them. But the dates are much debated, and presumably the language use preceded the invention of symbolism, probably by millennia.

There is evidence for anatomical specialisations which would allow humans better control over the vocal apparatus. Compared with other primates, modern humans have an enlarged spinal cord in the region where the nerves that control the diaphragm and the chest wall leave the spinal column; this would mean more control of the diaphragm to allow long steady speech-carrying breathing out. They also have a larger space at the base of the skull for the nerves that control the tongue and mouth, which could allow finer movements and better articulation. And there are differences between other primates and early and modern humans in the position of the hyoid bone and in the ear canals, which would help with the production and the perception of speech sounds.[156] The fossil record may date the possibility of speech that could have sounded like modern human speech to around 500,000 years ago; our ancestors would have shared this sort of speech with Neanderthals and probably earlier hominins. Dunbar also argues that the increasing size of social groups would have pushed for further language development (to communicate better) and encouraged some specifically human uses of language, for example to tell stories, to socialise, and to develop the idea of other people having minds like one's own. These last points I will come back to later.

Are there genetic bases for language development? Yes, obviously: from the anatomical level of being able to produce the sort of language that we do because of our hearing, our mobile faces and lips, and the structure of our larynx; to the abilities that we have to remember, to discriminate between other people, and to live in social groups; there have to be genetic programmes which make these things possible. There has also been evidence about genetic anomalies that seem to underlie some specific language impairments.[157] A mutation in the gene FOXP2 seems to be behind the language disorder developmental verbal dyspraxia. Individuals with this disorder have severe difficulties in planning and producing the delicate and complex facial movements required for speech. Animal studies find the same mutation causes changes in vocalisations in mice. FOXP2 has a role in controlling other genes, however, and other genes are certainly involved in building a brain and body that can produce speech. A recent study[158] reported on the 'JR' family, who had severe difficulties with language-based tasks such as naming pictures and defining words – 'I know what I want to say but I can't quite get to the word.' The pattern of which family members had difficulties suggested a genetic inheritance, and neuroimaging revealed that the individuals with the language problem also had abnormalities in brain regions known to be involved with processing the meaning of words. I would expect that future research may well uncover other links between serious language difficulties and brain development, though minor language variations may be harder to attribute to genetic anomalies.

What, if anything, is wired into the brain? Neuroscience studies have identified regions of the brain that are specially active in producing and understanding language, and from birth onwards, they are considerably more developed in humans than in other species. Specific regions (mainly in the left hemisphere) are specialised in dealing with particular aspects of language. Where language develops abnormally, it is sometimes possible to identify abnormalities in the brain too, as in the case of the JR family that I just mentioned.

We do know that very young babies selectively attend to the speech they can hear and can show discrimination between certain of its features. For example, consonant discrimination is probably a result of wired-in sensitivities in the brain's sound perception, as humans share it with some other species such as the chinchilla. But the brain's sensitivity to contrasts is altered by whether they mean anything in the native language. If they're not used, the potential to use them is gradually reduced. Babies during their first few months can differentiate between such consonant contrasts as /s/ or /z/, even if the community they are growing up in does not use this contrast. (English speakers distinguish between sit and zit, but Spanish speakers don't.) If the language that the baby hears does not use the consonant contrast, from around six months of age they seem to gradually lose the ability to hear it readily, and by adolescence they have difficulty in deliberately producing the consonants differently. This is part of what makes learning a new language difficult: the later that people try to learn a new language, the harder it will be for them to learn its sounds adequately. Exposure to more than one language will probably help children retain a wider range of discriminations between speech sounds.

Given that language has evolved and has genetic and brain bases, what else matters? Epidemiological evidence on language development suggests that simply the quantity and quality of language the child gets is associated with differences in the language that is developed. For example, the twins in the ALSPAC sample showed slightly retarded language development, as is often the case with twins. By carefully excluding other possibilities – such as health differences due to twins usually being smaller at birth and more at risk of perinatal complications, or twins talking to each other in their own invented language – the study team[159] established that the delay was probably due to each twin getting less involvement in talk with adults than a single child would. The parents living with twins increased the total amount of talk over what the average single child would hear, but they were unable to double it, so that on average the twins had enough less involvement in talking with adults to account for their slower language development.

Children who are brought up to be bilingual, so that they hear more than one language but not so much of each language as a monolingual child would do, tend to be slower in the initial growth of their language, especially their vocabulary, but in the end they have advantages in awareness of how language works (as well as the advantages of not having to rely on the patience of others when they travel abroad, or do the stereotypical English thing of speaking in English very slowly and expecting to be understood).

Large-scale American studies of language development in families across the range of social classes and educational levels have found that children who heard a larger amount of parental talk developed language faster; and there tended to be big differences between parents of different socioeconomic levels. But we need to be careful about interpreting this as 'more talk is better', for complex reasons.

At the extreme, children who are extremely neglected, who do not hear language, or who are not involved in language by their caregivers very often show serious deficits in learning language. 'Feral' children, whose early lives are spent without parental care and conversation, and the neglected children brought up in regimes like those in the Romanian orphan studies, typically have a serious lack of language when they are rescued. If the deprivation has been all-pervasive and lasted for a long time, the child may not develop normal language even after years of normal exposure to language. The famous case of 'Genie' is an example.[160] This little girl was isolated and abused by a psychotic father who had decided that she was defective. He confined her to a small room where she was tied into a crib and from before her second birthday to the age of thirteen she was rarely or never talked to or played with. When rescued, she had very little language. She was looked after by a succession of foster parents and observed by a succession of researchers, and in their care she developed better communication skills, but although her vocabulary increased and she understood other people's language better, Genie has not developed a grammatically organised language comparable with a normal child's. So, again, extreme deficit is a bad thing.

However, it would probably be a mistake to conclude that differences in amount of parental talk nearer the average lead to better or worse child language. In the first place, the relationship is likely to be two-way – more child talk inducing more parent talk. There is also the big issue of enjoyment. Being talked at is no fun compared to talking with, even when you are very young or incompetent at language. Being 'taught' and 'assessed' all the time is no fun either.

There are several sets of data which suggest the association between amount of involvement in language and developing language skills is not one-way. There are, for example, children who have heard much less language than usual because their parents are deaf, but have normal hearing themselves and develop language normally; and there are children who have been talked with a normal amount but have specific difficulties with language (SLI).[161] Their difficulties vary in type, but for a substantial proportion, their most obvious difficulties are with the rule-like aspects of language, for example phonology and syntax.[162] It seems possible that some children with SLI have got stuck on immature strategies of analysing words and so have only cumbersome attack skills for new words and an inefficient way of storing and retrieving familiar ones. The representations of language which underlie their behaviour may not work very well, which means they use up more processing capacity and are more likely to break down when the language system is heavily burdened with other tasks; reading is often fraught with difficulties for them.

Studies of brain development cast increasing light on the problems of children with SLI. They sometimes have obvious evidence of gross brain abnormalities, so it does seem possible that there are subtle differences in regions relevant to language functioning when comparing children with SLI and normal language users. Worse phonological awareness in young children seems to be associated with less asymmetry favouring Wernicke's area, a region critical for language comprehension. This might be a result of subtle genetic differences such that brain development is not quite set up for language development right from the beginning, so that the connections that are made in the brain are unusually arranged even prenatally. This explanation would fit in with the tendency for children with SLI to have parents and siblings with language impairments and with the fact that SLI is not as easily recovered from as localised brain damage. There is a strong environmental effect on both normal language development and the incidence of specific language impairment, but also considerable heritability for being in the bottom 5 per cent of the language ability distribution.[163]

Where there are neurological differences between children with SLI and children developing normally, these might be due to differences in development before birth, but they could also develop postnatally as a result of abnormal language input. If the child does not, for some reason, receive or attend to social interaction and parental communication, the regions of brain that are waiting for this input may not receive enough of it to have evidence to activate the left hemisphere brain mechanisms that normally analyse phonological or grammatical structure. Sometimes the regions crucial for phonological processing may be partly turned over to other tasks; deaf children who have learned to communicate with signs, for example, seem to use language regions of the brain for analysis of sign movements rather than the sounds they cannot hear and do not need to analyse.

Children use information about regularities in the language that they hear from birth. I've mentioned babies' recognition of familiar individual voices and of sounds characteristic of their own language; they also learn to pick up the stresses and emphasis that signal what's important and to use the gestures, facial expressions, and changes in pitch and volume that go along with parent–child conversation. With accumulating experience of language, of course, they become better and better at doing it.

Children's production of sounds and then words is highly predictable.[164] Its timing is a product of physical maturation increasingly modified by experience. It takes time for the infant's vocal apparatus to develop to the adult state. Initially, the larynx is high up in the throat, engaging the nasal passage, so that the infant is able to drink and breathe at the same time (very useful to someone who does a lot of suckling). By about three months of age, the larynx has descended in the throat, the pharynx has opened up, and there is scope for the tongue movements that are necessary to produce the full variety of vowel sounds (and increasing control of the complex set of muscles involved). Early sounds may unintentionally signal the baby's emotional states; parents, of course, use them as if they do.

Babies begin to play with sounds, producing a larger and larger range, play that appears to be for its own sake rather than involved in any attempt to communicate. How the parent responds to the baby's earliest practice with sounds doesn't seem to affect what sounds they make or the speed or direction of their later language development. If the parents want to make noises back, fine; if they don't, also fine, provided they are attending to the child in other ways, of course!

Around seven or eight months, babies start to combine vowels and consonants, usually producing ba-ba, ma-ma, da-da sorts of sounds. Many languages use these sounds as names for things relevant to babies, because they are babbled in much the same way across languages. A baby randomly producing a babbling noise which is also a name for a significant person in the native language may get a great deal of reward from its adults, who believe, or act as if they believe, that the baby is now addressing them by name. Quite a lot of parents enthusiastically babble back at their baby. This sort of social reward does not increase specific noises in babble, but it may increase the amount of general babble and the proportion of babble that is produced as a social activity rather than a solitary one. A wide range of sounds are produced in babbling initially, but by about ten months of age, the range is narrowing to include mainly those sounds which the baby hears produced by other people.

The stable sequence and timing of speech sound production to the babbling stage in virtually all children suggests that there is a high degree of genetic programming and maturation involved. However, experience is also necessary. Children born deaf start to make babble sounds but commonly give it up, presumably because they cannot hear themselves. If their parents are fluent users of a sign language and sign to the baby, the baby will 'babble' manually, probably at a slightly younger age than a hearing baby starts to babble vocally, perhaps because the muscular control needed for signing is easier for the baby than the muscular control needed to articulate speech. Signs may be invented as well as imitated.

From around the first birthday, infants begin to produce what we could call 'words', sounds which are consistently linked to a particular event or object and might be performing at least some of the same functions as an adult's word. You may remember me telling you that my daughter's first 'word' of this sort was /wow/, which we first noticed when she looked at a dog (in her father's talk to her, a 'bow-wow') running round in a local wood. Goodness only knows what exactly 'wow' meant to her at this stage: an imitation of the dog's noise or of her father's comment, or a true reference to the creature or something about it, or even the sort of superlative that 'wow!' is to an adult (she has grown up to be much keener on dogs than I ever was). But the 'word' being linked with a particular sight (dogs running about) and being a derivative of an adult's conventional word is pretty typical of first words.

Early words are commonly simplified in sound; indeed, the same sound may be produced in different contexts as different words – 'da' could mean dog, or duck, or daddy, depending on which of these interesting creatures is present. The context makes the word unambiguous. The 'first words' follow from a period where babies have shown understanding of words in adults' speech, have built up a vocabulary of twenty to fifty words that they understand but don't say, and may have produced idiosyncratic words (some of which go unrecognised).

By the second birthday, the vocabularies toddlers use will probably have upwards of fifty words, perhaps into the hundreds. Most early words are names of familiar people, objects, animals, food, toys, body parts and functions, and social routines, or social phrases such as 'bye-bye'. Importantly, they're used to get what the toddler wants, to regulate others' behaviour, to make or keep a social contact. The child saying 'ice cream!' probably means something like 'I can see a source of ice creams and I want one right now.' Only an unwise adult would think that the small child is disinterestedly naming the ice cream, rather than trying to bring about the desired outcome of getting some to eat. Children very quickly learn that words are powerful ways of controlling other people, fortunately for the adults who would like to use words to control the child; and eventually toddlers manage to use words to talk about themselves, to find out about the world, to inform others, and to pretend.

Parents' talk to children is often adapted to what the child can understand and produce, possibly because that is a specially good way of keeping communication working smoothly. From infancy onwards, parents often label the thing a child is already attending to: 'that's a doggie'. Or they may draw the child's attention to something by gesturing and labelling it at the same time: 'look at the doggie'. Establishing joint attention between oneself and the other person is one of the most important achievements of infancy (and one of the key problems of autistic children). Most young children monitor their parents' attention and react to new words accordingly.

Parents also talk about contrasts: 'you're not *big*, you're *little*' and 'that's not *nice*, that's *dirty*'. Differences in parents' use of such talk, and of labelling objects in picture books, are associated with differences in the rate of language development. But, as I just said, everyday talk involves parents adapting to the child's own language, so children who are already good at these things may get more of them, and children whose development has not advanced so far may get less. 'Association' is not water-tight evidence of cause.

If the adult has a particular interest, or recognises the child's interest and encourages it in the child, this may lead to enormous vocabularies in the special subject. There are numerous studies relating vocabulary content and rate of growth to the topics adults talk about with the child. Almost invariably, if the adult and child converse about a subject more than average, then the child's vocabulary in that area will tend to be larger and more useable than average. The child's thinking in the area may be more advanced, too; possibly having more vocabulary about a topic makes it easier to think about it. I think it's important to recognise the intertwining of children's language development and their cognitive development and their social interactions, with influence going in all directions between them. The enormous creativity of human language stems from vocabulary but also from the possibilities that it offers of new combinations of vocabulary items to say things that have never been said before. Word combinations are rule governed. There are rules about combining units of meaning smaller than words into words (for example *talked* combines *talk* and the past tense morpheme -*ed*, *handbags* combines the morphemes *hand*, *bag*, and -*s*); rules about combining words into grammatical phrases, clauses, and sentences; rules for combining sentences into more extended speech (or written text; these rules may be slightly different, typically more elaborate).

Children slowly construct grammar from the language they use and hear. Some early words look like grammatically constructed phrases but are more likely learned as unanalysed chunks. Social phrases such as 'How do you do' or 'S'il vous plaît' are examples. Or the child may often use 'fill the blank' structures. Children can become fluent producers of language using these sorts of slots, but they are skilled users of specific structures rather than possessors of an abstract or generalised grammar. What they have really learned is where to place words within certain familiar recurring patterns; progress towards an adult abstract grammar is piecemeal and gradual. Parental emphasis and systematic contrasting may help with both understanding and producing grammatical utterances, but in everyday life, the main criterion is whether the speech has the desired effect. Some syntax is more difficult for both children and adults; for example passive sentence structure and metaphor, which are rare in normal talk to children, continue to confuse them for years past the point at which they can deal with simple declarative sentences and questions.

Quite a lot of the support system for children's language development is outside language itself, in their interaction with more skilled language users who are keenly interested in talking to them and listening to them. Early joint attention, turn-taking, looking at picture books, and naming objects all figure heavily in the interaction of Western middle-class babies and toddlers with their parents. They facilitate vocabulary growth and knowledge about language, especially perhaps if they are accompanied by the specialised sort of language which has been called 'child-directed speech' (CDS). This is directed in two senses: it is addressed to children, directed towards them, and also it is in part directed by them, in that it is contingent on what they are heard to say and believed to understand, and on what they are known to enjoy.

Western middle-class parents are highly likely to use CDS to their babies and young children most of the time. The adult's language is closely linked to the child's current stage of cognitive and linguistic development because this is what works to keep everyone chatting happily. It is evoked by the child as well as provided by the parent. Parents adjust to what they can see the child understanding – after all, most talk is there to control, amuse, and communicate with the child, not to teach it language.

While the child is only at the beginnings of using language, the parent will do almost all the talking, playing both roles in the 'conversation'. For example, the talk that goes along with looking at a picture book will involve the adults saying 'What's that?' and straight away answering their own question with 'That's a teddy!' The next stage is to leave a little pause which the baby is expected to fill, but whatever noise the baby makes, the adult reacts as if the response was correct – baby says 'ba', adult says 'yes, it's a teddy!' Gradually the baby is given responsibility for producing closer and closer versions of the right answer, until the roles become more and more equal, and eventually the adult is asking genuine questions so the child has to give new information in full. This CDS is an example of 'scaffolding', a particularly useful parental frame.

All fruitful parental talk is based on what works and on beliefs about what children are like, how they should learn, and for what purposes and by what methods they should be socialised. There are different ways of talking with children besides CDS. In some societies, adults may ignore children conversationally until they are older. In other social settings, children are allowed to observe normal adult language, are encouraged to perform, and are challenged to use language in an adult way. They have a role to play and culturally appropriate ways to play it, and they learn these by imitating the social participation around them.[165]

Children grow up into normally competent language users apropos their culture even in groups which rarely or never use the sort of CDS that I have described, so it cannot be *necessary* for language development. Children are able and willing to learn from whatever language they encounter, to seek out meaning and knowledge actively as well as to imitate their partner's behaviour. They may have other interactional and conversational partners, such as siblings or older children who are their caretakers, and they are likely to have developed language which differentiates between partners of different skills and status and willingness to work to understand the child.

Child-directed speech and parental input may have different effects on different areas of the child's language. Vocabulary, topic understanding, and social routines do seem in many instances to be closely related to amount of parental input in that specific area. Elizabeth Meins,[166] for example, links mothers' talk about people's mental states with children's abilities to talk about minds. Specific effects on syntax have proved more elusive. It could be that the grammatical basics of language are more strongly wired in than other aspects of language or are even universal, as Chomsky and more recently Pinker argued.[167] But even here it's unquestionable that children get a lot of exposure to models that are at least approximately grammatical, over more years than Chomsky allowed for, and the basic programming might be simpler and not specific to language – memory for regularities and for what worked, for example.

Children learn that language is useful. It's a source of information, a means of expression, and a way of communicating with others – a rewarding social activity. Sooner or later, children who do not use language fluently, or who avoid language, will be at a disadvantage. Conversation with adults allows children to practice taking turns, listening as well as speaking, and other social routines, all socially valued skills and essential once you get to school. Practice in making yourself understood may help improve the intelligibility of the child's pronunciation, and it may be useful to have to reformulate utterances that have not been understood as the child desired. Conversations with interlocutors who do not know the child quite well enough to work out what an unclear utterance means could be particularly helpful here.

In the end, it would seem that different 'routes into language' result in a broadly similar sequence of language development and broadly similar levels of language competence. But the emphasis is on 'broadly': there may well be differences which seem small in themselves but have far-reaching effects. Differences in orientation to literacy are one example of a language difference with long-term developmental significance. The meeting of home language and the school is another. School is full of teachers who ask questions to which they, as teachers, know the answers; the point is to make children display whether they know the answer. Display questions are quite rare in ordinary talk and are socially tricky: if someone asks you something and you know they already know the answer, you're inclined to think that you're being tested (unpleasant) or that something hidden is meant (also unnerving). But CDS uses display questions in the naming game and the picture book game, so children who've grown up with this can take them for granted.

I think language learning obeys the general laws of cognitive and motor development. Like everything else that we do, it stems from and is shaped by both biological and social influences. Children have mouths, larynxes, and so forth that they can use to produce a tremendous range of sounds, and ears that can hear them. Under reasonably favourable conditions they are deeply curious and extremely interested in understanding, categorizing, and generalizing what they experience. They seek out contrast and notice equivalence. They observe and they imitate and they socialise. They have brains which allow and expect these sorts of behaviours. They use these proclivities when they are attending to other people's vocal behaviours and when they are producing their own. They want to communicate with others. Their caretakers are strongly interested in them acquiring the language of their community and using it in socially approved ways. Over the first year of life and during the preschool years, their ability to talk opens up all sorts of enjoyable possibilities for them – chattering, story-telling, narrating, memorising, arguing, sharing interests, and reading. These can be enjoyable possibilities for their parents, too.

We are all expected to become competent readers and writers nowadays, but we haven't evolved to be. Reading and writing are recent inventions. Although literacy is obligatory now in Western cultures, six generations or so ago most Europeans could not read much more than their own name, and only a very small minority would be literate in the way we expect everyone to be now. Evolution has not had time to select on the basis of an ability to read and write. We may be able to identify evolved characteristics that literacy is based on, but they evolved initially because they provided other advantages. Reading and writing may not be as easy as talking or walking, which have a longer evolutionary history. Experience, and especially socially provided experience, will be crucially important in how easy a child finds it to become literate.

Thus, it is completely unlikely that we will identify genes for reading, though we might identify genetic differences which are, say, associated with differences in distinguishing speech sounds and hence to differences in ability to learn to read.[168] It is unlikely that there are brain regions that are specialised for reading, though there may be brain regions which are heavily used when we read and these may work better in good readers than poor ones (but remember, however readers' brains are wired at birth, brains change in response to the experience they get).

The language that we read, when we read, is a visual representation of spoken words, and the spoken words are sound-based representations of things in the world or ideas. Both spoken words and written words are presented to us in organized sets – utterances, speeches, sentences, paragraphs – built up from smaller items to larger ones, and not necessarily built up in the same ways in written language as in the spoken language that we learn first. A spoken word will consist of one or more speech sounds (phonemes) and perhaps an intonation pattern and will be separated from other spoken words by a little bit of silence (generally). A written word will be built up of parts which represent speech sounds (graphemes),[169] and words will be separated from other words by a bit of white space. Spoken words are organised across time, not space, and pass by us just as the time passes by; written words are organized in space which we examine across time and can easily reexamine in more time.

All this means that reading written words is an activity involving links between the real world, conceptual worlds, and language structure, complicated by changes in sensory modality between hearing and seeing and in time scale from near-simultaneous to permanent. To be able to read, we need a lot of language knowledge, we need to make fine visual discriminations and identify the words we see written down, we need to move our eyes appropriately over the text, and we need to remember considerable quantities of information. Clearly it is, as Uta Frith says, 'a complex and astonishing accomplishment'.[170] And we expect all our children to learn to do it.

The first point I want to make is that there are different sorts of reading. We may only need to get the gist without worrying about implications, inferences, or sounds, or we may try to achieve exact pronunciation of the words, access to their deepest meanings, comparison with other texts. Reading is not a simple activity, though it does feel simple once you can do it.

Skilled readers with years of experience have read most of the words they encounter many times over. The links between the letter string c-a-t and its sound and what it refers to are so overlearned they are automatic and fast. Only when the text is very difficult or conditions are very adverse – too short a time, too little light, minute print, really distorted handwriting, poor motivation, tiredness – will skilled readers misread a word in the sense of not understanding it. They will probably not make a conscious analysis of words beyond the initial rapid recognition, and they will have difficulties spotting minor errors in spelling because they go from what is on the page to what it means so easily. Skilled readers rarely have to do more than scan the page, and they may well understand what is written there without having to process much of it consciously. Sometimes we have to deliberately slow down our reading in order to, for example, be sure we are being fair to the student whose work we are grading.

If skilled readers meet a new word, then they have to do something a little different from fast automatic recognition of word and meaning. Occasionally they may work out the sound of the word from its constituent units, recognising it as a word which is familiar as a heard word, though never before seen. (This is hard to illustrate in writing, but if we hear the commentaries on international football matches on television before we read the names on the footballers' shirts, we may perhaps process players' names in this way.) Skilled readers faced with a new word may find analogies in other words – *caterpillar*, for example, divides into familiar parts. If all this fails, the reader may not be able to do much more than guess or access the meaning from the context or use a dictionary.

Children at the beginning of learning to read do not have a large store of overlearned words where they can link written symbol, auditory symbol, and referent instantaneously. Nor do they have a large store of words whose sounds they know are analogous to each other. Nor do they have much practice in breaking down words into their constituent parts. This is particularly difficult in English. Some languages (for example Spanish) have a nearly unambiguous relationship between how a word is spelled and how it is pronounced, and children find it relatively easy to learn to read and spell in these languages. However, many English words break the normal correspondences between grapheme and phoneme. Almost every written letter can be pronounced in more than one way. Even combinations of letters can be pronounced differently, for example the -*ough* in *bough, cough, dough, through*, and so forth. The English spelling system is extremely informative for a native speaker who knows its rules and something of its history (as English has flourished by adopting words from other languages with something like their native pronunciation), but it is better suited to adult fluent readers than to children learning to read. Children bilingual in Spanish and English progress faster in reading Spanish than in English.

What do beginning readers do, then? Can we describe common strategies or common stages in becoming able to read? Normally, children begin to learn to read having already learned to use spoken language. They have a heard or spoken vocabulary of hundreds of words. They may have played with sounds as nursery rhymes do, and as some babies and children do spontaneously as they first learn to make speech sounds. Both vocabulary size and knowledge of nursery rhymes predict the ease with which children learn to read; in both cases, the children with the most limited knowledge are the most likely to have reading difficulties.

Epidemiological evidence shows significant associations between parents' and children's interest in literacy, particularly the frequency with which stories were read to the child during the preschool years and the child's progress in learning to read. Even when all sorts of other possible influential variables were allowed for, the amount that parents read to the child or taught education-relevant things, how often the public library was used, and the number of books the child owned made independent contributions to the child's reading readiness at school entry in the ALSPAC sample. (And it was also the case that more book use was associated with a lower level of behaviour problems.)

Children who learn to read early, and easily, have generally acquired very early a good understanding of what reading is about in general, and about such specific aspects as that you go along the lines from top left to bottom right; that the message is in the text, though the pictures may provide clues; what things called 'words' and 'sentences' are; and so on. Children who have had less opportunity to learn about books have ground to make up when they begin to have formal reading lessons; they have also had less opportunity, perhaps, to learn that reading gives you access to interesting information and enjoyable stories, and thus they may be less motivated to work at learning to read. I'm a lifelong reading addict. Sharing my family's interest in books is one of the positive memories of my childhood; reading to my daughter, from the earliest days until long after she could read herself, was one of the many delights of being a parent. An occasion when I looked up from reading The Hobbit to find her almost hidden under the bedclothes, her eyes like saucers, enjoyably terrified, is an especially proud example.

But although some children 'pick up' reading painlessly, many don't, so it's worth looking at why not. Which reading skills most often present problems? We have to see the differences between letters – rarely a problem. Unless the amount of text we have to deal with is very small (ten or twelve letters or spaces), we have to move our eyes over the text. Most children can perform the right sorts of eye movements. The necessary visual skills begin in infancy and run smoothly in most children. The uses to which visual processes are put may well change as development proceeds, but the basic visual capacities are functional very early. In fact, although poor readers are not so good at visual processing as good ones, this seems more often to be due to them having less experience as readers rather than being the cause of their poor reading in the first place. They do not read worse because they cannot distinguish letters, they distinguish letters worse because they read less.[171]

In the earliest stages of reading, most words which the child can read are in fact probably dealt with by recognising either their shape or their standard sequence of letters; many children are taught very early on to recognise their names, for example, and the environment has many written patterns such as 'stop' or 'exit'. Throughout later stages of learning to read, the presence of a particular letter or combination of letters which distinguishes a particular common word may be taken as a sign that the present word is the known one, even if the other letters in it are not quite right. There are many examples in *Winnie-the-Pooh*.[172] Pooh receives Piglet's urgent message in a bottle requesting rescue from a rising flood, but misreads the written word *Piglit* as his own name, because it begins with P. Consequently, he misinterprets the message as a personal message to himself, and it is only when it is taken to Christopher Robin, who is a more advanced reader, that it can be acted on appropriately. Similar errors are documented in the research literature about real children.

As I argued earlier, fluent adult readers read using their sight vocabulary, words they recognise at sight without analysing them much and often from only partial cues. Commonly, children begin reading by building up a sight vocabulary. Typically this includes interesting often-used words, such as their own names or the distinctive logo of some interesting place or product (commercial companies exploit this ruthlessly). Early reading schemes sometimes restrict themselves to a simple and repetitive vocabulary to enable children to build up sight vocabulary – we enjoyed a brilliant series by Allan Ahlberg when my daughter was small. Sight vocabulary is a useful basis for learning to read. Its problem is that it only works when the word that is met is already visually familiar. What can you do when you meet a new word that is not yet in your sight vocabulary?

If children are to extend their sight vocabularies, there are really only two ways to do this. One is memorizing each new word by rote, which typically takes a long, long time, but if your language is written in characters (Chinese, for example), it's what you have to do. The other method, potentially more generalisable, is to analyse the constituent parts of words in terms of sounds. Knowing that spoken words are made up of sounds, and written words are made up of letters, and having a writing system with a fairly simple correspondence between letters or groups of letters and the sounds they represent, enable the reader who meets an unfamiliar written word to make a good guess at how it should be pronounced and then to recognise the pronounced word and access its meaning.

To do this, the child has to recognise letters or letter groups and know what sounds are associated with each. There are a number of related skills. These include phonological awareness, which refers to the understanding that spoken words consist of individual speech sounds (phonemes) and combinations of speech sounds (syllables, onset-rime units); phonological decoding, that is the application of letter–sound correspondence rules; spelling ability; and verbal working memory. There's been masses of research, and although there is disagreement over details, there is an agreed general picture of poor phonological processes being very damaging to a child's chances of finding it unproblematic to learn to read, crucially in

English and to some extent even in languages with a more regular relation between written symbol and sound, and even in writing systems based on characters.[173]

Coping with a writing system that uses grapheme–phoneme correspondences is not easy unless you already know quite a lot about language sounds, even if the grapheme–phoneme correspondences are simple and predictable (as I said earlier, in English they are anything but simple). Before they read, children may delight in rhyme and alliteration and nonsense words. I don't think it's an accident that nursery rhymes so often play with word sounds – 'Baa baa black sheep', 'Sing a song of sixpence', 'Humpty Dumpty'. Children who've learned a lot of such rhymes seem to be advantaged when they come to learn to read; perhaps their brains have learned to be more aware of speech sounds than people who are not so experienced with them.

Children who are very poor phonological processors before beginning to learn to read are likely to have difficulties; training that improves phonological processing improves reading. These paired findings, that poor phonological processing precedes reading and that remedying it improves reading too, show that the poor phonological processing of poor readers is a cause not a consequence of their reading difficulties. Poor readers probably tend to have limited vocabularies, low enjoyment of reading, and low levels of educational success as *consequences* of their poor reading; poor phonological skills, in contrast, precede poor reading even though they may also be made even worse by it.

So, paradoxically, learning about phonics can help a lot with building a sight vocabulary so big that you will rarely need to use phonic analysis in order to read. This is why there has been such an emphasis on it in schools. Sometimes it's forgotten, however, that as readers get better, phonics will rarely be necessary, and it has also been forgotten that if a child is already reading well without phonics, having to do the phonic analysis may get in the way of the reading. The route between phonics and ending up as a good reader is largely through avoiding becoming a poor reader at an earlier stage.[174]

Reading includes many different activities at different perceptual, linguistic, and cognitive levels, and these may well operate in different ways as the reader tackles different tasks. I think it is important for parents to recognize this, and teachers too. It doesn't help children learn to read if too much of their experience of reading is them being under pressure to get every single word decoded correctly, and they rarely get to enjoy the text for its own sake. Virtually all children who feel books are enjoyable and useful learn to read successfully, and may like me be addicted. And reading together and discussing what you have shared in the reading can be a source of excellent bonding and discussion; you can get affiliations and attachments that in turn shape further activities and experiences, including more experiences with literacy.

Ever since the beginnings of literacy, adults have developed texts to social-ize children as well as to entertain them. Children often play out the story they have been read in social pretend play. My daughter at age three was very enthusiastic about pretending to be Sleeping Beauty and Snow White; both roles involved her lying on the floor with eyes tight shut and a smug smile on her face while her role-play partner had to do all the other parts, finally 'waking her' with a kiss. This irritated me immensely, so I provided an intensive course of stories with more feminist themes, such as Molly Whuppie who saved her family from the wicked ogre by tricking him into killing his own daughters, and various clever girls who outsmart the male baddies,[175] with probably some effect (she has grown up to be an ardent feminist who thinks that Molly Whuppie was lacking in sisterhood towards the ogre's daughters). Relationships between parents and children enrich and are enriched by sharing a bedtime story. Sharing out roles in pretend play, or identifying with the characters of a story, can be contributors to the life of the family or the friendship group.

You don't have to agree on the messages you draw from what you read, or even on what you read. To be honest, when my daughter loved a book that I despised, I did try to keep her preferred book out of sight or to negotiate that I would read it if I also got to choose a book I liked. As she has grown up, we have discussed why we thought something was good or bad, and tried out each other's recommendations; the birthday pres-ents she gives me always include some of the latest literary novels.[176] The social and emotional ties you have with your reading partners and the enthusiasm you have for the books you read may interact – we read some-thing because it is admired by someone we like or even revise our rating of a person because unexpectedly they like or dislike a particular author or text. Experiences such as these are part of forming one's view of one's self and of other people.

I turn now to look briefly at the psychology of parent control of children and children's self-control. There are many occasions when 'mother knows best' and parents need to control their children. But children also have a strong drive to function autonomously or to achieve mastery, all the way from 'I want to do it my own self' in the preschool years to the adolescent's desire to escape parental control of where they go, who they interact with, and what they eat, drink, and smoke. The crunch points occur when par-ents' attempts to direct children's behaviour come into conflict with the children's desires to develop their autonomy.

Parental control tactics come in many forms and are embedded in other qualities of the relationship, and parents use them with different degrees of consistency. Sometimes one discusses, reasons, negotiates, bargains, persuades; sometimes it is a matter of insistence or power assertion, or even force or punishment. Sometimes you are pleased that your little darling is thinking for herself, even if the result is a refusal to do what you want; sometimes you're not. I remember a moment of crisis and my partner saying to me, 'But you wouldn't have wanted a little pudding, would you'. At the time, blind unquestioning obedience would have suited me just fine. Longer term, he and I have both rejoiced that we have produced an autonomous, not to say feisty, daughter.

We all know from our own lives that no single technique always works or always fails. But the research literature from psychoneuroendocrinology, epidemiology, and psychology does suggest[177] that control which stems from a generally warm relationship, clarifies limits, and explains itself tends to have positive effects, while control which is rigid and insensitive, or which implies negative judgments of the child's rights, may be harmful. The warmth, the explanation, and the openness to negotiation of the participants may be what are positive about resolving the situation so conflict ends. It could also be that discussion and mutual respect are good beyond the control event because they allow us to practice a host of socially useful skills and demonstrate mutual positive respect. Both inside and outside the moments when parent and child are engaged in control issues, most individuals prefer some autonomy or at least the alternative of being a valued, if low-power, member of the community. We've already seen that this is good for cortisol levels.

However, there is one distinction between types of control that psychological theory makes.[178] This distinction is between behavioural control and psychological or emotional control. Behavioural control focuses directly on behaviour; there are rules for behaviour, and behaviour is monitored to ensure that the rules are kept, but if they are not, the matter can generally be dealt with as the breaking of a rule by an otherwise worthwhile, well-meaning person. The child who persistently fails to wear her hair tied back in school, for example, and gets nagged by her teachers and her mother, may be simultaneously very irritated by their insistence on a rule she sees as petty, and confident that their displeasure (or at least the mother's displeasure) is limited to this particular issue. Psychological control, in contrast, operates by working on the child's emotional state – inducing guilt, highlighting parents' emotional reactions, generalising to the worth of the child elsewhere in his or her life. The behaviourally controlling parent would say, 'You should tie your hair back, that's the rule and you just make your life more difficult if you rebel over it'; the psychologically controlling parent would say, 'You are shaming me', 'I can't love you if you don't do what I want', and so forth.

Some parents who use high rates of psychological control may act manipulatively and intrusively and undermine the children's sense of themselves as worthwhile, leading to children who are at risk of internalising problems such as low self-esteem, guilt, and anxiety. Whatever the sort of control, if it is felt to result from love and concern, it will not carry so much threat to the child's psychological well-being, and it may be accepted even if it sets a limit to autonomy. Sometimes explaining can help.

But it's not a simple picture on either side; in my example of the girl with the too freely flowing hair, there were some teachers who felt she was flaunting it at them – that the real issue was a much more pervasive one of a general disrespect for their authority. They may, looking back, have been absolutely right – I think there was some expertise here in behaviour which is subversive but hard to pin down and punish!

Parental control is of course moderated by other factors. Some children are more controllable than others. Having a highly active or an irritable temperament or a predisposition to negative emotions may mean that parenting which is harsh or intrusive is more than usually likely to lead to behaviour problems. This sort of the child needs patient calming control. Fearful children respond better to gentle, warm control. Almost all the time, it's likely to work out best if you can act before the situation gets really difficult, and preempt the conflict.

All this implies that control needs to be adjusted to the child. Parents find it easier to respond to a young child with simple direct control – saying 'no', moving the child away, using distraction – than to do so at later ages, when the child's persistence will have increased and prohibitions are more likely to be taken personally. Conversely, appeals to reason and the child's conscience would work better with an older child. The danger is that a history of conflict, hostility, and mutual negative expectations can build up, so that each little disagreement that occurs is reacted to in terms of the accumulated disagreement of several years of interaction. There is very interesting evidence[179] of this in families with a history of aggression and hostility; family members were prone to react to neutral or even well-intended behaviour as if it was hostile, and fights would ensue over the slightest thing. Adolescents with a chronic feeling of being disrespected seem to experience the world in the same, dangerous, way. The neuroscience on brain development in adolescence suggested that they might be a bit more confrontational than they were when younger or will be when older.[180] The comparison with other species suggests that adolescence is a phase of establishing autonomy and will often include a bit of riotous behaviour and risk-taking.

There are associations between control, monitoring, and children's behaviour, but they are complex. A substantial body of research suggests that poor parental monitoring may be associated with worse child behaviour.[181] Children are more likely to behave badly when away from parents' supervision or when parents do not know where they are, who they are with, and what they are doing. It has been argued from this that failures in parental monitoring gave their adolescents the space to behave badly, to hang out with deviant peers who will draw them into delinquency and other problem behaviours. But obviously there is room for a bidirectional effect here: children who wish to behave badly will undoubtedly seek to evade parental supervision while they do so. The girl who broke the rule about loose hair at school left home each morning with it tied back, or at least promising to tie it back en route. The child who wishes to steal, set a fire, or torture a cat will probably not do it where an adult can see. There is also room for earlier history to have an effect on monitoring; parents may not monitor a child who has always behaved impeccably, or they might try to monitor a troublesome child or a troublesome area of behaviour very much more closely; or, faced with a child who persists in behaving undesirably despite their monitoring, they may seek to preserve their relationship with the child rather than risk the child perceiving them as a gaoler: 'you never let me do anything'.

One issue to consider is how the parent might induce the child or adolescent *not* to want to engage in deviant behaviour. Earlier parental behaviour or cultural beliefs and practices might have induced a strong attachment between the child and the parent, so that the child wishes to avoid behaviour which will hurt or embarrass the parent or 'let down' the family honour (hence, it has been suggested,[182] the relatively low rate of delinquency in East Asian adolescents). Consistent parental explanation of why certain behaviours are undesirable may help if the family has discussed them and agreed on them. If the child has also internalised the controls that parents or culture offer, they may regulate and supervise themselves. This self-surveillance will be harder for the child to evade than parental surveillance; parents actually spend rather little time where their teenagers are, may have little information about what the teenagers are doing, and may receive only minimal and ungracious answers if they ask for too much information. I think it is very likely that the majority of teenagers prefer it that way. It is also the case that teenagers are likely to have other teenagers as a very important reference group. They may shift from wanting not to let down the family to wanting not let down the gang. Concerns with being disrespected loom large in how they see the world.

The psychology of control suggests that there are levels of self-control as well as reaction to control by others. One of the ways self-control has been examined is by putting children in a situation where they are tempted to break a rule or go against a prohibition or just wait to get a reward – famously, a test involving resisting taking one marshmallow in order to get two 'in a few minutes'.[183] There is a lot of evidence that how good the child is at deferred gratification is a strong predictor of later success, and probably mental health. Probably different abilities are involved in this: being able to focus attention and manage mood; willingness to commit to practice and not want instant results; better planning; confidence that reward will come, even if that takes a while.

Related ideas about focussing attention, planning, practice, and confidence apply also when we are thinking about control exerted on thinking tasks. There is a useful psychological model of 'working memory'[184] which is seen as a sort of 'desktop' related both to the input of our senses and the long-term memory stores holding our accumulated knowledge. This desktop is quite small, and the length of time we can hold information in it is limited, too – think of trying to remember a telephone number or a computer password long enough to use it – so we need to get on with things and coordinate the components of our solution to a task. Even babies learn and remember, as we have seen with their very early recognition of mother's voice or face; it seems possible that differences in babies' speed of learning predict their intelligence levels in the school years. As children get older, they normally become better at resisting distraction and organising information, and they simply know more; but most importantly, they become better at using strategies to remember what they need to remember and at knowing what their own strengths and weaknesses are. Going to school often has quite a lot to do with this, but home activities like Kim's Game or using shopping lists contribute, too.

Memory is also a major component of one's identity, and what we see children remembering or not illustrates how complex this autobiographical memory is. Our recollections of particular events early in our lives are usually fragmented and rarely include much before age five. Freud saw this as blocking about traumatic emotional events, but there are other (better) explanations in the psychology of cognitive development. One reason has to do with not having the 'labels' on our memory that help us retrieve it. For example: my three-year-old asking me for the videotape she wanted to watch in which 'he's in the snow, there's a monster, there's a robber lady' didn't work because my label was different – 'the tape with classic Chaplin films' – which is much more like the sort of label she would use now. The other reason why specific autobiographical memories are difficult is that we quickly and automatically generalise about events, building up a general script of what happens when we go to school, see a film, choose a book – and the generalised event representation obscures the individual details which are particular to an event.

One's own autobiographical memory builds up over time, often with contributions from others; it's part of developing a sense of oneself as an individual person. We don't know a lot about how a sense of oneself might have evolved. It's not been possible to identify anything much like this in other species; I used to think that my cat looked as though she was experiencing the self-conscious emotion of shame when I told her off for scratching the sofa, but the harder-nosed scientist who was my partner regularly told me I was anthropomorphising her. There are some fairly convincing demonstrations of primates recognising that the reflection in a mirror is their own. We do know that some primates have mirror neurons that react like our own, so that's one step towards self-consciousness. Damage to the frontal lobes tends to affect self-conscious emotions such as embarrassment. If there is a brain base for self-consciousness in the frontal lobes, adolescents being so extremely prone to being embarrassed might fit with their redevelopment.

Basic biological and perceptual processes which operate from quite early in the first year could begin a sense of oneself as an individual who does things.[185] For example, infants' attention to the visible bits of their bodies, and their special enthusiasm for events which are contingent on their own action, and their increasing interest in and pleasure in mastery show that they quickly learn that they can observe interesting things that are linked to their own actions. They add to this a capacity for imitation, perception of similarities between their own behaviour and other people's, and involvement in joint activity with their parents in games and routines. From later on, they use their attachment figure as a reference point about what they are doing. This all suggests their sense of existence in relation to the world and of agency within it could have roots very early in the first year.

We have goals of mastery, autonomy, and connectedness which lead to increasing subjective self-awareness on several fronts: awareness of oneself as able to do things, motivation to master things, and a sense of self-efficacy; ability to self-regulate, thus avoiding emotional distress; awareness of oneself as a social person, engaging in interaction with other social persons, and developing scripts of how such interactions should proceed; and awareness of oneself as someone who is judged by others. You can see that there are things here that will be a very good foundation for happiness if they go right, but a source of great risk if they go wrong.

Differences in infants' and children's experiences of emotion and the modulation of their emotions by parents and caregivers, in their experiences of social interaction games and routines with others involving reciprocal exchange and caregiver scaffolding, in the regularity of links between emotion and behaviour, in the early biographical narratives that parents offer to their children, in the development of autobiographical memory capacities, and in the stories children begin to tell would all feed into differences in their sense of who and what they are. In particular, individuals will develop a sense of self-efficacy of how capable they are of getting things as they want them. This is a massive component of educational success, so I am going to dwell on it.

As we develop, increasingly we accumulate labels applicable to us. We come to be able to experience ourselves as objects that can be described and classified as well as subjectively lived. Most theorists see this as being substantially a matter of labels offered to us or imposed on us by others, hence the phrase the 'looking glass self'.[186] We are constantly provided with labels – 'who's a pretty baby then', 'clever girl', 'bad boy', 'people like us just don't do such things', 'you've not just let the team down, you've let yourself down'. We seem to have a strong propensity to take on such labels, just as we seem to have a propensity to attend to and to imitate others. We live up (or down) to our labels. Sometimes we resist them. Adolescence provides a lot of crises in this.

What's important here is a long-lasting history of interaction between emotional tendencies and interpersonal relationships. Initially, this will be relationships with parents and with other significant figures. They tell us things about ourselves, and we build up our self-concepts from them. While we're very little, the labels we use are typically about physical and social characteristics. Often this involves putting ourselves in the same category as a person who is important to us; apparently at about age three I said, 'Mummy and Joe [my oldest brother] have curly hair; Daddy and I have nice soft straight hair', something which my adult self recognises as typical over a long time, both about the hair and about who I identified with most in my family.

Describing oneself in these terms tends to begin at the time when the child is also beginning to have autobiographical memory. Narratives of one's own life are often constructed in partnership with a parent. Everyday conversations about everyday events (and exceptional events, too) build into a story of who we are and what we're like.

Young school children tend to be positive in their self-descriptions, often unrealistically positive; possibly they have a sense of how rapidly they are learning new things and having new experiences, which gives them a sense of exciting possibilities being open for them. Being ahead of other classmates can be important; great prestige and self-satisfaction are sometimes attached to being the oldest in the class, for example (which may be one part of the reasons why summer-born children, the youngest in the class, tend to do a bit less well in terms of educational achievement). I know of a child who was happy at being one of the oldest and tallest in his primary school class, but became quite dismayed when classmates started to shed their baby teeth earlier, because they claimed this as a sign that they were more grown up than he was. A bit of discussion with parents of how long-lasting his own teeth were, and how his classmates were merely wearing out faster, restored his sense of superiority, but self-concept and prestige were vulnerable for a while.

As children move into school and spend more of their time with other children and with adults outside the family, their descriptions of themselves include more comparisons with others and incorporate more of others' views of themselves. Because schools are full of experiences of being assessed and evaluated, children show more sense of differentiating between the self they are and their ideal self. A substantial discrepancy may lead to dejection or anxiety. Small discrepancies that one thinks one can act on can be motivating, so a sense of what is a real possibility and what is unreasonably ambitious can be helpful. Some researchers think it is especially healthy to have a balance of a positive 'expected' self – what one can get to be – and a negative 'feared' self – I'm not like that and I know how to avoid being like that.[187] A mild overestimation of one's abilities is probably healthy and protective – depressed people tend to rate their abilities more realistically as well as more negatively.

Part of this can be linked[188] to what individuals think about intelligence; some see it as an attribute that you have a certain fixed and uncontrollable amount of, genetically determined, perhaps; others see it as something you could increase through practice. People in the first group, with an 'entity' theory, tend to focus on performance as evidence for their amount of intelligence and are oriented towards approval and avoiding negative feedback; their confidence is eroded if they fail, they then display learned helplessness, and they avoid challenges because of the risk that they might fail to meet them and so have their confidence reduced. The other group, 'incremental' theorists, who see intelligence as improvable, are more oriented towards learning rather than performance, are optimistic about doing better next time and resilient in the face of failure, and take on challenges with an expectation that they will have the skills to master them or at worst should learn from the experience. There's some evidence that entity theorists had too much feedback as children which praised their particular achievements in too general terms and located the causes of it in the individual rather than the individual's actions – 'Clever girl' rather than 'you did a really good job of remembering that'. Incremental theorists had more of this 'you did really well on that because you did such and such a thing' and consequently focussed more on what they had to do to complete tasks and less on the implications of success for a fixed and generalised view of their ability. Although there is not an enormous amount of scientific data on the issue, specific task-oriented feedback does seem to be more effective in motivating learners. I think it's worth trying to provide it to your children or pupils.

Whatever 'ability' is, the way you use it may have just as much to do with the results. The extremes of high performance probably do include 'ability', but they also invariably involve a lot of practice,[189] as we can see from outstanding athletes, musicians, artists. We learn most of what we can do from repetition and practice. We learn to do things well, and it may be especially helpful to learn to do things well in several different ways because these different ways are then available to fit in with variations in the task.

What does mastery mean for the well-being of the child? First, mastery is satisfying or even fun, as the grin of the baby shows, and it makes sense to see it as a natural part of our developmental machinery. Engaging in activities that involve mastery often leads to positive emotional states and feelings of satisfaction and relaxation. Second, mastery can itself be self-developing – we out-do our previous record, or increase our proficiency a bit, or become slicker and shinier and with more 'wow factor', or just reach the same result in a different way. (Though sometimes 'good enough' is good enough.) Third, we practice skills like planning and monitoring our own progress while we develop our mastery, and fourth, our own mastery and our own evaluation of it are situated in the middle of other people's evaluations of us and other people's degree of mastery. We compare ourselves with others. These comparisons offer us opportunities to learn from others' experiences, but they also have repercussions for our reputation and our motivation and our emotions as we experience emotions that are social and self-conscious, such as confidence, pride, shame, guilt, and embarrassment. These emotions all combine appraisal of oneself, of the situation, and of significant others, and the emotional consequences of the comparison – should I be pleased with myself, have I done something which will make other people think the worse of me – and may be powerful both in the particular situation and in general development, especially if we lose control over them.

You can see the beginnings of these emotions in toddlers. In one study,[190] researchers observed the reactions of children aged thirty-three to thirty-seven months to success and failure on easier and harder tasks and found that failure on the easier tasks was particularly likely to produce behaviour such as collapsed body posture, averted gaze, corners of the mouth drooping downwards, hiding one's face, and expressing a negative evaluation of oneself, and on the physiological level, there were cortisol changes similar to those in adults.

If there is a lot of it, an emotion like shame or anxiety may become more internalised and can come to be experienced as a deep sense of defectiveness and inadequacy: 'low self-esteem'. The way in which the child is socialised may affect how strongly this develops; people with fearful or preoccupied attachment patterns, people who have been abused, and people whose parents used shaming as a discipline technique may be more prone to it.

People who have low self-esteem, that is those who see themselves as being not nearly so good as they would like to be, are at high risk of all sorts of poor functioning, such as emotional and social difficulties, both contemporaneously and later. These may include depression and anxiety, substance abuse, suicidal behaviour, and social and adjustment problems. Biological bases in the regulation of the psycho-neuro-endocrinological systems and in position in the social group are likely to be relevant. Epidemiologically, having low levels of self-esteem in adolescence is associated with greater risk of later mental health problems (including depression, anxiety, conduct/antisocial personality disorder, and thinking about suicide), substance dependence problems (including nicotine and alcohol dependence and dependence on illicit drugs), and life and relationship satisfaction issues (including lower levels of life satisfaction, poorer perceived relationship quality, and lower levels of peer attachment). But it's unlikely there is a single simple causal sequence; possibly self-esteem plays a causal role in life outcomes, with an individual's level of self-esteem being critical in determining success and failure across a range of life tasks, or possibly it is a marker for problems elsewhere which lead to poor life outcomes. The epidemiological associations are moderate rather than strong. And they are very much reduced once confounding factors such as previous mental health problems, lower IQ, higher levels of neuroticism, and experience of a number of childhood adversities (including socioeconomic disadvantage, family dysfunction, child physical and sexual abuse, and impaired parental bonding) are allowed for.

Daily life stresses may have their effect via multiple levels. One such would be effects on the emotion-regulation systems of the central nervous system. As I have already discussed, if there is excessive, adverse input in early life, there may be long-lasting changes in the development of the brain and endocrine system responses to stress.[191] The plasticity of the child's brain development will allow for the establishment of central stress-responsive pathways which normally help the child to cope with the challenges of the environment by creating a central stress response pattern that can be evoked in subsequent times of stress. However, it is possible that this process may become maladaptive over the lifespan in those people exposed to excessive childhood stress; for example the child exposed to parental depression may on one level develop attachment problems and on another level build up a hypersensitive neural response to stressful stimuli.

One core factor in psychological development is self-regulation. Self-regulation of emotion, cognition, and action may be a key part of developing a set of responses to stress which prevent it from being an overly damaging experience. People whose behaviour is very low on self-regulation are less likely to show resilience in the face of adversity. Appraisal of a task is enormously helpful in carrying it out successfully. 'Planfulness' is a big component of educational success. Appraisal of a stressful situation, judgement of its emotional meaning, and regulation of emotions and arousal so that they do not impede problem-solving behaviour will all be useful components of positive coping responses and contribute to success and to resilience in the face of difficulties. Being better at self-regulation, at focussing on the task in hand, and at shifting tactics flexibly if necessary are all associated with greater resilience.[192]

Studies of adolescents in countries as different as the US, China, and Colombia[193] have found that those who were showing antisocial behaviour at age eleven showed less self-regulation than those whose antisocial behaviour emerged later, and that those who never showed antisocial behaviour had the highest levels of self-regulation. The effects of antisocial peer groups and adverse personal history were more powerful with the individuals who had poor self-regulation than they were with individuals who were better at regulating themselves. Individuals with poor self-regulation were more likely to be stressed and depressed. Finally, experience of parenting and opportunities to meet and rise to challenge are associated with later self-regulation and resilience. Other people's planning matters, too. In a classic study[194] of girls who had been 'in care' because of family breakdown, a substantial proportion of girls who had shown little ability to plan how their lives would go had poor outcomes, while girls who had planned were much more likely to turn out well. The peer group was important here, too; some girls who did not plan paired up with young men who were also in care and also lacked the skills and the support networks that might have helped them all to be better parents.

Poor impulse control is one of the risk factors for delinquency. Poorly functioning individuals suffering from psychological and social damage may show difficulties with regulating their emotions and their displays of emotion, with inhibiting risky or inappropriate behaviour, with orienting themselves towards the future rather than the immediate present, with thinking about consequences, and with the planning, initiation, and regulation of goal-directed behaviour. These consciously controlled behaviours or 'executive functions' are seen as being dependent on the functioning of the prefrontal cortex and connected regions, at least in adults; these are regions which are still maturing at adolescence, and which may be associated with the emotional volatility and waywardness that adolescents often show.

The obvious causal pathway from self-regulation and executive control to resilience is differences in coping strategies; children who are persistent and task-focussed, able to control impulse and delay gratification of their desires, and able to cope with the emotional arousal caused by struggling are more likely to work through to a satisfactory solution and to see themselves as able to succeed than children who have difficulty in focussing and persisting and give up easily. Children who are highly impulsive and do not reflect on their experience may suffer more adverse events such as physical injuries and may also be more at risk of substance abuse. Parents' feedback (and teachers' feedback) can help convince people that they can persist and improve, rather than that effort is futile. Obviously, it is possible to teach people to plan more and act on impulse less. Parents do this all the time with their children, and teachers do it with their pupils.

Although resilient people have often engaged in planful activity, and people who plan appear to be more resilient, there are issues about causation and about how much 'planfulness' is a good thing. The disadvantages of never being planful or controlled are fairly obvious, as I have just argued, but it may be possible to be too planful if it edges into rumination and excessive blaming of oneself. I spent much of my young adulthood thinking everything was my own fault; realising that most of it wasn't and that 'good enough' is good enough were among the many benefits of growing older.

Children whose approaches to life show positive emotions in response to minor life events show more resilience than those whose overall emotional tone is negative. Children whose characteristic temperaments show a positive sociable approach to new situations show lower levels of behaviour problems and higher levels of social competence and emotional adjustment than children whose temperament is low on approach and sociability. In a whole host of studies, children with a more open and optimistic outlook were more likely to show resilience than more pessimistic children. (We probably all know individuals who seem to expect the worst and then get it as expected, with every reaction being one of deep-dyed pessimism – Eeyore in the *Winnie-the-Pooh* books is a classic example. In some cultures, of course, expecting the worst and then having a good moan about it might be an acceptable coping strategy. There may be some cultural limitations to the evidence that justifies the assertion I have just made about chronic optimism being better for you than chronic pessimism.)

How does the association between a positive outlook and resilience come about? In a multiplicity of ways, but amongst these there are several that are of interest. It may be that children who are high on negative emotion or difficult temperament tend to get decreasing involvement with their parents compared with children whose behaviour is more smiley and sociable, which might mean that they get less parental support when a challenge comes along. Parents of children who are shy and inhibited may be protective rather than trying to promote their child's independence, which might increase the child's initial tendencies to be cautious and inhibited and decrease the likelihood that the child will become involved with and learn from more boisterous peers, and so be steeled against minor social stresses. Children high in negative emotionality may react more strongly to stress and negative events than more emotionally positive children. They may be more likely to employ passive avoidant coping strategies which reduce their opportunities to develop positive solutions to the problems they meet and less likely to use flexible, active coping strategies, all of which could make them a little more likely to face the next challenge with an anticipation of difficulty and defeat.

Similarly, children who are more socially oriented elicit more positive responses and support from their parents, peers, and other adults than unsociable individuals, which gives them more positive social experiences and more access to help and encouragement when things turn difficult. Children with better self-regulation and more supportive parenting had better cognitive, behavioural, and social outcomes following parental divorce, for example.

Psychology, like epidemiology, reminds us that resilience is going to be affected by multiple factors combining for better or for worse, and that some risks are just so big that everyone who encounters them is damaged. We are, historically, lucky if we personally don't encounter them. And we are morally obliged to try to minimise their effects for others.

9

◆

HOW TO MAKE THINGS BETTER

In which there is actually some advice

What use should we make of all this science? I began by saying this was not an advice book about how to bring up your children, that what I wanted to induce in you was simply enthusiasm for the science of child development. But in that enthusiasm is more detailed knowledge about what's happening as children develop – 'so that's what little kids are made of'. And implicit in that more detailed knowledge is understanding how development can go in ways which make life more difficult for individuals and their societies – too many slugs and snails, not enough sugar and spice. This leads (one would hope) to understanding what we could and should do to make things go better. I want to draw this last sort of understanding together now.

We are all in the current stage in a long history of evolution. Evolution is neither our friend nor our foe in our development and our lives; it's just the way things have worked. Nothing in evolution favours us; we are not its point, let alone its endpoint. We can't know if we are an early part of a lineage that will continue to flourish for thousands more years, or near the end of a lineage that is going to die off pretty soon, and the evolutionary process does not care. However, we have evolved, we have had ancestors who have coped with the challenges of life well enough to have descendants, and we have inherited from these ancestors genes that (in combination with other genes and with experience) build bodies, run bodies, and allow us a good prospect of adapting to the challenges we meet. We have to meet challenges, but many of them will be challenges that our ancestors faced, too, and for many of these challenges we are set up to be able to adapt appropriately using our inherited programmes.

We are, on the whole, quite robust. And we are also quite adaptable, quite committed learners, so that there is a fair chance we can cope with new challenges that our ancestors did not meet. We have a degree of plasticity so that we are not too thrown by change. We are less like the panda, who can only digest one sort of bamboo, and more like the seagull, who can catch small fish if there are small fish and also 'catch' the humans' fish and chips if they are left unattended by the beach. Most of us will get through to adulthood in more or less good enough shape to have descendants ourselves, and most of our descendants in each generation will, too.

For most of us, it's not our own imperfect genes and evolved physical characteristics that stop us from having a good enough life, it's too much environmental challenge and an insufficient capacity to adapt to that. In parts of the world and in parts of each society and in parts of history, some people face terribly severe challenges, and obviously if we mess up too much, future generations will have a harder time. Individual lineages and species do die out. There is a fair chance that most of us will survive and adapt and grow up sort of okay, given an averagely suitable environment. But evolution is not interested in individuals and wastage is not a problem for it. For a parent, and for a policy maker, on the other hand, bad outcomes and wastage *are* a problem, which implies that we shouldn't complacently leave everything to 'nature'.

But more specifically, looking at our evolutionary history shows that we are a species that has become very social, so we're all immersed in the lives of others. We have a reproductive strategy of having low numbers of offspring who are born immature and grow up slowly, needing a lot of parenting to survive. Our highly social lives and our need for parenting to be done can only work for us if we have all sorts of adaptations to help us live with others – mirror neurons, face recognition skills, self-awareness, memory, imitation, emotion regulation, language, planning, and so forth. As a species, we're also extremely likely to learn new skills, diversify our experiences, invent things, and invade new environments – in short, to add complexity to what we have to adapt to and to our ways of adapting to it. Our long period of being immature and protected and playful gives space for all this necessary learning and diversification. The availability of more skilled partners, in the shape of the people who parent us, can make the learning more efficient. It should be a matter of both personal and public policy to invest in our children, doing our best to give them good parenting frames and also to allow them room to grow up according to their own time scale. And we also need to support parents and institutions, such as schools, who take on parental roles. Intervening after things have gone wrong can work, but it will be easier and cheaper to get things working well early on than to put things right after a period of damaging experience. As social creatures, it's worth us all investing in all children, not just our own; the costs of the ones whose lives go badly spill over onto those who are doing better.

And what about children looked at from the neuroscience angle? We have brains that not only keep us going in all the basic mammalian ways but have also specialised to allow us to do complex learning and complex social adaptations. Our brains have enlarged regions which seem to be the focus of activities such as seeing faces, hearing and producing and understanding language; imitating other people's actions; and mapping the environment; and our brains can change in fine-tuned ways in response to their experiences, probably throughout all of our lives. Brains are built up over the long period from early in gestation to young adulthood (very possibly beyond that) in a genetically programmed way, but they are also dependent on experience. Subtle differences in brains' architecture and functioning give the individual a better or worse machine with which to learn and behave and adapt to life's challenges. Later development builds on earlier development, and complex skills are built on simpler ones, so there will be problems in the later stages if things have gone wrong in earlier ones. We need to facilitate good brain development through protecting developing brains from damage and malnutrition, through giving them useful experience (and not giving them too much counterproductive experience), through giving them repeated opportunities to learn and to discuss what they are learning, and through recognising that young children's brains seem to learn best from 'contingent reciprocity', where there are links between what the child's brain knows or is attending to and the new stimulation, where what is taught builds on the child's interests, and where child and adult take part in a 'scaffolded' interaction of each responding to the other's turn. Diet matters, health matters, a reasonable degree of consistent positive experience matters, and feedback and reflection matter. Children's brains are probably more adaptable than adults', so again, getting it right early on is a worthwhile investment. Adolescence may be another period of brain vulnerability, one reason why adolescents' use of drugs that affect brains can be a serious problem.

We also have mechanisms for managing stress and regulating our emotions. Many of these are shared with other mammals and are fine-tuned by experience. I've described how the same experiences seem to have the same effects across different species, how the nursing, licking, and grooming the mother rat does is so similar to the cuddling and grooming that primate mothers do and to the cuddling and stroking and talking and dandling that human parents do. Differences in these experiences show up in babies' hormone levels, the expression of their genes, their behaviour (as babies and as adults) when they are stressed, and how they mother the next generation. Rats, monkeys, and humans who are not cuddled are all at risk of being more stressed throughout life and of being worse mothers, should they become mothers, than those that have been stroked and licked and nursed. And stressed mothers are likely to be worse at cuddling, with stress while they're pregnant and stress after the birth both having negative effects. We should, both personally and as public policy, reduce stress on pregnant women and on parents and children after birth. Do everything possible to keep them calm and happy. Adjust the world to the parent or child, not the other way round. When parents or children are stressed, find ways to help them cope with it positively. And I do mean *ways* in the plural: better to have several tools in the stress-reducing toolbox. Get it right early and there's a good foundation for later;[195] get it wrong early and things will be harder to get right.

The evidence from epidemiology adds to this by teasing out patterns in the factors that affect development. Occasionally there is one factor that is all important, but more often there are many different ones which accumulate or counterbalance each other. One of the worst things about disadvantageous circumstances is that they often coincide; for example low income is associated with worse housing, worse health, worse parental education, worse parental mental health, more marital discord, and more stress for everyone. Each of these factors will impinge negatively on those who are poor, and the great difficulties that there are in parenting well under unfavourable circumstances may be at the centre of why social disadvantage can persist over generations. Intervening on only one may not have much effect. There needs to be 'joined-up policy' about reducing the negative effects of poverty and stress on children and their families. Interventions which support responsive parenting and a welfare system that means no one needs to be chronically ill or living in squalor or devoid of books would work. There have been examples: Nurse Family Partnerships, Sure Start, the Educational Maintenance Allowance, and benefits specifically targeted on doing good things for your child. Again, it's worth ensuring that support starts early so that things don't go down an unfavourable path. Again, we should act on the idea that inequality in society damages everyone in it, not just those at the bottom.

And what about the policy and practice that derive from psychology? I've just mentioned much of it: the protective effect of good attachment relationships, of ways of reducing stress, of learning to plan and self-regulate, of feeling just a little bit more optimistic and confident than is really realistic, of getting lots of thoughtful practice at any cognitive skills that are required, of getting clear and specific feedback. All of this comes most easily when embedded in positive social interactions, genuine discussions, conversations on shared interests, and mutually enjoyed joint activities. We should think about parental frames (and don't necessarily leave them to parents, anyone can operate them), balance patient support on the one hand and demands and challenges on the other, and not make children feel excluded or ignored. Negotiate where possible, and where not possible, explain why things have to be that way even when you insist on it, considering whether the 'not possible' is really justified or inevitable. Consider what opportunities this child has to learn whatever it is you hope is going to be learned, and consider also whether you are giving the child counterproductive opportunities to learn something contrary to what you want to be learned. Give feedback that highlights not just what has been achieved but also ways in which it has improved since last time and could improve in future. 'To jaw-jaw is always better than to war-war,' as Churchill said. It gives more practice on positive things such as thinking and listening and understanding others, quite apart from involving lower stress levels.

But the last point I want to make is pretty much the one I made first – the important one. The science inside the child is awesome and one's child can be more wonderful than anything else in the universe; both are endlessly fascinating. I hope I have convinced you that putting the science and the child together just increases the delight and amazement.

FURTHER READING AND NOTES TO CHAPTERS

◆

I've struggled a bit with how to manage the issue of suggesting further reading to substantiate, question, or extend the points I wanted to make. All my writing life, what I've produced has been designed for readers who would expect to do lots and lots of further reading before and beyond what they read in my text. The idea there is, basically, to ensure that the reader knows what I know; understands the field that my argument comes from; can test every assertion, procedure, and finding; can evaluate what I say in comparison with what other people say; and can build up a sense of what needs to be investigated next. Doing this is how science works, and a book about the excitement of science in understanding children should certainly try to model this. But in most of my books, what I've included as a list of references has been as long as the main text. I want someone reading this book to understand that this is how science proceeds, but I know that the reader may not have the time, expertise, motivation, or confidence to do this much further reading. There might be access issues, too; original papers may only be available via conferences or learned journals, and popular summaries are not always accurate. All in all, I can't expect the reader of this book to read everything that could be relevant, or even everything that is truly important.

So I have selected amongst possible reading. I have tried hard to concentrate on stuff that is likely to be accessible in every sense but also reliable. Fuller lists of references appear in two of my books.[196]

1   In all honesty, I identify with what Philip Larkin's poem 'This Be the Verse' famously said about parents.

2   Kaye, K. (1984) *The mental and social life of babies*. London: Methuen.

3   Kaye, K. (1984) *The mental and social life of babies*. London: Methuen; Meadows, S. (2010) *The child as social person*. London: Routledge; Bugenthal, D., and Grusec, J. (2006) Socialisation processes. In W. Damon (Ed.) *Handbook of child psychology* (6th edition) Volume 3. New York: Wiley.

4   Murray, L., and Andrews, L. (2005) *The social baby*. Richmond: The Children's Project. See also http://www.reading.ac.uk/pcls/people/lynne-murray.aspx.

5   Most famously, research by Andrew Meltzoff. See http://ilabs.uw.edu/institute-faculty/bio/i-labs-andrew-n-meltzoff-phd.

6   Baron-Cohen, S. et al. (2013) *Understanding other minds: Perspectives from developmental social neuroscience*. Oxford: Oxford University Press.

7   This phrase comes from the late nineteenth-century psychologist William James, writing about what babies experience; a lot of his psychology is still of interest, but in this instance he probably got it wrong.

8   Franklin, E. L. (2014) The journey of tandem running: The twists, turns and what we have learned. *Insectes Sociaux* 61: 1–8; Franklin, E. L., and Franks, N. R. (2012) Individual and social learning in tandem-running recruitment by ants. *Animal Behaviour* 84: 361–8.

9   For an autobiographical account of how this looks to the ambitious parent, see Chua, A. (2011) *Battle hymn of the tiger mother*. London: Penguin. For how it looks to the daughter working out her mother's ambitions, see Hong Kingston, M. (1975) *The woman warrior: Memoirs of a girlhood among ghosts*. New York: Vintage.

10 Chua, A. (2011) *Battle hymn of the tiger mother*. London: Penguin; Myerson, J. (2010) *The lost child*. London: Bloomsbury; Moss, S. (2010) *Nightwaking*. London: Granta; Fowler, K. J. (2014) *We are all completely beside ourselves*. London: Serpent's Tail.

11 Rogers, C. (1959) Persons or science (part 2). *Pastoral Psychology* 10(3): 19–26, p. 21.

12 Goldacre, B. (2008) *Bad science*. London: Fourth Estate; Goldacre, B. (2014) *I think you'll find it's a bit more complicated than that*. London: Fourth Estate.

13 Popper, K. (2002) *The logic of scientific discovery*. London: Routledge.

14 Ben Goldacre has been particularly worth reading on this.

15 Dawkins, R. (2010) *The greatest show on earth*. London: Black Swan.

16 You can still get a sense of his excitement and delight in *The Voyage of the Beagle*. Darwin, C. (2009) *The origin of species and the voyage of the Beagle*. London: Vintage.

17 Dawkins, R. (2005) *The ancestor's tale*. London: Phoenix.

18 Dawkins, R. (2010) *The greatest show on earth*. London: Black Swan; Ruse, M., and Travis, J. (Eds.) (2009) *Evolution: The first four billion years*. Cambridge, MA: Belknap Press.

19 For a recent discussion, see Dunbar, R. (2014) *Human evolution*. London: Pelican.

20 There is debate about when our ancestors really count as 'humans'. For convenience, I'm going to call the creatures that were marginally human as we understand it *hominins*, except where it is important to be more specific.

21 For example they've been uncovered at Laetoli in Tanzania and Happisburgh in Norfolk.

22 Dunbar, R. (2014) *Human evolution*. London: Pelican.

23 Dunne, J. et al. (2012) First dairying in green Saharan Africa in the fifth millennium BCE. Nature 486: 390–4. doi: 10.1038/nature11186.

24 More about this when I discuss stress systems in the chapter on psychoneuroendocrinology.

25 Working memory is an area of psychology that I flesh out a bit later. For the moment, think of it as what you need to remember or have on your desktop while you are engaged in a task, rather than as a library or archive.

26 Plotkin, H. (2004) *Evolutionary thought in psychology: A brief history*. Malden, MA: Blackwell.

27 Keynes, R. (2001) *Annie's box*. London: Fourth Estate.

28 Gould, S. J. (1977) *Ontogeny and phylogeny*. Cambridge, MA: Belknap Press of Harvard University Press.

29 Konner, M. (2010) *The evolution of childhood*. Cambridge, MA: Belknap Press of Harvard University Press.

30 Harden, A. et al. (2009) Teenage pregnancy and social disadvantage: Systematic review integrating controlled trials and qualitative studies. *British Medical Journal* 339:231–55. doi: 10.1136/bmj.b4254.

31 Mills, M. et al. (2011) Economic power and childbearing: Why do people postpone parenthood? Reasons and social policy incentives. *Human Reproduction Update* 17: 848–60.

32 Mackintosh, N. J. (1998) *IQ and human intelligence*. Cambridge: Cambridge University Press.

33 Vaz, J. et al. (2013) Dietary patterns, n-3 fatty acids intake from seafood and high levels of anxiety symptoms during pregnancy: Findings from the Avon Longitudinal Study of Parents and Children. *PloS One* 8(7): e67671; Hibbeln, J. et al. (2007) Maternal seafood consumption in pregnancy and neurodevelopmental outcomes in childhood (ALSPAC study): An observational cohort study. *LANCET* 369(9561): 578–85; Robinson, S., and Fall, C. (2012) Infant nutrition and later health: A review of current evidence. *Nutrients* 4: 859–74.

34 Parental conflict theory proposes that the genes you get from your father would try to increase the growth of the fetus so that it is born bigger and stronger and more likely to survive. If the danger to the mother is immaterial to him, bigger babies and Caesarean sections might be much in his interests. Conversely, the maternal genome would try to constrain the fetus's size in a

balance of allowing it to be strong enough to survive but small enough to be born safely. Because, on the whole, fathers do have a strong interest in the welfare of the mothers of their children, you would expect there to be genes that constrain the fetus's size.

35   Murray, L., and Andrews, L. (2005) *The social baby*. Richmond: The Children's Project.

36   Brunton, P. (2008) The expectant brain: Adapting for motherhood. *Nature Reviews Neuroscience* 9: 11–25.

37   For example see a body of work by Judy Dunn, especially Dunn, J., and Kendrick, C. (1982) *Siblings: Love, envy and understanding*. London: Grant McIntyre, and Dunn, J. (1993) *Young children's close relationships*. Newbury Park, CA: Sage.

38   For an interesting and moving set of interviews with parents whose children turn out to have unexpected characteristics, see Solomon, A. (2014) *Far from the tree*. New York: Vintage.

39   Lovell, J. (2011) *The opium war: Drugs, dreams and the making of China*. London: Picador.

40   Dunbar, R. (2014) *Human evolution*. London: Pelican.

41   Dunbar, R., and Shultz, S. (2007) Evolution in the social brain. *Science*. doi: 10.1126/science.1145463

42   Dunbar, R. (2014) *Human evolution*. London: Pelican.

43   By 'mentalising' I mean understanding that other people have mental lives like one's own and treating them accordingly.

44   Dunbar, R. (2014) *Human evolution*. London: Pelican.

45   Laskowski, K., and Pruitt, J. (2014) Evidence of social niche construction: Persistent and repeated social interactions generate stronger personalities in a social spider. *Proceedings of the Royal Society B-Biological Sciences* 281, article number: 20133166.

46   Darwin, C. (1871/2004) *The descent of man, and selection in relation to sex*. London: Penguin Books, p. 130.

47   Tomasello, M., and Vaish, A. (2013) Origins of human cooperation and morality. *Annual Review of Psychology* 64: 231–5.

48   Keltner, D. et al. (2014) The sociocultural appraisals, values, and emotions (SAVE) framework of prosociality: Core processes from gene to meme. *Annual Review of Psychology* 65: 425–60.

49   Dorling, D. (2011) *Injustice: Why social inequality persists*. Bristol: Policy Press; Wilkinson, R., and Pickett, K. (2010) *The spirit level: Why equality is better for everyone*. London: Penguin.

50   For interesting and accessible discussions of the basics, try Lane, N. (2010) *Life ascending*. London: Profile Books.

51   Which has, of course, revolutionised forensic attempts to identify criminals from samples of blood or other body fluids.

52   Chamowitz, D. (2012) *What a plant knows*. Oxford: One World Publications.

53   Knowledge here is moving fast, and anything I mention will be old by the time you read this. But I recommend Lane, N. (2005) *Power, sex and suicide: Mitochondria and the meaning of life*. Oxford: OUP, and Carroll, S. (2011) *Endless forms most beautiful*. London: Quercus. For an accessible review of research methods as well as findings, see Gu, J., and Kanai, R. (2014) What contributes to individual differences in brain structure? *Frontiers in Human Neuroscience* 8: 262.

54   Carroll, S. (2011) *Endless forms most beautiful*. London: Quercus.

55   For example the versions of the 5HTT genotype that you have may affect your risk of damage from abuse and deprivation; see Kumsta, R. et al. (2010) 5HTT genotype moderates the influence of early institutional deprivation on emotional problems in adolescence: evidence from the English and Romanian Adoptee (ERA) study. *Journal of Child Psychology and Psychiatry* 51: 755–62. See also Moffitt, T. et al. (2006) Measured gene-environment interactions in psychopathology. *Perspectives on Psychological Science* 1: 5–27.

56   Rutter, M. (2006) *Genes and behaviour*. Oxford: Blackwell. Mike Rutter (Professor Sir Michael Rutter) is immensely eminent and knowledgeable, and his website contains a lot of interesting material: http://www.iop.kcl.ac.uk/staff/profile/default.aspx?go=12692.

57   Gu, J., and Kanai, R. (2014) What contributes to individual differences in brain structure? *Frontiers in Human Neuroscience* 8: 262.

58   With momentous consequences for the history of Europe: the haemophilia of the only son of the last Tsar of Russia was a factor in the Russian revolution of the early 20th century.

59   Carey, N. (2011) *The epigenetics revolution*. London: Icon Books.

60   For simplicity, I've talked about methyl groups being added, but sometimes what happens is that there are fewer methyl groups than usual. This too has effects on how genes are expressed. See for example Labonté, B. et al. (2012) Genome-wide epigenetic regulation by early-life trauma. *Archives of General Psychiatry (JAMA Psychiatry)* 69(7): 722–31. doi: 10.1001/archgenpsychiatry.2011.2287.

61   Barker, D.J.P. (2012) Developmental origins of chronic disease. *Public Health* 126(3): 185–9.

62   Kaati, G. (2007) Transgenerational response to nutrition, early life circumstances, and longevity. *European Journal of Human Genetics* 15: 784–90.

63   There is a very interesting account of the food policies of the different governments involved in World War 2 in Collingham, L. (2011) *The taste of war*. London: Allen Lane. Collingham says that the Nazis had a policy of not trying to ensure that the population of countries they had occupied got adequate food. Their plan was, effectively, that non-Aryan populations could starve,

thus freeing up land for the Germans, and even if the conquered population was racially okay in Nazi eyes, they took little responsibility for looking after them. Indeed they expected their own forces to live off the local population and barely ensured that even their own soldiers were fed. The Japanese policies were even worse.

64 Many genes have boring acronymic names, but some are more memorable. The 'desert hedgehog' gene is one of an important family of genes called the hedgehog genes. They are so-called because they were found to affect the little body hairs that normally occur on the backs of fruit flies. Mostly the fruit fly's body is a long oval and the little hairs are in bands, but some mutant fruit flies have short stubby bodies and hair in different patterns resembling the spines on a hedgehog. Researchers identified the genes responsible and the variant genes were named desert hedgehog, sonic hedgehog, and mountain hedgehog. The cute name makes them memorable, but in case you think they are merely cute, there they are in humans too, and they seem to be involved in the formation of a lot of body parts in the embryo (not just the male genitalia but probably the development of fingers and toes, too) and probably in cancer and hair loss in adults.

65 Lewis, S., and Russell, A. (2014) Protecting children and young people from tobacco-related harm: A review. *Children and Society* 28: 140–51.

66 Northstone, K. et al. (2014) Prepubertal start of father's smoking and increased body fat in his sons: Further characterisation of paternal transgenerational responses. *European Journal of Human Genetics*: 1382–6. doi: 10.1038/ejhg.2014.31.

67 Northstone, K. et al. (2014) Prepubertal start of father's smoking and increased body fat in his sons: Further characterisation of paternal transgenerational responses. *European Journal of Human Genetics*: 1382–6. doi: 10.1038/ejhg.2014.31. See also Brion M. J. et al. (2010) Maternal smoking and child psychological problems: Disentangling causal and noncausal effects. *Pediatrics* 126 (1): e57–65.

68 Barker, D.J.P. (2012) Developmental origins of chronic disease. *Public Health* 126(3): 185–9; Meadows, S. (2006) *The child as thinker.* London: Routledge.

69 Anacker, C. et al. (2014) Early life adversity and the epigenetic programming of hypothalamic-pituitary-adrenal function. *Dialogues in Clinical Neuroscience* 16: 321–33.

70 Moffitt, T. et al. (2006) Measured gene-environment interactions in psychopathology. *Perspectives on Psychological Science* 1: 5–27.

71 Very recent advances in neuroimaging are extending descriptions of the connectivity of the fetus's brain back into the middle of pregnancy, for example Thomason M. et al. (2014) Intrinsic functional brain architecture derived from graph theoretical analysis in the human fetus. *PLoS One* 9(5): e94423. doi: 10.1371/journal.pone.0094423.

72 Gu, J., and Kanai, R. (2014) What contributes to individual differences in brain structure? *Frontiers in Human Neuroscience* 8: 262.

73 Measurement possibilities are improving all the time. For further references and discussion of the complexities of this research, see Gu, J., and Kanai, R. (2014) What contributes to individual differences in brain structure? *Frontiers in Human Neuroscience* 8: 262. doi: 10.3389/fnhum.2014.00262.

74 I think I should note in particular that there is little reason to think that bigger brains are better simply because they are bigger, and the notion that some brains are faster than others is even more ridiculous. Stephen J. Gould's classic *The Mismeasure of Man* is old now (Penguin, 1981) but still a salutary read.

75 Baron-Cohen, S. et al. (2013) *Understanding other minds: Perspectives from developmental social neuroscience.* Oxford: Oxford University Press

76 Karmiloff, K., and Karmiloff-Smith, A. (2001) *Pathways to language: From fetus to adolescent.* Cambridge, MA: Harvard University Press.

77 Blakemore, S.J. et al. (2014) Is Adolescence a Sensitive Period for Sociocultural Processing? *Annual Review of Psychology* 65: 187–207. See also https://iris. ucl.ac.uk/iris/publication/952352/2

78 For example see Hubel, D., and Wiesel, T. (1962) Receptive fields, binocular interaction and functional architecture in the cat's visual cortex. *Journal of Physiology* 160: 106–54.

79 Rahi, J. S. et al. (2011) Myopia over the lifecourse: Prevalence and early life influences in the 1958 British birth cohort. *Ophthalmology* 118: 797–804.

80 But there is some, for example Eluvathingal, T. et al. (2006) Abnormal brain connectivity in children after severe socioemotional deprivation: A diffusion tensor imaging study. *Pediatrics* 117: 2093–2100.

81 Radlowski, E. et al. (2013) Perinatal iron deficiency and neurocognitive development. *Frontiers in Human Neuroscience* 7, article number: UNSP 585; Zimmermann, M. (2013) Are mild maternal iodine deficiency and child IQ linked? *Nature Reviews Endocrinology* 9: 505–6; Bath, S. (2013) Effect of inadequate iodine status in UK pregnant women on cognitive outcomes in their children: Results from the Avon Longitudinal Study of Parents and Children (ALSPAC). *Lancet* 382(9889): 331–7. doi: 10.1016/S0140–6736 (13)60436–5.

82 Baron-Cohen, S. et al. (2013) *Understanding other minds: Perspectives from developmental social neuroscience.* Oxford: Oxford University Press.

83 Taylor, L. et al. (2014) Vaccines are not associated with autism: An evidence-based meta-analysis of case-control and cohort studies. *Vaccine* 32: 3623–9.

84 Crone, E., and Dahl, R. (2012) Understanding adolescence as a period of social-affective engagement and goal flexibility. *Nature Reviews Neuroscience* 13: 636–50; Blakemore, S. J. et al. (2014) Is adolescence a sensitive period for sociocultural processing? *Annual Review of Psychology* 65: 187–207.

85   For example Kumsta, R. et al. (2010) 5HTT genotype moderates the influ-
      ence of early institutional deprivation on emotional problems in adolescence:
      Evidence from the English and Romanian Adoptee (ERA) study. *Journal of Child
      Psychology and Psychiatry* 51: 755–62.

86   Romeo, R., and McEwen, B. (2006) Stress and the adolescent brain. *Annals of
      the New York Academy of Sciences* 1094: 202–14.

87   Laviola, G. et al. (2004) Beneficial effects of enriched environment on ado-
      lescent rats from stressed pregnancies. *European Journal of Neuroscience* 20(6):
      1655–64.

88   Happe, F., and Frith, U. (2014) Annual research review: Towards a develop-
      mental neuroscience of atypical social cognition. *Journal of Child Psychology and
      Psychiatry* 55: 553–77.

89   Hamilton, A., and Marsh, L. (2013) Two systems for action comprehension
      in autism. In S. Baron-Cohen et al. (Eds.) *Understanding other minds: Perspectives from
      developmental social neuroscience.* Oxford: Oxford University Press.

90   See, for example, Perry, A., and Shamay-Tsoory, S. (2013) Understanding
      emotional and cognitive empathy: A neuropsychological perspective. In S.
      Baron-Cohen et al. (Eds.) *Understanding other minds: Perspectives from developmental social
      neuroscience.* Oxford: Oxford University Press.

91   Macmillan, M. (2008) Phineas Gage – unravelling the myth. *The Psychologist* 21:
      828–31; Horne, J. (2011) Blasts from the past. *The Psychologist* 24: 622–3.

92   Hewitt, R. (2010) *Map of a nation: A biography of the ordnance survey.* London: Granta,
      p. 180.

93   For example Hibbeln, J. et al. (2007) Maternal seafood consumption in preg-
      nancy and neurodevelopmental outcomes in childhood (ALSPAC study): An
      observational cohort study. *Lancet* 369(9561): 578–85.

94   Williams, C. et al. (2001) Stereoacuity at 3.5 years of age in children born
      full-term is associated with prenatal and postnatal dietary factors: A report
      from a population based cohort study. *American Journal of Clinical Nutrition* 73:
      316–22. There is a useful review of the benefits of breastfeeding in Robinson,
      S., and Fall, C. (2012) Infant nutrition and later health: A review of current
      evidence. *Nutrients* 4: 859–74.

95   But this is not the only possible reason; see Meadows, S. (2006) *The child as
      thinker.* London: Routledge, pp. 99–100.

96   Rahi, J. S. et al. (2011) Myopia over the lifecourse: Prevalence and early life
      influences in the 1958 British Birth Cohort. *Ophthalmology* 118: 797–804.

97   Meadows, S. (2006) *The child as thinker.* London: Routledge.

98   See discussion later in this chapter of the children rescued from extreme
      deprivation.

99   Butterworth, B. https://iris.ucl.ac.uk/iris/browse/profile?upi=BLBUT84

100   Meadows, S. (2006) *The child as thinker.* London: Routledge.

101   Meadows, S. (2006) *The child as thinker*. London: Routledge.

102   Butterworth, B. https://iris.ucl.ac.uk/iris/browse/profile?upi=BLBUT84

103   For an introduction, see Schneider, B. (2014) *Child psychopathology*. Cambridge: Cambridge University Press.

104   Leis, J. et al. (2014) Associations between maternal mental health and child emotional and behavioral problems: Does prenatal mental health matter? *Journal of Abnormal Child Psychology* 42(1): 161–71; O'Donnell, K. et al. (2013) Prenatal maternal mood is associated with altered diurnal cortisol in adolescence. *Psychoneuroendocrinology* 38(9): 1630–8.

105   Calkins, S. et al. (2013) A biopsychosocial perspective on parenting and developmental psychopathology. *Development and Psychopathology* 25(4): 1399–1414.

106   For example Peters, E. et al. (2011) Peer rejection and HPA activity in middle childhood: Friendship makes a difference. Child Development 82(6): 1906–20.

107   Taylor, L. et al. (2014) Vaccines are not associated with autism: An evidence-based meta-analysis of case-control and cohort studies. *Vaccine* 32: 3623–9.

108   Sherriff, A. et al. (2002) Hygiene levels in a contemporary population cohort are associated with wheezing and atopic eczema in preschool infants. *Archives of Disease in Childhood* 87: 26–9. doi: 10.1136/adc.87.1.26.

109   A useful review of the benefits of breastfeeding appears in Robinson, S., and Fall, C. (2012) Infant nutrition and later health: A review of current evidence. *Nutrients* 4: 859–74.

110   For example Gilmer, W., and McKinney, W. (2003) Early experience and depressive disorders: Human and non-human primate studies. *Journal of Affective Disorders* 75(2): 97–113.

111   Kattman, A., and Meaney, M. (2007) Neurodevelopmental sequelae of postnatal maternal care in rodents: Clinical and research implications. *Journal of Child Psychology and Psychiatry* 48: 224–44.

112   Kattman, A., and Meaney, M. (2007) Neurodevelopmental sequelae of postnatal maternal care in rodents: Clinical and research implications. *Journal of Child Psychology and Psychiatry* 48: 224–44.

113   de Vries, M. (1984) Temperament and infant mortality among the Masai of East Africa. *American Journal of Psychiatry* 141: 1189–94.

114   Useful review of the benefits of breastfeeding in Robinson, S., and Fall, C. (2012) Infant nutrition and later health: A review of current evidence. *Nutrients* 4: 859–74.

115   Glover, V. (2014) Maternal depression, anxiety and stress during pregnancy and child outcome; what needs to be done. *Best Practice & Research Clinical Obstetrics & Gynaecology* 28(1): 25–35.

116   Before birth, the fetus may have some protection from the mother's stress hormones, but this may be in ways that increase the mother's risk of mood

disorders such as depression. Brunton, P. (2008) The expectant brain: Adapting for motherhood. *Nature Reviews Neuroscience* 9: 11–25.

117   Murray, L. (2005) *The social baby.* Richmond: The Children's Project.

118   Kattman, A., and Meaney, M. (2007) Neurodevelopmental sequelae of postnatal maternal care in rodents: Clinical and research implications. *Journal of Child Psychology and Psychiatry* 48: 224–44; Meaney, M. (2001) Maternal care, gene expression, and the transmission of individual differences in stress reactivity across generations. *Annual Review of Neuroscience* 24(1): 1161–92; Labonté, B. et al. (2012) Genome-wide epigenetic regulation by early-life trauma. *Archives of General Psychiatry (JAMA Psychiatry)* 69(7): 722–31. doi: 10.1001/arch genpsychiatry.2011.2287.

119   Moffitt, T. et al. (2006) Measured gene-environment interactions in psychopathology. *Perspectives on Psychological Science* 1: 5–27; Caspi, A. et al. (2003) Influence of life stress on depression: Moderation by a polymorphism in the 5-HTT gene. *Science* 301: 386–9.

120   Maestriperi, D. (2005) Early experience affects the intergenerational transmission of infant abuse in rhesus monkeys. *Proceedings of the National Academy of Sciences of the United States of America* 102(27): 9726–9.

121   Meadows, S. (2010) *The child as social person.* London: Routledge.

122   For example Goodyer, I. (2008) Early onset depressions – meanings, mechanisms and processes. *Journal of Child Psychology and Psychiatry* 49: 1239–56.

123   For example Eluvathingal, T. et al. (2006) Abnormal brain connectivity in children after early severe socio-emotional deprivation. *Pediatrics* 117: 2093–2100; Anacker, C. (2014) Early life adversity and the epigenetic programming of hypothalamic-pituitary-adrenal function. *Dialogues in Clinical Neuroscience* 16: 321–333.

124   Baron-Cohen, S. et al. (2013) *Understanding other minds: Perspectives from developmental social neuroscience.* Oxford: Oxford University Press.

125   Useful review of the benefits of breastfeeding in Robinson, S., and Fall, C. (2012) Infant nutrition and later health: A review of current evidence. *Nutrients* 4: 859–74.

126   Gomez-Pinilla, F. (2008) Brain foods: The effects of nutrients on brain function. *Nature Reviews Neuroscience* 95: 568–78; Northstone, K. et al. (2011) Are dietary patterns in childhood associated with IQ at 8 years of age? A population-based cohort study. *Journal of Epidemiology and Community Health* 66: 624–8.

127   Smoking is a major factor in many cot deaths. Another was sleeping position: babies asleep on their fronts were at risk, possibly because they more easily overheated than babies lying on their backs. Some epidemiological research from ALSPAC was amongst the first evidence on this; see Hunt, L. et al. (1997) Does the supine sleeping position have any adverse effects on the child? I: Health in the first six months. *Pediatrics* 100(1): E11. This research finding changed public policy.

128 Barker, D.J.P. (2012) Developmental origins of chronic disease. *Public Health* 126(3): 185–9.

129 Wilkinson, R., and Pickett, K. (2010) *The spirit level: Why equality is better for everyone.* London: Penguin.

130 Reilly, J., and Kelly, J. (2010) Long-term impact of overweight and obesity in childhood and adolescence on morbidity and premature mortality in adulthood: Systematic review. *International Journal of Obesity* 35: 891–8. doi: 10.1038/ijo.2010.222; Han, J. et al. (2010) Childhood obesity – 2010: Progress and challenges. *Lancet* 375: 1737–48; Robinson, S., and Fall, C. (2012) Infant nutrition and later health: A review of current evidence. *Nutrients* 4: 859–74.

131 Araya, R. et al (2009) Effects of stressful life events, maternal depression and 5-HTTLPR genotype on emotional symptoms in pre-adolescent children. *American Journal of Medical Genetics* 150B: 670–82.

132 For example Anacker, C. et al (2014) Early life adversity and the epigenetic regulation of hypothalamic-pituitary-adrenal function. *Dialogues in clinical neuroscience* 16: 321–33.

133 Kristenson, M. et al. (2001) Risk factors for coronary heart disease in different socioeconomic groups of Lithuania and Sweden – the LiVicordia study. Scandinavian Journal of Public Health 29: 140–50.

134 See the ALSPAC pages on the University of Bristol website (http://www.bristol.ac.uk/alspac/) for publications and information for participants. The ALSPAC twenty-first anniversary book (http://www.bristol.ac.uk/media-library/sites/alspac/migrated/documents/book-21-years-our-journey.pdf) is a very accessible summary of highlights so far.

135 Sherriff, A. et al. (2002) Hygiene levels in a contemporary population cohort are associated with wheezing and atopic eczema in preschool infants. *Archives of Disease in Childhood* 87: 26–9. doi: 10.1136/adc.87.1.26; Too much TV is also associated with wheezing, see Sherriff, A. et al. (2009) Association of duration of television viewing in early childhood with the subsequent development of asthma. *Thorax* 64: 321–325. doi:10.1136/thx.2008.104406.

136 Lack, G. et al. (2003) Factors associated with the development of peanut allergy in childhood. *New England Journal of Medicine* 348(11): 977–85.

137 O'Connor and Glover (2014) The persisting effect of maternal mood in pregnancy on childhood psychopathology. *Development and Psychopathology* 26(2): 393–403.

138 Barker, E. (2013) Prenatal maternal depression symptoms and nutrition, and child cognitive function. *British Journal of Psychiatry* 203(6): 417–21. doi: 10.1192/bjp.bp.113.129486.

139 For a brief account, see Meadows, S. (2006) *The child as thinker.* London: Routledge.

140 Bellinger, D. (2013) Prenatal exposures to environmental chemicals and children's neurodevelopment: An update. *Safety and Health at Work* 4(1): 1–11.

141   Bellinger, D. (2011) The protean toxicities of lead: New chapters in a familiar story. *International Journal of Environmental Research and Public Health* 8: 2593–628. doi: 10.3390/ijerph8072593; see also Bellinger, D. (2013) Prenatal exposures to environmental chemicals and children's neurodevelopment: An update. *Safety and Health at Work* 4(1): 1–11.

142   Lorenz, K. (1949/2002) *King Solomon's ring.* Hove: Routledge Classics.

143   Fearon, R. et al. (2010) The significance of insecure attachment and disorganisation in the development of children's externalising behaviour: A meta-analytic study. *Child Development* 81: 435–56; Groh, A. et al. (2012) The significance of insecure and disorganised attachment for children's internalising symptoms: A meta-analytic study. *Child Development* 83: 591–610.

144   Bowlby, J. (1973) *Attachment and loss: Vol. 2: Separation: Anxiety and anger.* New York: Basic Books, p. 412.

145   One landmark is Aries, P. (1973) *Centuries of childhood.* Penguin (originally published in French in 1960), which is a strong contrast with another view, Pollock, L. (1983) *Forgotten children.* Cambridge: Cambridge University Press. While I find Pollock much more convincing, one possible message from their disagreement is that people's views of children and how they treat them vary a great deal.

146   Gregg, P. et al. (2006) The effects of early maternal employment on child development in the UK. *CMPO Working Paper Series* No. 03/070.

147   Gregg, P. et al. (2006) The effects of early maternal employment on child development in the UK. *CMPO Working Paper Series* No. 03/070.

148   I mentioned some findings earlier when discussing neuroscience and endocrine research in the ERA study. There are summary chapters in *Monographs of the Society for Research in Child Development* 75(1), 2010.

149   *Monographs of the Society for Research in Child Development* 75(1), 2010. See also Fox, N. (2011) The effects of severe psychosocial deprivation and foster care intervention on cognitive development at 8 years of age: Findings from the Bucharest Early Intervention Project. *Journal of Child Psychology and Psychiatry* 52(9): 919–28.

150   Grotevant, H., and McDermott, J. (2014) Adoption: Biological and social processes linked to adaptation. *Annual Review of Psychology* 65: 235–65.

151   http://www.literacytrust.org.uk/assets/0000/2531/Buggy_research.pdf

152   Fearon, R. et al. (2010) The significance of insecure attachment and disorganisation in the development of children's externalising behaviour: A meta-analytic study. *Child Development* 81: 435–56; Groh, A. et al. (2012) The significance of insecure and disorganised attachment for children's internalising symptoms: A meta-analytic study. *Child Development* 83: 591–610.

153   For example Charles Dickens, Henry James, George Eliot. But also Stalin and Hitler.

154   Byrne, R., and Whiten, A. (1988) *Machiavellian intelligence.* Oxford: Clarendon Press.

155   See the earlier chapter on evolution, and especially Dunbar, R. (2014) *Human evolution.* London: Penguin, for a discussion of when language evolved.

156   Dunbar, R. (2014) *Human evolution.* London: Penguin.

157   Bishop, D. (2009) Genes, cognition, and communication insights from neurodevelopmental disorders. Year in cognitive neuroscience 2009 book series. *Annals of the New York Academy of Sciences* 1156: 1–18.

158   Briscoe, J. et al. (2012) A specific cognitive deficit within semantic cognition across a multi-generational family. *Proceedings of the Royal Society B* 279: 3652–61. doi: 10.1098/rspb.2012.0894.

159   Rutter, M. et al. (2003) Twins as a natural experiment to study the causes of mild language delay: I: Design; twin-singleton differences in language, and obstetric risks. *Journal of Child Psychology and Psychiatry and Allied Disciplines* 44(3): 326–41; Thorpe, K. et al. (2003) Twins as a natural experiment to study the causes of mild language delay: II: Family interaction risk factors. *Journal of Child Psychology and Psychiatry and Allied Disciplines* 44(3): 342–55.

160   Curtiss, S. (1977) *Genie: A psycholinguistic study of a modern-day 'wild child'.* New York: Academic Press; Rymer, R. (1993) *Genie: Escape from a silent childhood.* London: Michael Joseph.

161   Roulstone, S. et al. (2011) *Investigating the role of language in children's early educational outcomes.* Department for Education Research Report DFE-RR134; Bishop, D. (2014) When words fail us: Insights into language processing from developmental and acquired disorders. Introduction. *Philosophical Transactions of the Royal Society B-Biological Sciences* 369(1634), article number 20120403.

162   Bishop, D. (2014) When words fail us: Insights into language processing from developmental and acquired disorders. Introduction. *Philosophical Transactions of the Royal Society B-Biological Sciences* 369(1634), article number 20120403. See also http://deevybee.blogspot.co.uk.

163   Bishop, D. (2014) When words fail us: Insights into language processing from developmental and acquired disorders. Introduction. *Philosophical Transactions of the Royal Society B-Biological Sciences* 369(1634), article number 20120403. See also http://deevybee.blogspot.co.uk.

164   Meadows, S. (2006) *The child as thinker.* London: Routledge.

165   I very much enjoyed the description of children's language learning in this ethnographic book: Heath, S. B. (1983) *Ways with words.* Cambridge: Cambridge University Press.

166   For example Meins, E. et al. (2013) Mind-mindedness and theory of mind: Mediating roles of language and perspectival symbolic play. *Child Development* 84(5): 1777–90.

167   Pinker, S. (2000) *The language instinct: How the mind creates language.* New York: Perennial Classics.

168 Bishop, D. (2014) When words fail us: Insights into language processing from developmental and acquired disorders. Introduction. *Philosophical Transactions of the Royal Society B-Biological Sciences* 369(1634), article number 20120403. See also http://deevybee.blogspot.co.uk.

169 Or, in character-based languages, a written word will be built up of parts which are related to ideas (though some elements of characters may also carry information about speech sounds).

170 Frith, U. (1980) Reading and spelling skills. In M. Rutter (Ed.) *Scientific foundations of developmental psychology.* London: Heinemann.

171 Vellutino, F. R. et al. (2004) Specific reading disability (dyslexia): What have we learned in the past four decades? *Journal of Child Psychology and Psychiatry* 45: 12–40.

172 This book is a surprisingly good source of incisive observations of child development. Milne, A. A. (1926) *Winnie-the-Pooh.* London: Methuen.

173 Vellutino, F. R. et al. (2004) Specific reading disability (dyslexia): What have we learned in the past four decades? *Journal of Child Psychology and Psychiatry* 45: 12–40.

174 Bryant, P. (2014) The connection between children's knowledge and use of grapho-phonic and morphemic units in written text and their learning at school. *British Journal of Educational Psychology* 84(Pt 2): 211–25. doi: 10.1111/bjep.12030.

175 Leeson, R. (1993) *Smart girls.* London: Walker Books, is an excellent source of these.

176 Recently these have been the wonderful novels of Elena Ferrante, brilliant about the experience of being a child and adolescent and young woman.

177 Quite a lot of discussion of this in Meadows, S. (2010) *The child as social person.* London: Routledge.

178 Meadows, S. (2010) *The child as social person.* London: Routledge.

179 Patterson, G. R. (2002) Recent developments in our understanding of parenting: Bidirectional effects, causal models, and the search for parsimony. In M. Bornstein (Ed.) *Handbook of parenting* Volume 3. Mahwah: Erlbaum, pp. 59–88.

180 Crone, E., and Dahl, R. (2012) Understanding adolescence as a period of social-affective engagement and goal flexibility. *Nature Reviews Neuroscience* 13: 636–50; Blakemore, S. J. et al. (2014) Is adolescence a sensitive period for sociocultural processing? *Annual Review of Psychology* 65: 187–207; Laviola, G. et al. (2004) Beneficial effects of enriched environment on adolescent rats from stressed pregnancies. *European Journal of Neuroscience* 20(6): 1655–64.

181 Meadows, S. (2010) *The child as social person.* London: Routledge.

182 Meadows, S. (2010) *The child as social person.* London: Routledge.

183 Mischel, W. (2014) *The marshmallow test: Understanding self-control and how to master it.* London: Bantam Press.

184   Meadows, S. (2006) *The child as thinker.* London: Routledge.

185   Murray, L., and Andrews, L. (2005) *The social baby.* Richmond: The Children's Project. See also http://www.reading.ac.uk/pcls/people/lynne-murray.aspx.

186   Meadows, S. (2010) *The child as social person.* London: Routledge.

187   Meadows, S. (2010) *The child as social person.* London: Routledge.

188   For example Dweck, C. (1999) *Self theories.* Hove: Psychology Press. She has also written more self-help accounts of her theory.

189   The famous estimate of 10,000 hours of practice to become an 'expert' comes to mind.

190   Lewis, M. et al. (1992) Differences in shame and pride as a function of children's gender and task difficulty. *Child Development* 63: 630–38.

191   Leis, J. et al. (2014) Associations between maternal mental health and child emotional and behavioral problems: Does prenatal mental health matter? *Journal of Abnormal Child Psychology* 42(1): 161–71; O'Donnell, K. et al. (2013) Prenatal maternal mood is associated with altered diurnal cortisol in adolescence. *Psychoneuroendocrinology* 38(9): 1630–8.

192   Meadows, S. (2010) *The child as social person.* London: Routledge.

193   Brook, J. et al. (2007) Growing up in a violent society: Longitudinal predictors of violence in Colombian adolescents. *American Journal of Community Psychology* 40: 82–95.

194   Quinton, D., and Rutter, M. (1988) *Parenting breakdown: The making and breaking of intergenerational links.* Aldershot: Avebury.

195   Glover, V. (2014) Maternal depression, anxiety and stress during pregnancy and child outcome; what needs to be done. *Best Practice & Research Clinical Obstetrics & Gynaecology* 28(1): 25–35.

196   Meadows, S. (2006) *The child as thinker.* London: Routledge; Meadows, S. (2010) *The child as social person.* London: Routledge.

INDEX